2/2010

THE NEXT
HUNDRED
MILLION

ALSO BY JOEL KOTKIN

California, Inc. (with Paul Grabowicz)

The Valley

*The Third Century: America's Resurgence in the
Asian Era* (with Yoriko Kishimoto)

*Tribes: How Race, Religion, and Identity Determine
Success in the New Global Economy*

*The New Geography: How the Digital Revolution
Is Reshaping the American Landscape*

The City: A Global History

THE NEXT
HUNDRED
MILLION

AMERICA IN 2050

JOEL KOTKIN

THE PENGUIN PRESS | *New York* *2010*

THE PENGUIN PRESS
Published by the Penguin Group
Penguin Group (USA) Inc., 375 Hudson Street, New York, New York 10014, U.S.A. •
Penguin Group (Canada), 90 Eglinton Avenue East, Suite 700, Toronto, Ontario, Canada
M4P 2Y3 (a division of Pearson Penguin Canada Inc.) • Penguin Books Ltd, 80 Strand,
London WC2R 0RL, England • Penguin Ireland, 25 St. Stephen's Green, Dublin 2, Ireland
(a division of Penguin Books Ltd) • Penguin Books Australia Ltd, 250 Camberwell Road,
Camberwell, Victoria 3124, Australia (a division of Pearson Australia Group Pty Ltd) •
Penguin Books India Pvt Ltd, 11 Community Centre, Panchsheel Park,
New Delhi – 110 017, India • Penguin Group (NZ), 67 Apollo Drive, Rosedale,
North Shore 0632, New Zealand (a division of Pearson New Zealand Ltd) • Penguin Books
(South Africa) (Pty) Ltd, 24 Sturdee Avenue, Rosebank, Johannesburg 2196, South Africa

Penguin Books Ltd, Registered Offices: 80 Strand, London WC2R 0RL, England

First Published in 2010 by The Penguin Press, a member of Penguin Group (USA) Inc.

LIBRARY OF CONGRESS CATALOGING-IN-PUBLICATION DATA
Kotkin, Joel.
The next hundred million : America in 2050 / Joel Kotkin.
p. cm.
Includes bibliographical references and index.
ISBN 978-1-59420-244-5
1. Social prediction—United States.   2. Population forecasting—United States.
3. Cities and towns—United States—Growth—Forecasting.
4. United States—Forecasting.   I. Title.
HN60. K68 2010
307.760973'0112—dc22   2009030609

Printed in the United States of America
1   3   5   7   9   10   8   6   4   2

DESIGNED BY NICOLE LAROCHE

For Ariel and Hannah, and their future

CONTENTS

THE NEXT
HUNDRED
MILLION

CHAPTER ONE: FOUR HUNDRED MILLION AMERICANS

This book is inspired by a remarkable fact: in stark contrast to its more rapidly aging rivals in Europe and Asia, America's population is expected to expand dramatically in coming decades. According to the most conservative estimates, the United States by 2050 will be home to at least four hundred million people, roughly one hundred million more than live here today. But because of America's unique demographic trajectory among advanced countries, it should emerge by midcentury as the most affluent, culturally rich, and successful nation in human history.

The addition of a hundred million more residents also will place new stresses on the environment, challenging the country to build homes, communities, and businesses that can sustain an expanding and ever-more-diverse society. America will inevitably become a more complex, crowded, and competitive place, highly dependent, as it has been throughout its history, on its people's innovative and entrepreneurial spirit.

The United States of 2050 will look very different from the country that existed just a decade ago, at the dawn of the new millennium. Between 2000 and 2050 the vast majority of America's net population growth will be in its racial minorities, particularly Asians and Hispanics, as well as in a growing mixed-race population.[1] Our experiment with creating what Walt Whitman described as "the race of races" will continue to evolve.[2] By midcentury the United States will be a predominantly "white country" no longer but rather a staggering amalgam of racial, ethnic, and religious groups, all participants in the construction of a new civilization whose roots lie not in any one country or continent but across the entirety of human cultures and racial types. No other advanced, populous country will enjoy such ethnic diversity.

These demographic changes will affect America's relations with the rest of the world. The United States likely will remain militarily preeminent, but it may well be wary of its long experience in "leading" the world through force or through overweening economic or political power. America's wars of the late 20th and early 21st centuries—in Vietnam, Iraq, and Afghanistan—have shown the limits of superpower status in a world marked by technological diffusion, fierce economic competition, and ever-more-sophisticated unconventional warfare.

Instead the future United States will seek to exercise its influence primarily through technological and cultural innovation and through the dynamism of its diverse society. The election of Barack Obama, the nation's first African-American president, displayed the changing nature of the country to the world. In this sense the primacy of America in 2050 will rest, as Thomas Jefferson saw back in 1817, "not on conquest, but in principles of compact and equality."[3]

Such long-term optimism may seem out of place in the wake of the great economic recession that began in late 2007. The downturn has devastated the national economy and appears to some Americans to be the prelude to a new dark age. Many critical elements of the American dream, such as home ownership, have slipped away from millions of families, at least for the short term. Confidence in the financial system and capitalism itself has fallen to historic lows, as has belief in the political parties, despite the immense popularity in some quarters of the current president. Huge parts of the country's industrial base, most notably the automobile industry, have experienced a massive contraction while many other critical concerns—from health care and education to basic infrastructural needs—still remain to be fully addressed.

Yet this book looks beyond short-term hardship and seeks to illuminate the paths that can lead to a potentially brighter future. America's robust population growth represents just one reason to believe that the United States will remain ascendant in this new era. With proper dedication to its ancient ideals and an embrace of new technology, the United States can emerge as a land of unprecedented opportunity: a youthful, evolving nation amid an advanced industrial world beset by old age, bitter ethnic conflicts, and erratically functioning economic institutions.

This surge in growth, like previous boom eras, will impose itself on the national landscape and reshape the national geography. Scores of new communities will have to be built to accommodate the next hundred million Americans. This will create a massive demand for new housing, as well as industrial and commercial space.[4] This growth will be variously expressed, from the widespread "infilling" of once-desolate inner cities, to the creation of new suburban and exurban towns, to the resettling of the American Heartland—the vast, still sparsely populated regions that constitute the vast majority of the U.S. landmass. In order to accommodate the next hundred million Americans, new environmentally friendly technologies and infrastructure will be required, to reduce commutes by bringing work closer to or even into the home and by finding more energy-efficient means of transportation.

But technology represents only one critical aspect of this successful future. Only a society rooted *both* in traditional values and in social tolerance can support such vast changes in the physical landscape. The country's ever-more-diverse population will generate many of our future society's new ideas, technological innovations, and cultural expressions. They will supply the critical manpower to run the increasingly automated and highly specialized factories, efficient farms both large and small, and scientific laboratories of the 21st century. And they will be a primary source for the teachers, caretakers, and hospital workers needed to both raise large numbers of children and cope with an increasing number of the aged.

The America of 2050 will be radically transformed, but it will still reflect the basic ideal that has driven its evolution from the beginning— a rejection of the fatalism and hierarchy characteristic of most older societies. The central government and giant private institutions can play a critical role in helping meet what will no doubt be daunting obstacles, but basic faith in the individual, family, and community will remain the fundamental instruments for securing the country's future.

DEMOGRAPHICS AS DESTINY

Nothing better illustrates the basic vitality of the United States than the essential factor that drives our analysis: the addition of another hundred million Americans by 2050. The percentage of childless women continues to rise, but compared to other advanced countries, America still boasts the highest fertility rate: 50 percent higher than Russia, Germany, or Japan and well above that of China, Italy, Singapore, Korea, and virtually all of eastern Europe. To these fertility numbers one must add the even greater impact of continued large-scale immigration from around the world.

This pattern places the United States in a radically different position from that of its historic competitors, particularly Europe and Japan, whose populations are stagnant and seem destined to eventually decline. The shift between the United States and Russia, America's onetime primary rival for world power, is even more dramatic. Thirty years ago

Russia constituted the core of a vast Soviet empire that was considerably more populous than the United States. Today, even with its energy riches, Russia's low birth and high mortality rates suggest that its population will drop by 30 percent by 2050, to less than one third that of the United States. Even Prime Minister Vladimir Putin has spoken of "the serious threat of turning into a decaying nation."[5]

Even more remarkably, America will expand its population in the midst of a global demographic slowdown. Population growth projections made around the time of *The Population Bomb*, Paul Ehrlich's widely acclaimed 1968 Malthusian tract, still shape public perceptions, but those forecasts have turned out to be well off the mark. Global population growth rates of 2 percent in the 1960s have dropped to less than half that rate, and projections of the number of earth's human residents in 2000 overshot the mark by over two hundred million. This pattern is likely to continue: growth rates will drop further—to less than 0.8 percent by 2025—largely due to an unanticipated drop in birthrates in developing countries such as Mexico and Iran. These declines are in part the result of increased urbanization, the education of women, and higher property prices. The world's population, according to some estimates, could peak as early as 2050 and begin to fall by the end of the century.

One of the most dramatic demographic shifts has been in East Asia, particularly in China, where the one-child policy has set the stage for a rapidly aging population by midcentury. Fertility is particularly low in highly crowded Asian cities like Tokyo, Shanghai, Tainjin, Beijing, and Seoul. By 2050, according to the United Nations, roughly 30 percent of China's population will be over sixty years old. South Korea, meanwhile, has experienced arguably the fastest drop in fertility in world history, which perhaps explains its extraordinary, if scandal-plagued, interest in human cloning.

Over the past few decades a rapid expansion of their workforce fueled the rise of the so-called East Asian tigers, the great economic success stories of the late 20th and early 21st centuries. However, within the next four decades most of the developed countries in both Europe and East Asia will become veritable old-age homes: a third or more of their populations will be over sixty-five, compared with only a fifth in America.[6] Like the rest of the developed world, the United States will have to cope with an aging population and lower population growth, but in relative terms it will maintain a youthful, dynamic demographic.

History has much to tell us about the relationship between demographics and national destiny. People do not line up to occupy deck chairs on a sinking ship, and if they find themselves stuck on one, they certainly do not start having children. Population growth has a very different effect on wealthy and poor nations. In the developing world a slowdown of population growth can offer at least a short-term economic and environmental benefit. But in advanced countries a rapidly aging or decreasing population does not bode well for societal or economic health, whereas a growing one offers the hope of expanding markets, new workers, and entrepreneurial innovation.[7]

Throughout history low fertility and socioeconomic decline have been inextricably linked, creating a vicious cycle that affected such once-vibrant civilizations as ancient Rome and 17th-century Venice and that now affects contemporary Europe, South Korea, and Japan.[8] The desire to have children is a fundamental affirmation of faith in the future and in values that transcend the individual. This is particularly true in affluent societies, where technology has made the decision not to have children simple and socially acceptable.

The increasingly common decision not to have children reflects a profound moral dilemma that will have long-term consequences. In some countries a sense of diminished prospects, combined with a chronic lack of space, appear to be the root causes for plunging birthrates. As Italians, Germans, Japanese, Koreans, and Russians have fewer offspring—one recent survey found that only *half* of Italian women 16 to 24 said they wanted to have children—they will have less concern for future generations. One British writer, noting that more than one out of every three Scottish women born in the 1960s is now childless, commented, "This looks like a society that has lost the will to live."[9]

AMERICA'S FUNDAMENTAL STRENGTHS

Why does America diverge so dramatically from this global demographic slowdown? The answer lies in the country's unique and fundamental assets—its deep-seated spirit of ingenuity, its robust demographics (including a resourceful stream of ever-assimilating immigrants), and the world's largest, most productive expanse of arable land.[10]

The ability to adjust to economic challenges is the essence of the American story. To be sure, the current housing collapse has created many problems for the financial system and for families, but for millions of others, particularly in high-cost states, it could eventually create new opportunities for home ownership. Although many Americans may be renters for the time being, lower house prices will allow both family balance sheets and communities to regenerate.

This prospect offers a valuable first lesson for those contemplating the likely path of the American future. Throughout our history America has responded to crises—notably, the inevitable excesses of capitalist growth—by reforming itself, both in Washington and at the local level. Between 1900 and 1950, after the traumas of rapid industrial development, the Depression, World War II, and the onset of the Cold War, successive waves of reform—first under the Progressives, then during the presidencies of Franklin Roosevelt and Harry Truman—helped restore public confidence. The public schools and the GI Bill opened up opportunities for the children of immigrants. By the end of World War II, the supposedly unassimilable newcomers had integrated into America in a way that would have been unimaginable to most turn-of-the-century pundits. In addition American capitalism, reformed but also emboldened, proceeded to create both enormous wealth and a pattern of upward mobility unprecedented in world history.

But it would be a mistake to see these successful transitions predominantly as a product of government action. Much important change took place at the family, community, and entrepreneurial levels. Over the centuries American society has drawn its adaptive power from the grassroots, through the efforts of communities, churches, entrepreneurs, and families.

On the street level, lonely reformers at urban missions, in religious institutions, and in political parties paced the integration of an ever-more-heterogeneous population.[11] Whether on the Great Plains or in the densest cities, immigrants made their place in a new society by building up their own businesses, churches, and community institutions.

These traits provide the United States with what Japanese scholar Fuji Kamiya has described as *sokojikara:* a reserve power that allows it to overcome both the inadequacies of its leaders and the foibles of its citizens.[12] This power can be seen throughout America's evolution, as the country faced daunting challenges but found the means to overcome them.

THE RISE OF DECLINISM

The optimism that underlies this book's thesis may seem out of place in a time of recession and war. Americans feel increasingly anxious about many facets of contemporary life, in particular the future that their children will inherit.[13] The reasons are not hard to discern: a profoundly disturbed economy, the threat of environmental disaster, the rise of lethal terrorist organizations, multiple foreign wars, and pervasive political corruption. Many prognosticators see these developments as harbingers of an inevitable American decline.

One common conceit among recent major historians has been to see analogies between America today and the Roman and British empires in their dotage. Perhaps the most influential statement of this thesis was Yale history professor Paul Kennedy's 1987 tome, *The Rise and Fall of the Great Powers*.[14] A host of more contemporary thinkers have also adopted, to some degree, the notion of American decline.[15]

The best the United States can do, according to this pessimistic view, is downscale its expectations and emulate the modesty and economy of other countries.[16] "There is much to be said for being a Denmark or Sweden, even a Great Britain, France or Italy," Andrew Hacker suggested in 1971.[17] More than thirty-five years later author Parag Khanna envisions a "shrunken" America that is lucky to eke out a meager existence between a "triumphant China" and a "retooled Europe."[18] America, notes critic Morris Berman, "is running on empty."[19]

This pessimism extends to the highest perches of business and government, even to those who have benefited most from our national fecundity. Both Microsoft founder Bill Gates and investor Warren Buffett have declared the United States to be a nation in decline, as they shift their own assets to China, India, and other rising countries. In 2005 Gates expressed his enthusiasm for China's state-directed, market-oriented authoritarianism by describing it as a "brand-new form of capitalism," seeming to endorse, or at least condone, that country's rapid but centrally controlled form of economic competition.

For a generation now much of the American intelligentsia has embraced the notion of American decline sometimes with something akin to glee. Historian Immanuel Wallerstein, for example, asserts that the United States has been "a fading global power" since the 1970s. The only question now, he suggests, is "whether the United States can devise a way to descend gradually, with minimum damage to the world, and to itself."[20] Nor is such pessimism the exclusive preserve of left-of-center academic elites. Wall Street power brokers Jeffrey Garten and Peter Peterson, as well as military analyst Edward Luttwak, have all suggested that the United States has become unmoored from its traditions and is now economically and politically weak.[21]

Many prominent conservatives also believe the nation is on a downward path, a belief that has been exacerbated by the political ascendancies of Barack Obama and, at least temporarily, of liberal Democrats in Congress. Pat Buchanan, Paul Craig Roberts, and Samuel Huntington have all recently expressed concern about erosions of republican virtue, entrepreneurial ingenuity, or our supposed Anglo-Saxon national ethnic identity. Huntington in particular writes powerfully of the "immediate and present challenge" that multicultural assaults pose to "the American cultural identity," including fealty to the Constitution and our historic ties to Western civilization. As conservatives have done throughout history, they mourn the perceived fading of a glorious past, and they fear for the future.[22]

Perhaps more influential have been concerns about environmental deterioration, the depletion of natural resources, and the threat of global warning. A looming environmental crisis has been widely predicted since the energy crisis of the 1970s. Ehrlich's *The Population Bomb* (1968) and the Club of Rome report *The Limits to Growth* (1972) became prophetic gospel to many in the academy, the media, and the policy world. Predictions of mass starvation, as well the imminent depletion of all gold, mercury, tin, zinc, petroleum, and gas, went largely unchallenged.[23]

Nearly four decades later such prognostications have proved at best premature, yet the notion of an inevitable environmental collapse and of profound shortages in basic commodities has, if anything, gained adherents. Not surprisingly, the prospect of an additional hundred million Americans by 2050 worries some environmentalists, who see in such growth the expanded "ecological footprint" of a wasteful, profligate nation. Some environmentalists have even joined traditionally conservative xenophobes and anti-immigration activists in calling for a "national population policy" aimed at slowing population growth by severely limiting immigration.[24]

The notion of inevitable American decline, although often accurate in its critique of aspects of American society, consistently underestimates America's proven adaptability, its *sokojikara*. The United States still possesses the fundamental tools—human and material resources, entrepreneurship, and stable political institutions—to overcome the likely potential threats to its preeminence. Perhaps the greatest danger would be to take the notion of inevitable decline to heart and in the process lose the motivation to meet the coming challenges.

THE UNITED STATES AND ITS COMPETITORS

For much of the 20th century many Americans were deeply pessimistic about the nation's ability to compete against foreign countries and against economic systems, especially (at different times) Germany, Japan, and the Soviet Union. In the mid-1950s a majority were convinced that we were losing the Cold War. In the 1980s Harvard's John Kenneth Galbraith thought the Soviet model successful enough that the two systems would eventually "converge." In the 1970s and 1980s George Lodge, Lester Thurow, and Robert Reich all pointed to Europe and Japan as the nations slated to beat the United States on the economic battlefield.[25] "Japan is replacing America as the world's strongest economic power," Lawrence Krause, a scholar at Brookings, told a Joint Economic Committee of Congress in 1986. "It is in everyone's interest that the transition goes smoothly."[26]

Yet the record of American economic adjustment repeatedly has shown that despite occasional periods of turbulence, the country is far more adaptable than its competitors—and it is likely to remain this way. By the mid-2000s, according to a European Commission survey, the

EU at its current rate of innovation would take fifty years to catch up technologically with the United States.[27]

When the financial crisis hit in 2008, observers on both sides of the Atlantic quickly embraced the belief that Europe possessed a more adaptable economic system. But in a matter of months these economic assumptions unraveled, as the recession sparked more overt social unrest in Europe than in the United States and equal, and, in some countries, more precipitous, declines in employment and gross domestic product.

This fact is all the more remarkable since the economic crisis started in the United States; but European financial institutions too had been deeply involved in the purchase of mortgage-based securities and other risky investments. Nor are the future prospects for Europe's ascendancy particularly bright. Overall, according to the European Central Bank, the Euro-zone's overall growth potential is now roughly half that of the United States.[28]

Today most political prognosticators identify China and India as posing the greatest challenges to American predominance. In 2009 British author Martin Jacques, former editor of the defunct publication *Marxism Today* and now a columnist for the *Guardian* newspaper, published a book called *When China Rules the World*. Based largely on projections from recent growth rates, Jacques predicts that by 2050 China will easily surpass America economically, militarily, and politically. A dominant, racially homogenous, communalistic "Middle Kingdom" of unprecedented global power, Jacques warns, will emerge.

But China, like America's former great rival, Russia, lacks the basic environmental protections, the reliable legal structures, the favorable demographics, and the social resilience of the United States. Inequality, a growing issue in most countries (including America), has been rising even more quickly in theoretically egalitarian China, which could further undermine its long-term social stability. China's tendency to ascribe superiority to the Han race, so critical to Jacques's thesis, will also limit its ability to project itself onto a world that will remain predominantly non-Chinese.[29]

Some have predicted that China will become the world's largest economy as early as 2020, but this too is far from certain. Earlier predictions of eventual Soviet, European, and Japanese preeminence, after all, proved staggeringly off the mark. And as David Kampf, a former USAID official, points out, even at overall parity in economic output, China is certain to lag far behind in per capita income. The country's lack of democratic institutions, its cultural homogeneity, its historic insularity, and the rapid aging that will start by the 2020s do not augur well for its global preeminence.

India, for its part, still has an overwhelmingly impoverished population as well as ethnic, religious, and regional conflicts. The vast majority of the population remains semiliterate and lives in poor rural villages. Divisions by caste, religion, and region remain deeply embedded in the culture. India's stockpile of engineers and other scientists appears to be vastly exaggerated. The United States still produces far more engineers per capita than does either India or China.[30]

To be sure, India and China will likely emerge as the greatest powers to reckon with in 2050, far more so than Europe. They may well be America's most important economic competitors and even its political rivals. But given their stages of development and deep-seated challenges, they are not likely to surpass the United States in economic prowess and overall global influence.

THE FUTURE ECONOMIC LANDSCAPE

Above all, America's continuing demographic vitality will drive its economic resilience in the coming decades. As many other advanced countries become dominated by the elderly,[31] the United States will have the benefit of a millennial baby boomlet: in the decade 2010–20 the children of the original baby boomers will start having offspring. This next surge in growth may be delayed if tough economic times continue, but over time the rise in births, producing a generation slightly larger than the boomers, will add to the workforce, boost consumer spending, and allow for new creative inputs. It could well lead to an American economy twice the size of Europe's, making the United States a primary market for firms from around the world.[32]

Perhaps more important, America's flexible business culture will be able to tap these demographics in order to meet the challenges of competitors both new and traditional. The failures of Wall Street's investment banks and other financial institutions do not signal the end of American capitalism. New investment vehicles will emerge, as will the dynamic locally based banks that avoided the most arcane and dangerous financial instruments. Some of these banks are now quite small or not even in existence, but as the country grows, they will evolve, both in traditional financial centers like New York and elsewhere.

Immigrants will no doubt play a leading role in the next economic transition. Recent newcomers have already distinguished themselves as entrepreneurs, forming businesses from street-level *bodegas* to the most sophisticated technology companies. Between 1990 and 2005 immigrants started one-quarter of all venture-backed public companies. Large American firms are also increasingly led by people with roots in foreign countries, including fourteen of the CEOs of the 2007 Fortune 100. Even corporate America—once the almost-exclusive reserve of native-born Anglo-Saxons—will become as post-ethnic as the larger society.[33]

Many of those who used to be considered of "retirement age" also will likely play a greater role in the 21st-century economy, in part due to home-based work and less-rigid retirement schemes. Freed by new technologies and a culture that rewards entrepreneurship, many Americans, including those in their fifties and beyond, will locate where they wish and consistently reinvent what they do.[34]

Tough economic times and shrunken pensions, of course, may also keep people in the workforce far longer than they ever expected. According to recent research by the Kauffman Foundation, people in their fifties are already the most likely to start new companies, either by choice or by necessity, due to weakened pensions and layoffs. In early 2009 RetirementJobs.com, a major career site for job-seekers over fifty, claimed that its visitor count had nearly quadrupled in the previous six months.

This process is likely to continue, even with an economic recovery. Prior to the recession of 2008, nearly one in four Americans reported they did not intend to retire when they hit their sixties, as was once considered the norm. Some of these seniors may end up in full-time jobs, but many others will work part time or may serve as mentors to younger businesses. In any case, the seniors may well prove less of a burden and more a powerful reserve force for the American economy.[35]

HOW WE WILL LIVE IN 2050

America's population growth will continue to change our lifeways, creating huge opportunities for new communities, goods, and services. An ever-more-diversified country will produce numerous thriving submarkets, from immigrants to aging boomers to superaffluents.

Suburbia—currently the predominant form of American life—will probably remain the focal point of innovations in development. Despite criticisms that suburbs are culturally barren, energy inefficient, or suitable only for young families, 80 percent or more of the total U.S. metropolitan population growth has taken place in suburbia, confounding oft-repeated predictions of its inevitable decline.[36]

By the mid-21st century this pattern will likely accelerate. The reasons are not hard to identify: suburbs experience faster job and income growth, far lower crime rates (roughly one third), and much higher rates of home ownership. While cities will always exercise a strong draw for younger people, the appeal often proves to be short-lived; and as people enter their thirties and beyond, they generally prefer suburbs. This pattern will become more pronounced as the huge millennial generation—those born after 1983—enters this age cohort.[37]

Over the next few decades, however, suburban communities will evolve beyond the conventional 1950s-style "production suburbs," vast housing tracts constructed far from existing commercial and industrial centers. The suburbs of the 21st century will increasingly incorporate aspects of preindustrial villages. They will be more compact and self-sufficient, providing office space as well as a surging home-based workforce.

As a result, they will be less reliant on major cities and on long-distance commuting. Boasting traditional urban functions like markets, churches, museums, monuments, and culture, they will be more like traditional villages. Their primary advantage will be quality of daily life, but with a huge added difference—instantaneous communication links with the rest of the world.

To be sure, some aspects of suburban life—notably long-distance commuting and reliance on fossil fuels—will gradually have to be changed, but this transition will be carried out primarily not by government fiat but by market forces and the introduction of new technologies, particularly energy-efficient cars. The growing use of the Internet, wireless phones, video conferencing, and other communication technologies will allow even more people to commute from home: at least one in four or five will work full or part time from their residence. After the 1970s "oil shock" Americans turned to smaller, fuel-efficient cars; similarly, advances in transportation technology and new fuel sources will make suburbs more sustainable and prevent their much-anticipated decline.

Surveys of housing preferences consistently show that if given the choice, most Americans, particularly families, will still opt for a place with a spot of land and a little breathing room.[38] Despite the coming population growth, most Americans will probably continue to resist being forced into density; and even with one hundred million more people, the country will still be only one sixth as crowded as Germany.[39]

Most indications suggest that aging baby boomers will stay in the suburbs until very late in life or move farther out into the countryside. A movement of seniors back to the city has been much ballyhooed; one *Newsweek* article said it had turned into a "steady stream." Seniors en masse, it reported, were "forfeiting regular tee time in favor of loft living, opera tickets and bistros."[40]

But surveys and analyses of demographic patterns show that this movement is, in fact, small. A 2008 Pew study found urbanites to be less satisfied with where they live than those living in suburbs or rural areas.[41] Of course, aging suburbanites will also require new kinds of housing, with smaller lots and more restaurants, shops, religious institutions, and cultural venues within walking or shuttle distance than is common in today's suburbs. The suburbs of the 21st century will also be more diverse than in the past, with more seniors, singles, and minorities.[42]

Maintaining this dispersed lifestyle in an environmentally responsible way will be a critical challenge. In countries where education levels have risen and housing has become both expensive and extraordinarily dense—Japan, Germany, South Korea, and Singapore—birthrates have become very low.[43] Preserving suburbs is thus critical for our demographic vitality, not least for attracting immigrants. Suburbs serve, in many ways, as nurseries of the nation and epitomize much of what

constitutes—particularly for immigrants and the aspiring middle class—
the American dream.[44]

THE FUTURE OF CITIES

The persistent appeal of suburbia does not mean that America's urban
centers are doomed—on the contrary, the United States will remain a
nation of great cities. Throughout the history of civilization, cities have
been engines for social, cultural, and economic activity. The market for
dense urban existence is likely to remain small compared to suburbs,
but there will still be massive opportunities to provide for as many as
fifteen to twenty million new urban dwellers by 2050.[45]

In the coming decades cities will perform some new functions. Some
will continue to serve as what Wharton business professor Joe Gyourko
has called "superstar cities." San Francisco, Boston, Manhattan, and the
western edge of Los Angeles already function as "productive resorts"—
places adapted both to business and to recreation—for the elite and
those who work for them. By 2050 Seattle, Portland, and Austin could
join their ranks. These elite cities are becoming too expensive for the
middle class, who will seek other places to buy homes, find employment, and raise families elsewhere.

Although lacking a large middle class, these cities will continue to
draw the affluent, particularly those with inherited wealth, as well as
nomadic groups like college students and recent immigrants. After all,
these cities contain many of the nation's most vibrant cultural institutions, research centers, colleges, and universities and much of its most
attractive architecture. They will remain irresistible for millions of people under thirty and, given some reasonable reform, could grow their
populations and economies.

Superstar cities will sit atop the urban economic food chain, somewhat aloof from the rest of country, and will experience modest growth.

But for most Americans the focus of urban life will shift to cities that are more spread out and, by some standards, less intrinsically attractive.[46] These new "cities of aspiration"—Phoenix, Houston, Dallas, Atlanta, and Charlotte—will perform many of the functions as centers for upward mobility that New York and other great industrial cities once did.

Over time these cities will compete with the "superstars" for finance, culture, and media industries and the amenities that typically go along with them. Money and commercial success has already turned Houston, once considered the ultimate backwater, into "an art mecca," as the *Wall Street Journal* called it. Similar progressions will be seen in other dynamic cities in the decades to come.[47]

ENERGY, CLIMATE CHANGE, AND THE HEARTLAND

One of the least anticipated developments in the nation's 21st-century geography will be the resurgence of the American Heartland, often dismissed by coastal dwellers as "flyover country." For the better part of the 20th century rural and small-town communities declined in percentage of population and in economic importance. In 1940, 40 percent of Americans lived in rural areas; within three decades that percentage fell by half.[48]

But as the nation gains one hundred million people, population and cost pressures are destined to resurrect the nation's vast hinterlands. This trend has already begun in parts of the South and the Intermountain West, to which there has been a large-scale migration from the expensive, crowded coasts. The growth capacity for "megacities" like New York, Chicago, and Los Angeles, as well as their residents' desire for more crowding, may be limited. As conditions in the urban megalopolis of cities, suburbs, and exurbs become more crowded and expensive, more Americans will be pushed farther out.[49]

As happens with dispersion in general, these Americans will leave because they prefer to. According to recent surveys, as many as one in three American adults would prefer to live in a rural area—compared to the 20-odd percent who actually do. Most Americans perceive rural America as epitomizing traditional values of family, religion, and self-sufficiency and as being more attractive, friendly, and safe, particularly for children.[50]

As high costs, crime, congestion, and other woes have spread beyond inner cities, the movement out of the Heartland has shown signs of slowing and likely will reverse.[51] One critical factor in the Heartland's growing relevance is the advent of the Internet, which has broken the traditional isolation of rural communities. As the technology of mass communications improves, the movement of technology companies, business service, and manufacturing firms into the hinterland is likely to accelerate. This will be not so much a movement to remote hamlets, but to the growing number of dynamic small cities and towns spread throughout the Heartland.[52]

Pressing concerns over global energy and hydrocarbon emissions will bolster the importance of America's interior regions. As world competition for energy supplies intensifies, the primary advantage for the United States—in contrast to China, India, Japan, and the European Union—will be the vast natural abundance of its Heartland regions.

The belief that America was commodity rich faded in the 1950s, when the nation first became a net importer of raw materials.[53] But in relative terms, the United States retains enormous energy resources, including coal and other fossil fuels, notably natural gas. Louisiana, Montana, Wyoming, the Dakotas, and the great Permian Basin of West Texas possess huge stockpiles of carbon-based energy. By 2009 new large-scale discoveries of natural gas—a relatively clean fuel—boosted estimates of future domestic supplies to enough to last one hundred years. These energy finds will probably be exploited as energy technology improves.[54]

Overall, North America is the world's second-largest reservoir of conventional energy. In the coming decades dependence on less reliable, distant sources such as the Persian Gulf, Venezuela, Russia, and Nigeria will be understood to present a clear danger to the national interest, in terms of both security and finance. New investment will flow back into the Heartland to tap previously difficult-to-access resources, while new technologies will reduce their negative environmental effects.[55]

Over the longer term the Heartland is likely to play a pivotal role in the century's most important environmental and economic challenge: the shift to renewable fuels. By 2030, due to incentives for new energy sources, even Exxon expects oil demand to have weakened by 22 percent. Fortunately, the American Heartland is well positioned to foster this transition.

Recent estimates suggest that the United States has enough productive capacity to produce more than 1.3 billion dry tons of biomass a year, enough to displace 30 percent or more of the current national demand for transportation fuels. This amount could be produced with only modest changes in land use, in agricultural and forest management practices, and in production of food and fiber.[56]

The Heartland, consigned to the fringes of American society and economy in the 20th century, is poised to enjoy a significant renaissance in the early 21st. Not since the 19th century, when it was a major source of America's economic, social, and cultural supremacy, has the vast continental expanse been set to play so powerful a role in shaping the nation's future.

AN EVER-MORE-DISTINCT POPULATION

By the middle of the 21st century, America will have no clear "majority" race; rather, the dazzling and complex composite will include a large and growing population with mixed racial heritages. Latino and Asian populations are expected to triple. Today 30 percent of the U.S. population is nonwhite; in 2050 this figure may reach nearly 50 percent. Today, due to high Latino birthrates, one in five American children under the age of five is Hispanic; future growth of the Latino and Asian populations will be based less on immigration, which could ebb somewhat, than on childbearing. At the dawn of the new millennium American-born Latinos accounted for roughly half of the group's growth, and by 2009 the percentage was estimated as over two thirds. The multiracial society now emerging in a few places—such as southern California—will become ever more commonplace in the rest of the country.[57]

One critical factor is the continuing movement of minorities and immigrants into the suburbs, where racial enclaves are fewer than in urban neighborhoods. The best places to find America's Hindu temples and new mosques are not in the teeming cities but in the outer suburbs of Los Angeles, New York, and Houston. But these areas are rarely dominated by one ethnicity, and alongside the temples and mosques you will also find churches and synagogues.[58]

In contrast, the nation's chief global rivals seem far less able to accommodate this level of immigration. China, Japan, and Korea are culturally resistant to diversity and unlikely to welcome large-scale immigration even if much of their labor force has to go to work in walkers and wheelchairs. Given Europe's current considerable problems integrating its immigrants, particularly Muslims, the continent seems ill disposed to open its doors further; Denmark and the Netherlands are considering measures to sharply restrict immigration.[59]

At the same time European influence on America's ethnic character, although proportionately less, will continue to play a role. Indeed, many talented young Europeans have escaped the continental nursing home by heading to the United States. One influential social commentator, Richard Florida, has claimed that the bright lights and "tolerance" of Europe attract skilled American labor to the point that an exodus threatens, but actual migration trends tell quite the opposite story: the large net flow of immigration is crossing the Atlantic westward to the United States and Canada or going to Australia.[60]

By far the largest groups of immigrants to the United States come from Latin America, Africa, China, and other developing countries. The United Nations estimates that two million people will move to developed countries annually until 2050, and more than half will come to the United States.[61] The United States also remains by far the world's largest destination for educated, skilled migrants. In 2001, according to the Organization for Economic Co-operation and Development (OECD), an association of thirty democratic, free-market countries, the United States was home to nearly eight million skilled immigrants, equaling the combined total for the entire EU, Australia, and Canada. Although this critical migration slowed after 9/11, it picked up again in 2006. The migration again ebbed in 2009 due to the recession, but will likely pick up with future economic growth.[62]

Some of best educated and most successful will then go back home, as has been case through most of American history. But many more will stay, often for very mundane reasons, such as the chance to live in a dwelling larger than a shoebox or to have more than one child. Others will cherish the chance to live without worrying about the depredations of some party bureaucrat, *caudillo*, or religious fanatic. These immigrants are not seeking a spot on the *Titanic*. They realize that, despite its many failings, America is uniquely able to reinvent and re-energize itself—a country with *sokojikara*.

So what will hold this society together? It will not be bloodlines but the ideals and attitudes shaped by a uniquely diverse society. The percentage of Americans of mixed race is growing significantly among people under eighteen; in California and Nevada mixed-marriage rates are at more than 13 percent; and in the rest of the Southwest a heavily Latino population increasingly intermarries with other ethnic groups.[63]

More important still will be changes in racial attitudes, which we can already see among younger Americans. According to market research firm Teen Research Unlimited, 60 percent of American teens say they have friends of different ethnic backgrounds. Even more telling, a 2006 Gallup Poll showed that 95 percent of young people (ages 18 to 29) approved of interracial dating—compared to only 45 percent of respondents over the age of 64. Likewise, a *USA Today*/Gallup Poll conducted in 2008 among teens showed that 57 percent have dated someone of another race or ethnic group—up 40 percent from when Gallup last polled teens on the question, back in 1980.[64]

THE EXCEPTIONAL AMERICANS

America's cultural uniqueness will also be evident in its attitudes toward work and child rearing, and in its moral and religious values. Demographically at least, America may have more in common with Third World countries than with the developed world. The greater presence of children may be the most important point of commonality. Countries where adults' primary concerns center on saving and investing for their offspring and for their offspring's offspring are likely to view the future differently than nations dominated by aging, childless adults.

Importantly, even childless aunts and uncles may share this concern, as they choose to play a supporting role in the lives of their nieces and nephews. In sharp contrast, by 2050, at current rates, 60 percent of Italians will have had no personal experience as a brother, sister, aunt, uncle, or cousin. The extended family may well dissipate into a collection of autonomous individuals such as the world has never before seen.

This commitment to having children, and to the primacy of the family, is connected to a different religious and spiritual orientation. In all countries including the United States, growing affluence and mass education have a dampening effect on people's willingness to have children.[65] But in America it has occurred to a much lesser extent, in large part due to a greater religiosity. Religious people, here as elsewhere, tend to have children more than nonbelievers.[66]

In contrast, a majority of Europeans (apart from Muslim immigrants) appear indifferent or hostile to religion. One analyst, David Hart, has spoken of Europe's "metaphysical boredom." Half or more of Europeans never attend church, compared to barely 20 percent in the United States. Among younger Europeans, the loss of traditional Christian identity—with its focus on long-term commitments, sacrifice, and responsibility—is virtually complete; according to one Belgian demographer, barely one in ten young adults in the EU maintains any link to an organized religion.[67] Korea, Japan, and China show much the same tendency. The vast majority of Japanese do not believe in God or Buddha. South Korea and Taiwan have seen similar drops in religious belief along with their plunging birthrates.[68]

In contrast, Americans retain a much higher tendency toward spirituality and religious belief. Some observers, both in America and abroad, see it as an indication of what one British journalist has called America's "neo-fascist" tendency. But religious belief in America is remarkably varied, extending beyond groups that are easily classified as liberal or conservative. And it is not only conventional religious practice that is exceptionally popular in America. A "spiritual" tradition that extends beyond regular church attendance—dating from the earliest founders and continuing through the transcendentalists and Walt Whitman—persists as a vital force.[69]

BEYOND THE EUROPEAN "MODEL"

Daily life in mid-21st-century America will increasingly diverge from that in other advanced countries. Americans tend to work longer hours and be more career-oriented than their European counterparts. In 2003 Americans worked over 300 more hours than did the average resident of the EU. Hard work appears to be an ingrained American attitude, out of proportion to other countries. This is not to argue that one model is superior to the other, but to point out essential differences between cultures.

As one writer puts it, Europeans "emphasize quality of life over accumulation" and "deep play over unrelenting toil." Some have argued that this attitude is better for people and keeps the production of greenhouse gases down.[70] Even in Japan and Korea, countries long known for a fevered work ethic, concern about the younger generation's tolerance for hard work is now widespread.[71]

In contrast, an America with an additional hundred million citizens seems unlikely to relax its work ethic, especially as more and more Americans try to carve out a place for themselves and their families in a more crowded country. Significantly, despite working more, Americans seem no less satisfied with their harried way of life than do Europeans. In fact, according to polls, they appear much more content than their counterparts in France, Germany, or Italy. As a people, Americans retain an essentially different set of assumptions, maintaining a deeper faith in the future and holding to the notion that success lies fundamentally in their hands. All indications suggest that this basic philosophical difference between Americans and Europeans is likely to grow even more pronounced over time.[72]

THE GREATEST CHALLENGES FACING AMERICA IN 2050

In coming decades the most critical challenge facing the nation may be maintaining the prospect of upward mobility. The promise that "anyone" can reach the highest levels of society has been and remains fundamental to the American ethos. Social mobility is particularly critical as the population grows and the citizenry becomes ever more diverse.

Over the past century the United States has done a remarkable job of fostering the ascent of former outsider groups—Catholics, Jews, southerners, Asians—into the top echelon of business and political leadership. For African-Americans, Latinos, and other nonwhite groups, progress has continued apace, albeit at slower rates, and it will likely continue in the next four decades. It is difficult to imagine the nation ever reverting to the Anglo-Saxon elite structure that predominated before the Second World War, as the recent changes in political leadership, with minorities in elite positions under both presidents George W. Bush and Barack Obama, suggest.[73]

But in America as elsewhere, a globalized society based on knowledge and information has an inherent tendency to create wider class divisions: an expanding affluent class of the highly educated, a stubbornly impoverished population, and a shrinking middle class. Such an economy cannot be easily organized into labor unions, or stopped by workers refusing to work. In many cases, workers who ask for too much in pay and working conditions, or who are too hard to manage, can be replaced by other workers, not only in factories but also in call centers and research labs.

Although American society still experiences considerable mobility, both up and down, wealth has concentrated in fewer hands, with relatively fewer benefits to the working and middle classes. The vast difference in the quality of schooling between poor and affluent areas is a key contributing factor. Perhaps even more disturbing, younger people with degrees have lagged behind in wage growth, suggesting an acceleration of inequality. This could become a longer-term trend, particularly for some of the large millennial generation, as they crowd into a labor market that may be far tougher than the one their boomer parents faced.[74]

Over the long term, as the reformers of the late 19th and 20th centuries knew, class polarization is the greatest threat not only to an essentially egalitarian society but also to society's prosperity and long-term social stability. Impediments to upward mobility, which some studies reveal are occurring, constitute a direct threat to the national ethos. The loss of aspiration could become particularly acute among younger workers, who even before the 2008 recession were suffering diminishing economic prospects.[75]

As the nation moves further toward 2050, to a society that is ethnically less European, larger, and more complex than it is today, another critical question will arise: how can the United States maintain a common ethical center? Ultimately, this unique society will find its binding principle in the notions that have traditionally differentiated it from the rest of world: a common belief system and spiritual core, a sense of a shared destiny, a culture of opportunity, and a recognition of the importance of community and family.

Most other countries—whether in Europe, Asia, or the developing world—rely for unity upon a substructure of racial identity and a distinct cultural heritage or even on the manipulations of colonial mapmakers. America can continue its evolution only to the extent that it fulfills some of its historic mission as a purveyor of classical liberal values. This effort will become more, not less, important as the new powers of the 21st century, notably China, export what has been called their "illiberal challenge" to America's more inclusive and democratic system.[76]

As the British writer G. K. Chesterton once put it, the United States is "the only nation . . . that is founded on a creed." This faith is not, and was not initially meant to be, explicitly religious; rather, it is a fundamentally spiritual idea of a national raison d'être. As George Washington said in his first inaugural in 1789, the fate of the republican "experiment" lay in how the country would live up to "the eternal rules of order and right."[77]

This creed will become ever more important as the United States attempts to cope with its growing diversity, differentiate itself from other nations, and meet the challenge of new aspiring powers. In this emerging future America will need to present to the world a model of a successful society.

Tracking the successful evolution of this emerging society is the primary concern of this book. *The Next Hundred Million* is not a story of power brokers, policy disputes, or media perceptions. Rather, it is an inquiry into the evolution of cities, towns, and neighborhoods, and of industries, churches, and families, both in newly emerging regions and in venerable older ones. It is in these more intimate units, in what Jefferson called our "little republics,"[78] that mid-21st-century America— a nation of four hundred million souls—will find its fundamental sustenance and its best hope for the brightest future.

CHAPTER TWO: THE CITIES OF ASPIRATION

On a warm spring night Tim Cisneros is driving me in his Chevy truck through the wide streets of Houston. Districts and neighborhoods unfold in what seems like an undefined pattern. We started on Westheimer Road, amid the glitter of the River Oaks neighborhood, and are heading over to the Galleria mall, with its towers and shopping centers—glistening monuments to unexamined consumption.

The big engines of Tim's truck growl as we enter nondescript areas filled with the ubiquitous Houston restaurant chains that offer everything from Cajun seafood to tacos, sushi, and barbecue. Then comes a mishmash of ethnic areas—some Hispanic, others Asian—rising suddenly from the flat expanses along Bellaire Road, a sprawling boulevard that cuts through a constantly shifting landscape of middle-class white, Latino, and Asian neighborhoods.

Romulo "Tim" Cisneros grew up in an intensely Mexican-American family in San Antonio. His brother, Henry, rose to become the city's first Latino mayor in recent history. Tim has little time for politics, though, and it's not Houston's Mexicanness that enchants him. Rather, it's the surge of grassroots dynamism that has taken hold in recent years. "Houston is my favorite third-world city," jokes Cisneros, an architect who has offices in the trendy Montrose Section but whose clients include a motley crew of largely suburban Nigerian, Mexican, Chinese, and Indian entrepreneurs. "But it is all changed by capitalism. It's becoming a new city with new opportunities."

Most of his fellow architects, urbanists, and planners detest Houston's seemingly hodgepodge patterns of development, Tim acknowledges. But the tall, lanky Cisneros thinks this is precisely the kind of ever-evolving city that can absorb the next generations of Americans who will seek urban homes. Talking in a rapid-fire way, with an accent that reveals a South Texas twang, Cisneros speaks of an evolving urban constellation of moderately dense nodes—homes, town houses, condos—connected by a network of roads, bus lanes, and fiber-optic cables.

As we head down the city's ethnically diverse Bellaire Road, Cisneros even sings praises for Houston's ubiquitous strip malls. These low-cost areas, he argues, provide opportunities for ethnic restaurateurs and other entrepreneurs who could never afford the kind of carefully planned dense spaces that most urbanists favor. They offer close-by services and sometimes the land for the new town house developments that he and his partners have put up.

To Cisneros, what makes a city great is opportunity—not only for himself but for the Indian-American doctors, Columbian and Mexican restaurateurs, and Chinese mall-builders who keep him busy even in tough times. People come to Houston not simply to live for a phase of their lives but to improve their economic station. As he recounts:

> It's amazing. Every time I go out there's something new out there. You have seventy thousand people moving here every year, and some of them are young, like the engineer making $80,000 a year who'd live like crap back east or in California but here can buy a cool condo. Houston is so big that you don't have to worry about the dream getting too expensive because there's so much new product. It will take a generation to fill it in.[1]

FROM ANTI-CITY TO NEW CITY

Urbanists have been frequently decried cities like Houston, with their dispersed economic and residential patterns, as "anti-cities." Jane Jacobs, despite her considerable genius, never understood or appreciated such places; she never recognized that vast, multipolar Houston, Phoenix, and Los Angeles represented a vital new urban form. Instead, she saw sprawling Los Angeles as "a vast blind-eyed reservation."[2]

Such attitudes have proven as shortsighted as it would have been for a 19th-century Florentine to view then-new industrial Manchester as an "anti-city." Like industrial Manchester, today's new American cities have embraced a new form of urbanism, shaped by factors unique to their historical development. Manchester arose from the mechanization and power of the early industrial age; the new American cities are products of a vast availability of land, technology growth, and the high level of affluence enjoyed by late-20th-century Americans who could afford to purchase cars and homes.

In many ways this postindustrial model hearkens back to preindustrial patterns of settlement, reinforced by advances in transportation and, increasingly, telecommunications. It represents both a return to older traditions of an organic, unplanned urbanism, but with a new technology-enabled freedom in terms of distance.

The dominant form of 21st-century urbanism has developed under conditions markedly different from those of earlier eras and from European models. Demographics and timing, notes urban theorist Ali Modarres, shaped America's urban patterns in ways not seen in previous civilizations. For example, over the second half of the 20th century America's population grew by 130 million, essentially doubling, while the populations of France, Germany, and Britain together increased by 40 million, or 25 percent. This growth, Modarres suggests, took place during a period in which the automobile became more dominant.

America's population is also younger than Europe's, which led to an emphasis on single-family homes and suburblike development.[3]

This population increase sparked the growth first of Los Angeles and later of Phoenix, Dallas, Houston, Atlanta, Miami, and Las Vegas. Such fast-growing cities have virtually no European equivalent, for America's pattern of urban growth also reflects the country's enormous land mass, so different from that of its European counterparts. American urbanism, like all other aspects of America, continues to be shaped, as Tocqueville noted in the 1830s, by "the nature of its territory."[4]

The profound shift in the nation's urban geography toward these enormous new cities has exceeded the expectations of many observers. In 1967, for example, the prominent futurist Herman Kahn correctly predicted the rise of huge, sprawling megaregions, but he projected that one in four Americans would live between Boston and Washington; in fact, less than one in five were living there in 2000.[5]

Kahn's predictions about enormous, sprawling megalopolitan regions, including cities, suburbs, and exurbs, were correct, but he underestimated their number and the extent of their dispersion. By 2030, according to one recent estimate, the nation will be dominated by ten different so-called megalopolitan areas, but only two—New York and Chicago—will be located in the traditional urban bastions of the Northeast and the Midwest. The vast majority of these giant regional centers will be in the South and the West; most of the growth will take place around late-20th-century boomtowns such as Los Angeles, Phoenix, Houston, Dallas, Atlanta, and Miami.[6] All of them will share the basic characteristics of L.A.: they will be multipolar, auto-dependent, and geographically vast.

In this century the urban landscape will continue to evolve in ways that few 20th-century observers could have predicted. Phoenix, Houston, Dallas, and Atlanta, for example, are now four of the nation's top ten largest metropolitan areas; not one of them would have made that list as recently as 1960.[7] Although this growth tends to slow during periods of economic stagnation, the long-term trajectory seems likely to continue. Indeed, according to census projections, these areas are expected to enjoy the most robust growth of all U.S. regions.

In the 21st century individuals, families, and businesses will have ever more freedom to locate where they wish. This trend will accelerate the expansion of some cities as well as the development of diverse environments, from gritty downtowns to low- and moderate-density inner-ring communities, and from dense suburbs to ever-farther-reaching outer rings. But most of the urban growth will take place not on the older model of New York or Chicago but along the lines of Los Angeles, Houston, and Phoenix.

THE LOS ANGELES MODEL

Los Angeles evolved as the archetype for this new kind of city. Rising out of a broad, dry basin along the Pacific, L.A. has confounded aesthetes for almost a century. In contrast to its urbane rival, San Francisco, the sprawling city possesses few charms for observers from the East Coast and Europe. Its unorthodox settlement pattern has led observers to describe the place as "nineteen suburbs in search of a metropolis" or "less a city than a perpetual convention." Some writers have been even harsher. Aldous Huxley deemed it "the city of Dreadful Joy," while William Faulkner dismissed it as "the plastic asshole of the world."[8]

Yet Los Angeles, which possessed a mere hundred thousand inhabitants at the turn of the 20th century, has emerged as the essential model for the 21st-century city. Conceived as a bucolic collection of suburbs, it has matured into a dense network of communities, organized more like the random-access memory of a computer than the linear, hierarchical pattern that was common to cities for millennia.

Long before the emergence of other Sunbelt and southern cities,

Los Angeles initiated a fundamental change in urban development. In the early 20th century, rising cities generally aspired to become the "next" New York or Chicago; Los Angeles created a completely different model that rejected the legacy of crowded slums and belching factories. Blessed with a mild climate, clear vistas, ample land, and a lightly industrialized economy, the city, according to one prominent local cleric, hoped to become "a place of inspiration for nobler living."[9]

The L.A. vision—shaped by real estate developers, civic leaders, and even some religious figures—was indeed a radical one: it replaced the traditional, critical urban core with a constellation of smaller subcenters. Manufacturing plants would be "transferred" to the city's outskirts. The working class would live, not in crowded tenements, but in neat, single-family homes.[10]

To realize this novel vision, in 1908 Los Angeles enacted the nation's first comprehensive urban zoning ordinance, one that encouraged decentralization, single-family homes, and dispersed industrial development.[11] Unlike New York, Los Angeles developed its economy in tandem with its housing. Early on, downtown was relegated to relative unimportance. Los Angeles, noted historian Carey McWilliams, was "the first modernized decentralized industrial city in America"—but it would not be the last.[12]

Los Angeles's natural attractions, and its leadership's willingness to develop critical infrastructure, fostered the growth of new, future-oriented industries. After all, it lacked the traditional prerequisites for a successful city: a natural harbor, a significant river or lake, even an adequate water supply. L.A.'s ascendance represented, as two historians put it, "a remarkable victory of human cunning over the so-called limits of nature."[13]

The first of these new industries was the film business. By the Second World War the movie business had grown to be one of America's eleven largest industries. It was a perplexing business, as McWilliams noted in 1946, one that "required no raw materials, for which discriminatory freight rates were meaningless, and which, at the same time, possessed an enormous payroll."[14]

The second component of the emerging Los Angeles economy was science-based development. Robert Millikan, the visionary president of Caltech, argued that the new city must "use more resourcefulness, more intelligence, more scientific and engineering brains."[15] Exploiting Los Angeles's nearly perfect flying weather, he and others built one of the world's densest concentrations of aerospace development. They were aided by World War II, which boosted aircraft employment to over 120,000 workers.[16]

The region's novel industries generated explosive growth. Between 1900 and 1940 the population rose by a phenomenal 1,500 percent.[17] From 1940 to the mid-1970s the number of technical and professional workers there jumped at five times the rate of the East Coast.[18] "Technologies exploded," recalled Tex Thornton, a former aide to Howard Hughes and founder of Litton Industries. "Technologies that went first to the military would then spill into new products like computers, calculators, and other devices."[19]

The beneficiaries of these technologies were in no way limited to L.A.; they would play a critical role in the expansion of Houston, Miami, Phoenix, Atlanta, and eventually the vast sprawl that grew around Washington, D.C. But in all these cities, from the swamplands of Florida to the deserts of Arizona, the model was not New York or San Francisco but Los Angeles.

L.A. AFTER L.A.

Despite Los Angeles's influence, it was not the culminating version of this new model. Like many experiments, this one had ample opportunity to go awry—and it frequently has. Throughout the 1950s and

1960s the reach of Los Angeles extended ever farther across and then over the coastal plain, but the racial riots that erupted in 1965 and again in 1992, as well as a persistent problem with air pollution, led many to reject Los Angeles as the harbinger of a new urban model.

Instead of representing urbanity's best hope, L.A. became increasingly identified as its worst nightmare. Cities, both traditional and new, frequently have pledged not to become "another Los Angeles." Others simply saw Los Angeles as the culminating disaster of capitalism, existing, as Marxist writer Mike Davis put it, "on the hard edge of postmodernity."[20]

In addition, the fact that much of the 1992 rioting took place in older, working-class suburbs—places that once epitomized the promise of the "better city" for the aspiring middle class—provided fodder for those who saw in Los Angeles's vast sprawl a failed urban model. These areas, suggested UCLA historian Eugen Weber, were now "suburban badlands, ageing garden cities" well on their way to becoming "crabgrass slums." Rather than a new and improved model for human habitation, these areas, he claimed, "offer only junk-food versions of urbanity."[21]

Despite these setbacks, Los Angeles has created the template for the development of virtually all major American cities in the 21st century. We are, after all, unlikely to see any future New Yorks or Chicagos, metropolitan regions dominated by thriving centers, skyscraper skylines, and huge expanses of tall apartment blocks. Some developments in selected urban cores—particularly those formerly given over to industrial or commercial activities—may expand to accommodate growing populations, but the notion of a Houston, Charlotte, Phoenix, or Dallas replicating the centralized model of Manhattan seems highly unlikely, given resistance from largely lower-density communities close to the core and a transportation grid fixed primarily on the automobile.

On the contrary, we will see much more exportation of Los Angeles–style urbanism, in the rise of master planned communities such as Irvine and Valencia, in the faux downtown landscapes of Century City, Universal Citywalk, and their offspring, and in the processions of ethnic-oriented minimalls. Even modern "urban entertainment centers"—areas packed with cultural institutions, restaurants, and sports arenas like those in downtown Indianapolis and Phoenix—draw their inspiration from southern California or from its more outrageous progeny, Las Vegas. Fundamentally these centers are cramped versions of family-oriented theme parks like Disneyland and of the lifestyle centers associated with L.A.'s suburban mall developers.[22]

"VOTING WITH YOUR FEET"

Los Angeles's troubled bout with its own maturity—especially with rising land and housing prices during the 1990s and in the first six years of the new millennium—also unintentionally accelerated the development of new burgeoning centers that embraced, consciously or not, it as a model. Starting in the 1960s, the "new Los Angeles" was Phoenix. Like its Californian counterpart, Phoenix epitomized all the clichés of plasticity and impermanence associated with the new American city. And like Los Angeles, it drew ambitious newcomers seeking a better life, particularly in the form of mild winters and ease of getting around. In the 2000 census, almost a third of residents had arrived within the previous five years.[23]

Local entrepreneur Deb Weidenhamer, who came to the Valley of the Sun in 1970 and opened an auction business, says the rapid growth and basic openness to newcomers has created unprecedented opportunities for her: "We came with nothing. We came here because it had wealth that was increasing. You can find opportunities. People come here for a new start and come with ambitions. Longevity here doesn't matter here. You can be here ten years and it's like you're an old fogy—in the East Coast you'd be like a newcomer."

Virtually all of Weidenhamer's employees, she notes, also come from outside the region. They create what she calls a "multiplier" effect, with each person bringing new ideas and new energies. "In San Francisco or New York you would have to compete with entrenched companies. Here you can always market the new people," she suggested at her crowded warehouse. "There's always a new zip code to service."[24]

As in Los Angeles, the Second World War accelerated the development of new technology and business-service firms in Phoenix. Initially the desire was to base more production farther from potentially vulnerable sites on the coasts; that brought several thousand skilled engineers and scientists to the area.[25] But later the city itself—with its low-density lifestyle, its brilliant sunshine, and its lack of social constraints—brought waves of high-technology firms to the region.

Many leading urban thinkers, however, have been less than impressed. Much like Los Angeles, Phoenix has often been criticized from within and without as lacking the finer aspects of civic life, including style and culture. Its sprawling array of separate districts and its relatively weak downtown have led some, like the prominent new urbanist Andres Duany, to conclude that Phoenix is a place where "civic life has ceased to exist." Duany, like Emerson a century earlier, hailed Boston as an example of a superior kind of community.[26]

But in the next few decades Phoenix, not Boston, will represent the predominant form of urbanization. Like many older metropolises, Boston and its environs have been either losing residents—particularly middle-class families—or growing slowly. The same can be said of Chicago, San Francisco, and even Washington, D.C., whose population growth rate has remained well below that of cities like Phoenix. Although this growth likely will slow in response to the housing downturn that began in 2007, the historic pattern—with ever-growing L.A.-style multiple centers—is likely to recur eventually, as people begin to purchase or rent increasingly affordable homes, condos, or apartments.[27]

THE NEW URBAN MODEL: BEYOND THE "BIG IT"

Phoenix and Los Angeles epitomize the new urban model, wherein the downtown core plays a relatively minor role. This dispersion is particularly evident in employment patterns. Despite billions of dollars spent on public investment, less than 3 percent of all workers in the L.A. and Phoenix regions work in the downtown area, compared to some 20 percent in the New York and Washington regions.

Most urbanists view this dispersion as reflecting an essentially dysfunctional metropolis that needs to be saved by heavy investment in the central core.[28] Much is made of the symbolic role of downtown in the urban psyche. According to former Milwaukee mayor John Norquist, "In almost any metropolitan area in the country, the local news begins with an aerial view of the downtown skyline. Why? Simply because the downtown is the most striking visual aspect of a city. Imagine starting the news each night with an image of a suburban strip mall and its parking lot. . . . Celebrations, charity races, parades and festivals—incongruous in malls or edge cities—are usually held downtown."[29]

Some in the new multipolar cities have adopted these aspirations—with decidedly mixed results. One prominent Phoenix consultant describes its downtown as "the glorious goose that's laying the gilded egg" that will turn the city into a dynamic trend-setter of a new urban paradigm. In contrast, the burgeoning suburbs and surrounding independent cities "make us big, but do not make us strong." Phoenix, he opined, "won't be a place of renown till it has the Big It." In other words, Phoenix will not be a true metropolis until it has its own Times Square, Eiffel Tower, Space Needle, or other grand attraction.[30]

But in the newer cities the quest for "big it" is often delusional. In New York, Boston, and San Francisco, the central core provides a kind of "sacred space," a place with a hold on the collective memory of a large part of the population. In the newer cities a large proportion of the population arrived decades after the original downtown lost its primacy.[31] People have their own notion of what "it" is, and many times "it" could be in a different center or in more than one center spread across the metropolitan fabric.

In coming decades, the quest for the core is likely to seem anachronistic. Although Sunbelt cities may see some (likely highly subsidized) growth in their downtowns, cutting-edge 21st-century metropolises will continue evolve without a large dense core or a dominant economic, cultural, and political center. Los Angeles managed to become a "big it" without much of a thriving downtown. San Jose, another late-20th-century growth city, has also failed to develop a strong central core, despite its investment of billions of dollars on condominiums, stadia, and cultural institutions.

Like some of the newer suburbs on the urban fringe, many such developments have shown themselves to be economically unviable. In Los Angeles, Phoenix, and Atlanta, much-ballyhooed central city developments have failed or been cut back due to lack of fundamental demand.[32]

In the fastest-rising cities, new telecommunications and transportation technologies simply render industrial-age downtowns functioning as economic, cultural, and demographic hubs anachronistic. The public may perceive these city cores as prominent, but their importance will be cultural or symbolic more than economic. Any such newly created core will be largely ersatz. Suggests social scientist Andrew Kirby, "While I am no great fan of the 21st-century city, it strikes me as hubris of the highest order to keep trying to turn our new cities into jury-built versions of the old ones—the need to create a downtown where none has emerged naturally is a nostalgia reminiscent of Las Vegas."[33]

BACK TO THE FUTURE—BUT IN A CAR

The relative insignificance of the urban core does not mean that the 21st-century city will be a collection of featureless suburban communities. Rather, cities like Phoenix have urbanized according to the prevailing multipolar model. While the much-subsidized downtown area has experienced only modestly successful growth since the 1950s, the Phoenix area has been developing a series of dense, vital centers. Some, like the Camelback Corridor, a largely upscale area roughly surrounding the Arizona Biltmore Hotel, are near the core, but others are in suburbs and independent small towns. Many of them—for example, Scottsdale and Tempe, both in the greater Phoenix area—retain more characteristics of a functioning urban "core" than does the center itself.[34]

Viewed from a longer historical perspective, this dispersed pattern reflects a return to preindustrial urban traditions. The great cities of the past—London, Paris, Tokyo—did not and to a large extent still do not center on "downtowns." Rather, they were composed of many different districts, each one dominated by the church, by merchants (such as the Paris Bourse or the City in London), or by specific trades and specialties.

In contrast, the notion of downtown as the dominating business, cultural, mercantile, and transport hub is a relatively recent one. The earliest reference to the term *downtown* appeared in 1836; it did not make its way into common usage until the early 1900s. The first real downtown was the dense industrial and trading district of lower Manhattan, a model that replicated itself in Chicago as well as many other cities throughout the early 20th century.[35]

What is emerging in places like Phoenix, then, is not so much a rejection of urbanism as a redefinition of the notion of "city life" that encompasses both a move back into the preindustrial past and a move forward into the postindustrial future. This model of urbanism, created on a new scale and with a newly possible mix of transportation and communications technologies, thrives in large part because for most commercial and industrial purposes it is as efficient in the contemporary era as the dense walking city was in its epoch. Indeed, even with their much-derided traffic jams, Phoenix, Houston, Atlanta, and even Los Angeles have shorter average commute times than denser, more transit-dependent New York and Chicago.[36]

BUILDING THE NEXT AMERICAN CITY

Much of the coming population growth in the nation's cities will take place in those that lack a strong center. These places will become denser as well as more multipolar, essentially creating a new urban paradigm that is neither suburban sprawl nor traditional city. The demand for such development will be propelled by many factors: the overall rise in population and immigration, energy-related concerns, the desire for shorter commutes, and rising land costs.

These forces will converge particularly across the newer cities' large and often underdeveloped "inner rings." In Phoenix the trend has been for growth to become slightly denser, less in the inner core than in the surrounding outer rings.[37] These areas often have more job opportunities than the traditional cores.

Starting in the 1990s, Houston experienced a huge surge in multifamily home construction within its central 610 loop, which circles the inner-ring neighborhoods. Density grew to levels seen in more traditional Portland or San Francisco but took place across a much wider area.[38] In comparison, the city districts of Portland, Seattle, Boston, Philadelphia, Chicago, and San Francisco all either lost population or accounted for 5 percent or less of regional growth.[39]

In coming decades the inner rings of Houston, Phoenix, and Los Angeles will continue to grow denser. But they will not adhere to Manhattan or Chicago Loop models; rather, they will follow a far wider, more diverse pattern dependent on the existence of more than one job center and on people working increasingly at home.

Although some of this denser growth has occurred in the old downtowns, it will just as likely locate in dispersed places within the metropolis.[40] This new kind of urban growth will be diverse, indeed protean in nature. Some pockets of Houston have long been neglected but now are experiencing growth. These include predominantly African-American areas such as the Third Ward, as well as Latino neighborhoods, and the more upscale, largely Anglo areas near the Galleria, and some closer to downtown. Between these neighborhoods will be stretches of more suburban areas, as well as industrial zones, hospital complexes, and university-dominated sections.

Under no circumstances will these pockets of dynamic urban growth physically resemble older American or European cities. Not dependent on access to their cores, these dense zones will be ad hoc, constantly shifting, and ethnically diverse. Their prevailing characteristic will be their multiple poles, range of functions, and ethnic diversity. One possible model, Houston's Harwin Corridor, along a long, auto-reliant boulevard, has evolved as a kind of wholesale-goods bazaar dominated by Asian businesses.

AMERICA'S MODEL: THE CITY OF ASPIRATION

The road that is leading to this explosive new urban growth is a distinctly American one. It is a product of a protean and nontraditional urban culture that flourished in America from the earliest times, allowing power and influence to move from place to place with astonishing speed. The loci of this growth could well change over the next few decades, but the fundamental process of seeking out new places with greater opportunity seems likely to continue at least to 2050.

The primary force driving these rapid changes is the aspirations of American urbanites. Unlike most urban cultures, American culture has been dominated not by dictates of princes or priests but by the efforts of ambitious entrepreneurs and migrants. Indeed, until late in the 20th century our national capital remained something of a backwater compared to the commercial and cultural centers of New York and Chicago.

Despite early expectations that Washington would become "the Rome of the New World," the city did not achieve significant scale until the New Deal and the Second World War. For much of the 19th century Washington, compared to other American cities, remained a laggard in growth. Widely reviled as a fetid, swampy place with atrocious cuisine—"hog and hominy grits" were its staples—it offered little in the way of commerce, industry, or culture. Even its great buildings were compared to "the ruins of Roman grandeur."[41]

This lack of a dynamic imperial center, noted the great sociologist E. Digby Baltzell, contrasted with other great capitals and cosmopolitan centers, which became irresistible lures of national elites. Baghdad, Cairo, Paris, London, Berlin, Vienna, Rome, Beijing, Seoul, and Tokyo may have also been places of opportunity for the ambitious, but their fundamental strength rested on political or ecclesiastical power.

Not until the 1960s did Washington and its region begin to emerge as something like a traditional national capital, with a large permanent population of well-educated and cultured citizens as well as a robust economy based on the defense industry and the expanding welfare state. The financial crisis of 2008, and the consequent expansion of federal power, will likely further elevate Washington's status, at least for the near future.

Even if Washington's role expands, however, the nation's demographic and economic vitality, its protean, ever-shifting commercial and middle-class culture will likely continue to drive the growth of American cities. This pattern emerged, as Baltzell noted, clearly by the early 19th century: New York and other American cities were neither aristocratic nor sharply defined by class but were "heterogeneous from top to bottom."[42] Social mobility has been the key driving force in American urban development; it is what has made American cities different and allowed for the rapid adoption of new models and the constant emergence of new centers of power.

NEW YORK: THE ASPIRATIONAL ARCHETYPE

The earliest precursors of the American urban model were the commercial cities of the Low Countries, notably Amsterdam. Descartes observed in the 1630s that this great Dutch city represented an "inventory of the possible."[43] Its greatness grew from allowing a highly differentiated and mercantile-oriented population to accomplish what they could never achieve elsewhere.

By the mid-17th century its namesake, a tiny settlement on Manhattan Island, had lured an astoundingly diverse mix among its one thousand residents. Eighteen languages were spoken and numerous faiths practiced. Appropriately, the counting house, not the church or any public building, stood as the most important civic building. Even after the Dutch were pushed out by the more powerful British military, the bustling island city—renamed New York—retained its character as fundamentally commercial. After the transfer of power most of the Dutch, Walloons, French, Jews, and Africans saw the greater opportunities before them and, under British rule, chose to remain and continued to increase their numbers.[44]

Those who followed came chiefly because they saw in New York an ideal environment for employment, particularly for skilled artisans and traders with high expectations. The primary source of its preeminence—it served only briefly as the new nation's capital—rested not on political power but on its role as the leading port for both goods and immigrants. Philadelphia and Boston also offered opportunities, but for those who sought to improve their lives, New York emerged as the principal North American bastion.[45]

New York's 19th-century growth was rapid and mostly unplanned, the result of minimally restrained entrepreneurial energies. It was to that century what Los Angeles, Phoenix, and Houston would be to the next. The sense of opportunity and lack of class stability startled many Europeans. As the French consul to New York complained in 1810, "The inhabitants . . . have in general no mind for anything but business. New York might be described as a permanent fair in which two-thirds of the population is constantly being replaced; where huge deals are being made, almost always with fictitious capital; and where luxury has reached alarming heights."[46]

Early aspirational New York was not inherently pleasant or culturally edifying. Although its wealth would one day propel it to become the world's cultural capital, visitors from more genteel Philadelphia and Boston often regarded 19th-century New Yorkers as crass and money oriented. In 1861 the Bostonian Ralph Waldo Emerson conceded the greater economic importance of New York, but Boston, he declared, was still "appointed" by destiny to "lead the civilization of North America."[47] This conflict between the "cultured" historic city and the dynamic aspirational city has continued into the current era and will define differences among our urban centers well into the 21st century.

"MISERABLE AND UGLY CITIES"

By the late 19th and early 20th centuries, as America's aspirational urban culture was creating a new kind of city, dense downtown districts arose in most major cities. A distinctly American phenomenon, the down-town was a product of both rapid growth and a relative lack of tradition. Its evolution would have been far more difficult in a European setting, where the relics of an older urban culture—great cathedrals, palaces, historical monuments—impeded the wholesale transformation of the city center.

As with today's sprawling cities, the 19th-century innovations in American urbanism were the result of massive migration and the swift adaptation of new technologies. Population shifted massively westward: during the first two decades of the 19th century, as much as 15 per-cent of New England's population migrated outward.[48] Many thousands of immigrants, most often from Germany, Ireland and Great Britain, joined them.

The new cities, due to their rapid growth and their ability to take prompt advantage of trains and the telegraph, innovated rapidly. The growth of railroads, allowing the massive movement of people to cen-tral points, facilitated the creation of dense, all-purpose downtowns. This in turn led to the demand for ever taller buildings and ever denser business districts. Chicago, the ultimate railroad city, pioneered the first steel skyscraper in 1895, but New York and others soon followed with their own massive towers. Anchored by their superior rail connections, each downtown would also become home to the leading cultural and retail establishments, most notably the department stores, which one writer called "Cathedrals of commerce."[49]

These innovations in form were complemented by equally dynamic societies. The dictates of hereditary leaders did not design the great American cities, as was the case in Paris and Vienna; rather, they were the cumulative result of small initiatives by merchants of modest origins, as well as the strenuous efforts of immigrants, who by 1890 accounted for as much as half of the nation's urban dwellers.[50]

The immigrants were joined by Americans fleeing the rural coun-tryside, including by the early 20th century many African-Americans.

The "Great Migration" of African-Americans from the rural south, noted Gunnar Myrdal in 1944, created "a fundamental redefinition of the Negro's status in America." Urban life had its horrors, but in the cities it became increasing difficult to restrict a person into "tight caste boundaries." African-American migrants from the South may have been different in many ways from newcomers from Italy, Ireland or Russia, but their fundamental aspirations were often very much the same.[51]

HIDEOUS BLOSSOMS

In the early phases of urbanization, Americans migrated to cities for economic necessity, where living conditions were, if somewhat better than those in Europe, still far from pleasant. The period that followed between the New Deal and the 1970s turned out to be a kind of golden age of the aspirational city, both in the Northeast and farther west, as the middle and working classes made unprecedented gains.[52] In the current era and beyond, the urban experience is likely to become both less essential and more volitional.

Modern urbanists might romanticize life in the traditional dense, crowded inner cities, but for millions of urbanites the cities' outward expansion—spurred by rail construction and then by highways— bequeathed the gifts of more space, greater personal mobility, and at their best, contact with the natural world. This early dispersion—much of it within the confines of existing city boundaries—allowed the middle class access to the urban economy as well as a chance to live in a more bucolic, family-friendly setting.

The evolution of a new kind of urbanity began in areas closely tied to the inner city. In New York the massive public works constructed under Robert Moses allowed Queens, long a rural backwater, to become transformed into new bedroom communities.[53] In 1939 the construction of the Bronx-Whitestone Bridge opened up then-fairly exclusive northwestern Queens to settlers, many of whom came from the highly congested working-class neighborhoods of the Bronx and Manhattan.

The rapid growth of the outer boroughs not only relieved the burgeoning inner city (New York's population nearly doubled in the first half of the 20th century) but also created a new kind of urban life, which added the pleasures of the single-family home and the automobile to older patterns of settlement. Tracts of Tudors, ranches, and colonials rose chock-a-block. Critics derided them as tasteless; in his Pulitzer Prize–winning biography of Robert Moses, Robert Caro described these new communities as "blossoming hideously."

But to their willing occupants, these new neighborhoods, simultaneously urban and suburban, offered a fine alternative to the tenement life they had experienced in Manhattan, the older parts of Brooklyn, and the South Bronx. In the 1920s alone more than a million people joined the exodus outward. The movement was accelerated by highway construction, which brutalized many neighborhoods and worsened conditions for the urban poor who were now left behind.[54] Yet at the same time the new neighborhoods offered urban Americans affordable homes in a "middle landscape" of tree-lined streets, parks, and broad, car-friendly boulevards. [55]

"JUST LIKE HELL"

The development of roads and the "car culture" ushered in a remarkable shift in population and economics, not only within existing large urban regions but from them to previously obscure cities in the South and West. Accelerated by the availability of cheap fuel for transportation as well as air-conditioning, these locations served as "safety valves" for the pent-up aspirations of 20th-century Americans, much as New York and Chicago had once played that role for the "surplus" masses of the European continent.

Few of these southern and western cities owed their origins to conscious government planning, or to efforts of the upper class or even "the respectable middle." Arizona, according to U.S. Senator Benjamin Wade, was "just like hell, all it lacks is water and good society."[56] Phoenix's city fathers included "Jack" Swilling, an often-inebriated Confederate Army deserter turned promoter, and a sturdy group of Mormon farmers who shared Swilling's outsider status, if not his taste for alcohol.[57]

Similarly, Tim Cisneros's adopted hometown of Houston (by 2005 the nation's fourth-largest city) had less-than-auspicious beginnings. Founded by New York real estate speculators, it appeared to early visitors an unlikely candidate for greatness. "Heat is so severe during the middle of the day, that most of us lie in the shade and pant," physician Ashbel Smith wrote in 1838.[58]

More than a hundred years later Houston's stock had not risen much in the national eye. In 1946 journalist John Gunther described it as a place "where few people think about anything but money." It was, he added, "the noisiest city" in the nation, "with a residential section mostly ugly and barren, a city without a single good restaurant and of hotels with cockroaches."[59]

Gunther's distaste reflected established urban elites' contempt for these newer cities. In 1940 the "high society" of Los Angeles, Houston, Dallas, Charlotte, and Phoenix were barely present on the *Social Register*.[60] Their later rise to national prominence was evidence, as Marxist scholar William Domhoff observed, that America's "open class system is almost the opposite of a caste system."[61]

The shift of headquarters and economic power to these cities has been remarkable. In 1950 Atlanta did not rank among America's most important economic centers; fifty years later it was one of the most popular cities for large corporations and their subsidiaries. After the great oil bust of the early 1980s, Houston rose to become the nation's—and the world's—great energy capital, surpassing New York, Los Angeles, and San Francisco combined in the concentration of top energy company headquarters.[62]

THE RISE OF LUXURY CITY

Though the most dynamic growth in coming decades will take place in these new cities of aspiration, another urban model likely will define some of urban America in 2050—what Wharton's Joe Gyourko has called the "superstar city." New York mayor Michael Bloomberg has also expounded this notion, dubbing the new urban form the "luxury city."

The luxury or superstar city is not an engine of opportunity but rather a natural abode for those who already reside at the apex of society—or expect to soon due to inheritance or education. Such cities are no longer for the masses of middle-class families but instead are a preserve primarily for the pleasure and edification of society's higher orders.

This idea well predates the Bloomberg era in New York, but it evolved first amid the decline of the traditional cities—New York, Boston, Chicago—that became obvious by the late 1950s. As the vast middle class and many corporations headed to the suburban periphery or to the new cities of the West and South, leaders of older cities looked for ways to retain their predominance.[63] The new approach focused decisively on the elite sectors of industry and society and was often expressed in boldly conceived "redevelopment" projects. These often involved ripping up older, industrial, white working-class areas, such as Boston's West End, in order to replace them with housing for the professional class, or with office towers.[64]

Perhaps nothing reflected this phenomenon better than the push for the construction of the ill-fated World Trade Center. Constructed between 1966 and 1977, the twin towers not only displaced as many as 33,000 small businesses in the old electrical district but essentially cut whole sections of New York off from one another. Minoru Yamasaki, the architect of the World Trade Center, believed that such structures reflected "a society such as ours, which is one of large scale and grand achievements."[65]

The symbolism was revealing. The two soaring towers epitomized New York as occupying "the commanding heights" of the global economy, notably the finance, design, and information industries. The new international economy, Saskia Sassen suggests, would be run from such towers in a handful of "global cities" ranging from London and Tokyo overseas to New York and Chicago.

In this vision central cities would function not as broad-based providers of goods and services but rather as specifically elite centers. Even if they lost headquarters-related jobs and population, Sassen argued, such cities would occupy "new geographies of centrality" that would provide "the strategic sites for management of the global economy."[66] Population and job growth would be slow, even negative, since the highest levels of global business rely on the skills of only a handful of people.

The denizens of these "geographies of centrality" do not greatly depend on the public institutions (like schools) or the private ones (like churches) that were once so critical to the traditional working- and middle-class urbanities. Their wealth allows them to avoid the poor public schools, high tax payments, and onerous regulations that drove lower-end players to other cities and the outer suburbs. Instead they purchase critical amenities—such as child care and open space—on the private market, without dependence on grassroots social networks.

Maintaining and even expanding this well-educated, well-heeled society requires no major reform of the ways cities are run. These cities need merely cultivate what Sassen calls "the urban glamour zone" and host firms specializing elite services such as finance, media, and design.[67] Such areas would take on some of the characteristics of exclusive resorts, with extremely expensive real estate and concentrations of high-end amenities, like Aspen and Telluride.[68]

Many of the residents of such metropolitan areas will be intrinsically nomadic; they live in the city for a while, say while they are young, and move away later. Others can afford to purchase urban pied-à-terres while also owning homes in other parts of the country that appeal to them for, say, the climate. A growing number of apartments are owned by nonresidents—in 2007 nonresidents made up to 10 percent of all Manhattan apartment purchases, up from 5 percent eight years ago. (In the short run, this pattern will most likely decrease due to the economic crisis.) Nonetheless, in some newer buildings, nonresidents are more than half of new buyers. "Living in a superstar city," a Wharton study concludes, "is like owning a scarce luxury good."[69]

As Terry Nichols Clark points out, these cities may no longer serve as vehicles for class mobility, in the ways they once did; their raison d'être is to serve as an "entertainment machine" for the privileged. For these elite residents, the lures are not only job opportunities in the financial and creative fields but also "hip restaurants, bars, shops, and boutiques abundant in restructured urban neighborhoods."[70]

Such urban districts, of course, can still serve as places of upward mobility for those who possess the education, family wealth, and connections to afford residence there. A small number of people in the service sector—for example, restaurant owners, top chefs, even skilled physical trainers and medical personnel—could also build thriving careers in these cities. But for the most part, the middle and working classes will not be able to improve their standards of living in such places.

A DEMOGRAPHIC DEAD END?

The superstar or luxury city represents the culmination of a certain kind of urban development, but it is also a demographic dead end. In recent years virtually all of these cities have seen the continuing loss of middle- and working-class families with children over the age of five.[71]

In the coming decades the "luxury city" may be a place with a significant increase in high-end dwellings but not many more people. In the new urban landscape high-rise towers for the rich predominate, some of them in refurbished office buildings that formerly employed the middle class. The funds for this city come largely from the global economy, but its needs are cared for by residents of outlying areas who eke out a low-wage existence in the city.[72]

An individual from Houston who earns $50,000 would have to make $115,769 in Manhattan and $81,695 in Queens to live at the same level of comfort, according to Council for Community and Economic Research's Cost of Living Calculator. Similarly, earning $50,000 in Atlanta is the equivalent of earning $106,198 in Manhattan and $74,941 in Queens.[73] Over the past few decades even educated workers, particularly when they enter their thirties, have tended in increasing numbers to leave more expensive cities for less expensive ones like Phoenix, Dallas, Atlanta, and Raleigh-Durham.[74]

THE FUTURE OF THE URBAN MIDDLE CLASS

As the nation grows by another hundred million people, it should have ample room for a handful of these highly expensive and glamorous metropolitan areas, but their model of urbanism will ultimately limit their long-term economic and social vitality. Many companies and industries depend on the presence of a broader array of talent than can afford to live in such places; that talent will continue to relocate to less exclusive places, either in the suburbs or to different regions. Charlotte, suggests local real estate developer John Harris, can compete against an expensive metropolitan region not only at the top levels of management but across the board. "It's hard to be a mass employer in San Francisco," he notes.[75]

American urbanism has always centered on notions of aspiration and upward mobility. As Jane Jacobs once wisely remarked, "A metropolitan economy, if it is working well, is constantly transforming many poor people into middle-class people, many illiterates into skilled people, many greenhorns into competent citizens. . . . Cities don't lure the middle class. They create it."[76]

By its nature the luxury city abandons this traditional focus on upward mobility and the middle class. A large working class remains, but for the most part its members are trapped in low-wage jobs with relatively little opportunity to move up. And when they do move out of the working class, their usual course is to move farther out into the periphery, or out of the region altogether.[77] Immigrants too have tended to move, once established, out of New York and Los Angeles and to head for less expensive areas in the suburbs or in cities such as Atlanta and Charlotte.[78]

The trend is particularly marked in Manhattan, where the new demographics have tilted toward a large permanent upper class, serviced by poorer people living in the surrounding boroughs and suburbs.[79] The elite group is supplemented by a constantly rotating, nomadic population of younger, often highly educated people who come to the city for school or for the early part of their careers, then leave as they reach middle age.[80]

This diminishment of the permanent middle class has also been occasioned by a loss of broad economic diversity. In recent decades the financial sector, for example, has accounted for an ever-larger proportion of all income in New York, reaching 35 percent of the revenue generated in the city in 2007. Such enormous wealth was beneficial to the city's fiscal position, at least when Wall Street was booming, and proved a boon to an array of luxury services, from high-end restaurants to dog-walkers, but it did little for the city's middle class.

Indeed, since the 1990s virtually all the gains made in New York's economy have accrued to the highest-income earners. In 2005 the city's middle class—households making between $35,000 and $150,000 a year—stood at 53 percent, well below the national average of 63 percent.

Overall New York has the smallest share of middle-income families in the nation, according to a recent Brookings Institution study, and its proportion of middle-income neighborhoods was smaller than that of any metropolitan area other than Los Angeles.[81]

Ultimately the future luxury city is limited by its lack of affordability and by its overdependence on a few high-wage sectors. In the 1990s crime and urban decay were driving people out of New York; today the primary cause is the absence of opportunities for people to earn enough to afford the exorbitant cost of living.[82]

"Can you live a middle-class life in New York, even in Brooklyn, when it costs $650,000 to buy a two-bedroom apartment in Fort Greene?" asks Jay Greenspan, a writer living in rental housing in Brooklyn. Greenspan and his wife, who works for a nonprofit, have a combined income of about $160,000. But because they can't afford to buy a place in one of the Brooklyn neighborhoods they like, they are going to relocate, most likely to western Massachusetts. "We've just decided to move. It's heartbreaking because we want to stay."[83]

The situation is even more dire for many minorities and immigrants. Back in the 1960s Jane Jacobs could predict that Latino immigrants to New York, mainly from Puerto Rico, would inevitably make "a fine middle class." But four decades later in the Bronx, the city's most heavily Latino county, roughly one in three households lives in poverty, the highest rate of any urban county in the nation. On the other extreme, in Manhattan, where the rich are concentrated, the disparities between the classes have been rising steadily. In 1980 Manhattan ranked seventeenth among the nation's counties for social inequality; by 2007 ranked first, with the top fifth of wage earners earning 52 times that of the lowest fifth, a disparity roughly comparable to that of Namibia.[84]

This bifurcation can be seen in other cities that have great concentrations of wealthy and well-educated people.[85] In the coming decades Portland, Seattle, and possibly Austin could evolve along similar lines. In all these areas ever-higher housing prices may increasingly push low-wage workers to congregate in the closer-in suburbs, as has happened in many cities, not only in the United States but in Europe, such as Paris.[86]

THE GLAMOROUS ROAD TO DECLINE

If the aspirational city like Houston offers one model of an urban future and the "glamour zone" cities another, what about those older cities that have undergone decades of decline and now lack the requisite amenities, high-end industries, and global cachet to become either? Unfortunately many of them have focused very little on their primary economic functions, preferring instead vainly to ape the "luxury city" strategy of places like New York or San Francisco.[87]

This desire to imitate superstar cities led many older industrial cities to adopt urban revitalization efforts, the results of which have been tragically unsuccessful. During the 1960s and 1970s, as historian Jon Teaford notes, "the proposed rebuilding seemed to be a cookie cutter designed to make Cleveland, Detroit, Akron, and Dayton look like every renewed city in the nation." Along with adopting an "international style" of architecture, the basic strategy was to ape what was happening in New York, Chicago, Boston, and the great California metropolitan economies.[88]

Since the 1990s this approach has focused less on gleaming corporate headquarters than on bolstering the amenity offerings—museums, concert halls, and luxury condos—that are thought to appeal to what social thinker Richard Florida calls "creative class." This group is purported to be driven largely by cultural concerns, such as access to the arts and recreation, and by a generalized "bohemian" sensibility. To lure this group, some cities have created what amounts at best to Potemkin Villages—amenity-rich urban theme parks—that form a small *cordon sanitaire* of upscale urbanism while the city around them has shrunk or stagnated.

The attempted "renaissance" of downtown Philadelphia, for example, in the 1990s and early 2000s did little to reverse the continued decline of that metropolis: thousands of deserted houses stand testament to the failure of the civic enterprise. Massive expenditures went into an $800 million convention center and ball stadia, and some limited gentrification spread through parts of the central city, but the city's overall health and vitality ebbed, as the tourist economy generated few middle-class jobs. In the first seven years of the new millennium Philadelphia's population declined 4.5 percent while jobs, income, and wealth continued to shift to the periphery.

As longtime political consultant Dennis Powell observes, the city had become, for a large proportion of its middle class, "an opportunity-free zone." To be sure, the center city has been revived, with better restaurants, more cultural offerings, and ever more students. But Philadelphia has largely failed to become a place that encourages long-term residence by middle-class families and entrepreneurs, particularly in the neighborhoods outside the core.[89]

But Philadelphia is a stunning success story compared to other rustbelt cities that have attempted urban renewal. Cleveland, another supposed "comeback" city, also tried to use a culture-based approach to redevelopment. It spent millions to build the Rock and Roll Museum, much celebrated when it was launched in 1995. But a decade after the museum's opening, the city's population had sunk to its lowest point since 1900, its poverty rate was among the highest of any major American city, and its graduation rate among the lowest. Even more than Philadelphia, Cleveland has suffered considerable population loss— 8 percent between 2000 and 2008—and its income growth lags behind national averages.[90] Instead of a comeback, Cleveland has experienced ever-escalating decline.

There may be no more tragic example of this kind of misplaced investment than New Orleans. Once ranked among America's great commercial centers, the city went on to lose most of the industries that had employed the middle and working class, in part due to its notoriously corrupt government. Throughout the latter decades of the 20th century, New Orleans ignored the needs of its traditional industries such as those tied to the port, to manufacturing, and to energy.[91] Even as critical infrastructure such as levees declined, the city chose to invest in arts, culture, and tourism as sources of civic salvation.

Unfortunately, tourism does not readily provide middle-class employment or social mobility. Before Katrina, nearly 40 percent of New Orleans households—nearly all of them African-American—earned less than $20,000 a year. The culture-first strategy might have worked well for Garden District elites and for the operators of the tourist hotels, but it failed the rest of the city's population.[92]

Ultimately, the blame for the Katrina crisis lies in the absence of policies that focused on basic infrastructure, industrial development, and modernization of transportation. Although the federal government failed to react swiftly or provide aid after the disaster, local levee boards and politicians blocked the construction of improved levees and other basic protective structures. The city provided money for convention centers, stadia, and other ephemera but not for the basic necessities.[93]

After Katrina, not surprisingly, a hundred thousand former residents of New Orleans relocated permanently to Houston and other cities, revealing the extent of the city's failure to provide opportunity for its residents. "We are the bottom for poverty," sums up Sonya Heisser, a graduate student in social work from Southern University and herself a product of New Orleans hardscrabble streets. "People work in low-wage industries. We have a poor school system, and the politicians keep getting indicted. It's the worst situation."[94]

As Heisser's comments suggest, New Orleans and the state of Louisiana, with their inefficient and often corrupt governments, have had much to answer for. The city and state had no real plan to evacuate its huge, impoverished population, 30 percent of whom did not own cars. Corruption may also have had something to do with the dramatic failure of the levee system itself. Even worse, much of the post-Katrina efforts in New Orleans are once again focused on tourism, high-end urbanism, and culture, with relatively little attention to the basics that can nurture and expand a middle class.

Although New Orleans may be an extreme case, similar decay in other cities will only be accelerated by local initiatives that try to imitate the "glamour zone" cities. Marketing Detroit as "a cool city" might generate the odd glowing media report, but it cannot resolve its many deep-seated problems.[95] As demographer Bill Frey once remarked, "There are not enough yuppies to go around to save Detroit."[96]

THE POWER OF PLAIN VANILLA

American cities cannot secure long-term viability simply by expanding the "glamour zone." Contrary to what some boosters believe, cities, glamorous or not, cannot thrive on hopes that "empty nesters" will move back or that high energy prices will "force" Americans back into inner cities. Nor can they prosper due to the imagined dynamics of the "creative" economy based on arts, culture, and high-technology research, which provides relatively little employment for the city's middle and working classes.

Concentrations of highly educated professionals are certainly important, but cities still must provide affordable and desirable places to live, or most people will seek opportunities elsewhere. The notion that the postcrash economy will decimate the suburbs and help the priciest cities contradicts not only a generation of migration patterns but also the reasons why people settle for the long term.[97] These suggestions miss the fundamental point that most people move for relatively prosaic reasons: a good job, a decent school, proximity to relatives, a safe neighborhood.[98] Although much will change in the coming decades, these basic priorities will likely not shift dramatically.

In order to capture the additional twenty million or so who can be expected to locate in urban areas over the next four decades, cities will need to nurture neighborhoods that are a bit more "plain vanilla"; that is, areas that are distinctly urban but share certain traits with suburbia, like a canopy of trees, an attractive but low-key shopping street, a place for a spacious apartment, a townhome, or even a single-family residence.

Such neighborhoods still exist in some parts of San Francisco, Boston, and Manhattan, but for the most part they are farther out in the periphery. Many of these districts—Bay Ridge, Whitestone, and Middle Village in New York; the Sunset in San Francisco; Chicago's Bridgeport; parts of northeastern Philadelphia; the west side of St. Louis; and sections of Los Angeles's San Fernando Valley—have long stood out as urban stalwarts, places that managed to resist the urban decay of the 1970s. They are not glamorous or well-known neighborhoods that receive extensive coverage in the global or national media. "Queens," observes writer Ian Frazier, "specializes in communities nonresidents have heard of but could never place on a map."[99]

Such communities provide a critical middle ground between the exclusive precincts of the "luxury city" and the most destitute, neglected neighborhoods. Although some urbanists—and many developers—would seek to make such areas denser, their very appeal is based on their relatively low density and the proximity of work areas, shopping streets, new schools, and parks. As Beth DeBetham, a community activist in the southeastern Queens community of Laurelton, notes: "What we see is that the issue is not about race, black or white, but about squeezing the middle class. We like the trees and the small-town community. That's what keeps the middle-class family here."[100]

America's cities—particularly in the rustbelt and the cores of Sunbelt cities—could be well suited for creating and even expanding such middle-class neighborhoods. Over time these could become the critical small building blocks with which future great urban areas can be built and nurtured. As the renowned urban historian Lewis Mumford suggested over a half century ago, "We shall never succeed with dealing with the complex problems of large units and differentiated groups unless at the same time we rebuild and revitalize the small unit. We must begin at the beginning; it is here where all life, even in big communities and organizations, starts."[101]

Keeping such "small units" together will require substantial input. They cannot be sustained by the subsidies that developers often receive for luxury mega-developments, new museums, or performing arts centers. Instead, they require attention in the fundamentals that no longer draw much interest from city officials or scholars of urban policy: transportation, public safety, education, and sanitation.

A challenge for "plain vanilla" urban neighborhoods will be to create economic opportunities for their residents, as well nurturing the basics of middle-class life—good schools, safe streets, and thriving churches and civic institutions. Cities tend to be expensive and overregulated, which has discouraged job growth. But some places still have remnants of the old economy, with smaller firms engaged in such activities as food processing, furniture making, and garment production.

Such small specialized businesses once constituted a critical aspect of these cities' competitive advantage. The great French historian Fernand Braudel described these firms as they existed in New York as late as the 1950s: "the little firms, sometimes employing thirty or fewer people, which made up its commercial and industrial substance—the huge clothing sector, hundreds of small printers, many food industries and small builders—all contributing to a truly 'competitive' world whose little units were both in competition, yet dependent upon each other."[102] Traditionally these industries were run and staffed by immigrants; Germans, Poles, and Italians; increasingly West Indians, Latinos, and Asians do this work today.[103]

In the 21st century such businesses still have a role, serving local markets; for example, bakeries catering to Manhattan restaurants or specialty construction firms tied to the needs of changing urban markets. But the future middle class will also include a new kind of urban artisan, one who works in small firms or independently in growing fields like information, education, health, and culture, as well as specialists in a wide array of business services.

These professions have continued to grow in older cities, even as other fields declined. By 2006 San Francisco had an estimated 70,000 home-based businesses and a thriving culture of self-employed "Bedouins" working in postindustrial professions: film and book editors, fashion designers, freelance software writers, and business consultants. These self-employed people, noted one study, were critical to helping the city withstand the ill effects of the post-2000 dot-com collapse.[104]

Similarly, the communities of the San Fernando Valley—particularly those close to the studios in Burbank, Glendale, and Studio City—are home to large contingents of entertainment-industry workers, many of them self-employed. According to studies by Dan Blake, up to 60 percent of all Los Angeles–area workers in this highly dispersed industry reside somewhere in the sprawling Valley.[105] Workers in media, graphic arts, and other specialized services have also been among the few groups of middle- and upper-middle income-earners to see rapid growth in New York's outer boroughs.[106]

Such workers are critical to the future of the cities, but those who paint them as unreconstructed bohemians or as high-end consumers of arts, culture, and fashion often mischaracterize their needs. They may well have been somewhat bohemian in their twenties and early thirties, but their priorities change enormously as they age, make commitments, start businesses, and perhaps even raise families. They may still frequent jazz clubs or museums, but more practical issues—stable employment, taxes, safety, schools, and housing affordability—tend to assume a greater priority.

CITIES OF THE FUTURE

These postindustrial age artisans—along with more traditional middle-class workers like civil servants, teachers, and nurses—could provide the critical residential base for "plain vanilla" urban neighborhoods. Neither rich nor poor, these artisans could use the new telecommunications net to access clients in the sprawling suburban rings, throughout the United States, or overseas.

Earlier generations of urban residents stayed in a city to be close to an industrial job or, as with immigrants, to remain near other members of their community. But these newcomers will be urbanites by choice. Unlike students or the nomadic rich, their reasons for staying in the city will have less to do with cultural cachet than with family-friendliness and social cohesion. Nelson Ryland, a film editor with two children who works part time in his sprawling turn-of-the-century Flatbush house, suggests, "It's easy to name the things that attracted us—the neighbors, the moderate density. More than anything it's the sense of the community. That's the great thing that keeps people like us here."

This "sense of community" will become the key to sustaining urban communities. Cities cannot survive by appealing only to "creative" types; nor can they serve as merely "communities in cyberspace" or lifestyle centers. This is particularly true in an era when technology allows many functions, like financial services, to move seamlessly across global boundaries. Work that was once the province of Silicon Valley, Hollywood, or Wall Street can now easily be accessed in smaller, bucolic cities like Greenwich, Connecticut. It can also flow to rival centers, be they older ones like London and Hong Kong or newer ones such as Mumbai, Singapore, or Shanghai.[107] In such a highly competitive environment, cultural hipness is not enough to draw and retain residents.

In the 21st century, as in the 20th or 19th, successful, sustainable urban centers will be those that nurture individuals, families, and businesses across generations and life stages. The sustainable city in 2050 will depend in large part on the revival of traditional institutions that have faded in many of today's cities. Religious institutions—albeit often in reinvented form—help maintain and nurture such communities. Extended family networks will be critical. As Queens resident and real estate agent Judy Markowitz puts it, "In Manhattan, people with kids have nannies. In Queens, we have grandparents."[108]

In the coming decades technology could boost this sense of community. Social networks can facilitate contact in different parts of a city among artists, families, and neighborhood groups, enhancing existing mechanisms offered by churches, political machines, or homeowner associations.[109] It is out of these dense networks of communities that America's great cities, both new and old, can continue to grow and flourish.

CHAPTER THREE: THE
ARCHIPELAGO OF VILLAGES

Except for a brief period during the rainy season, when the hills turn a kind of Astroturf green, the rangy scrublands northeast of Los Angeles unfold in chalky waves. Broken only by the occasional tree or scraggly bush, the dry lands—a classic western landscape of cattle ranches, oil wells, and dried-up riverbeds—reach toward the abruptly rising San Gabriel Mountains.

Until 2004 this harsh terrain, thirty miles north of downtown Los Angeles, was controlled by the Newhall family. But then Los Angeles, with its great outward reach, pushed through the San Fernando Valley and licked its edges. In only a short matter of time, it seemed, the jumbled landscape of the San Fernando Valley, with its tract homes, massive shopping centers, and office parks, would reach the Newhall lands and rapidly engulf it.

Victor Gruen, an Austrian émigré who was hired to plan the area's development, had no intention of following the conventional script. Vienna-born, Gruen declared that suburban America was "an avenue of horrors" that was "flanked by the greatest collection of vulgarity—billboards, motels, gas stations, shanties, car lots, hot dog stands, wayside stores—ever collected by man."[1]

Gruen's notion of suburbia was distinctly European. He believed it should provide a "middle landscape" combining access to nature with what he considered "the advantages of urban life." His goal was to build a new American town with mixed housing organized into neighborhoods, a well-preserved natural environment, and a thriving town center.[2] He saw his efforts, as USC researcher Patrick Wirtz put it, as "suburbia redeemed," a place combining both the urban and the rural spirit.

In Valencia, California, Gruen developed a community with a mix of homes, many with red tile roofs, suggesting the area's historical tie to Mexico and its natural Mediterranean-like setting. The vibrant village core has attractive shops and offices and serves as a natural meeting place for those who work and live in the area. An elaborate network of twenty-eight miles of car-free *paseos* make the community accessible to the residents.

He also recognized the commercial appeal of such an environment. A 1992 ad for Valencia featured a smiling girl saying, "I can be in my classroom one minute and riding my horse the next. I don't know whether I'm a city or country girl."[3]

Valencia is no longer owned by the Newhall family; it was sold in 2004 to the housing giant Lennar. But by almost any standard it must be considered a success. Its town center, *paseos*, and housing stock have evolved beyond any traditional notion of a bedroom suburb. In 1987 an incorporated city, Santa Clarita, was founded in this area of north Los Angeles County; today, with a population of over 150,000, Valencia can be seen as its heart.[4]

Perhaps the greatest testament to Gruen's vision lies in the fact that Valencia residents consider their town far from the usual Los Angeles "sprawl." Santa Clarita boasts a thriving industrial base and an ethically diverse population, most of whose incomes range from middle to upper middle class. The vast majority of the population are homeowners.[5]

Valencia residents are far more likely than other suburbanites to work, shop, and play close by; according to some estimates, nearly one in ten work from home.[6] Valencia is certainly not a conventional suburb but a place that combines aspects of the urban and rural life. "We are embedded in the community," observes Julie Weith, a resident and director of Human Resources at UVDI, a local manufacturer. "The allure of the place is the community, and that's the key for us."[7]

THE SUBURBAN FUTURE

Valencia offers a glimpse into a future that breaks traditional boundaries between urban and rural, city and suburb. Instead of either densely packed cities or sprawling, characterless suburbs, a landscape may emerge that resembles the network of smaller towns characteristic of 19th-century America. The nation's landmass is large enough—less than 5 percent of it is currently urbanized—to accommodate this growth, while still husbanding critical farmland and open space.[8]

Gruen and other suburban visionaries have been criticized for facilitating migration out of the city, but as one author commented, "Americans were headed for the hills anyway"; at least these developers "tried to channel the flight into something constructive."[9] In many parts of the United States the development of planned communities has accelerated since the 1990s and seems likely to continue.[10] By one count, as many as fifty million Americans already live in such "master planned communities." As they have often proved more viable commercially than conventional developments, those constitute a potential market-based solution to accommodating the country's growing population.[11]

Such developments represent one of the most sustainable ways—economically and socially as well as environmentally—to accommodate the next hundred million Americans. Rather than be forced to cluster in cities, Americans are likely to increasingly opt for communities that blend the single-family housing patterns of suburbia with basic urban amenities. These suburbs of tomorrow will have a diversity of housing types, thriving town centers, and growing cultural and religious institutions. They will provide more opportunities to walk, ride bikes, and work at nearby companies.

But what makes these suburban villages so different is not so much design as their vibrant economic and social self-sufficiency. They testify not only to the fundamental attraction of lower-density living but also the growing role of suburban communities as cultural, religious, entertainment, and business centers.

FUTURE SLUMS?

The prospects for suburbia have been widely debated for generations. Starting in the 1950s intellectuals, drew a prevailing picture of suburbanites as "an uneducated, gullible, petty 'mass' which rejects the culture that would make it fully human," wrote Herbert Gans in *The Levittowners*. The suburbanite, according to Gans, displeased "the professional planner and the intellectual defender of cosmopolitan culture." The 1960s counterculture spread this critique, viewing suburbia as one of many "tasteless travesties of mass society," along with fast and processed food, plastics, and large cars. It represented the opposite of the cosmopolitan urban scene; one critic even termed it "vulgaria."[12]

Since the 1980s the new urbanism has had a major impact on thinking about the suburban future. Espousing a greater reliance on walkways, public transport, and bikeways, and commingling office, residential, and commercial space, the new urbanism has provided many helpful suggestions about making suburbia more intimate and human-scale. But many adherents of new urbanism are also fundamentally hostile to backyards, cul-de-sacs, and single-family houses, the aspects often favored by families for their safety, privacy, and children's play opportunities.[13]

The housing crash that began in 2007 has led some to contend that the age of suburban growth has come to an end and that "the gospel of urbanism" will become the predominant faith. The early phases of the subprime mortgage bust were heavily concentrated in newer developments in the outer fringes, in part because these communities had a disproportionate number of new buyers using unconventional mortgages.

The distress in the outer suburbs attracted much of the media attention and delighted many who had long detested suburbs. One leading new urbanist, Chris Leinberger, actually described suburban sprawl as "the root cause of the financial crisis." Leinberger and other critics have described suburbia as the home of the nation's future "slums." Others portray suburbs as serving at best as backwaters in a society dominated by urbanites.[14]

In one economist's estimate, by 2025 the United States will have a "likely surplus of 22 million large lot homes"—that is, residences on more than one-sixth of an acre.[15] Unwilling to let natural forces do their work, many advocates seem ready to impose policies to discourage single-family homes and promote denser kinds of development, just in case the inevitable destruction does not come about quickly enough.[16] Some have predicted that many prosperous middle-class suburbs will turn into "new slums" inhabited by the poor and minorities.[17]

But cities themselves have not been immune to the downturn in real estate values that developed after 2007. Just like the new exurbs at the fringe, many new dense condo units in New York and Chicago and Denver have lost value, and residents. Other areas hard hit by the crisis include heavily minority neighborhoods in Boston and New York. The large new stock of housing in downtown and inner-city condominium projects was devastated.[18]

Still, the longer-term trends continue to favor suburbs. On average they remain far more affluent than cities. While some cities have seen the growth of an upper-class educated segment, the 2000 census showed that over the 1990s per capita income growth in suburbs was twice that of the cities, while poverty rates remained twice as high in urban areas as in suburbs.[19] The suburbs remain the preferred home for the vast majority of the middle class.[20]

Equally critical jobs have also been moving farther outward. A 2009 study by the Brookings Institution found that between 1998 and 2006, in 95 out of 98 leading metropolitan regions, jobs shifted away from the center and to the periphery. This was the case not only in "sprawl" regions like Dallas, Los Angeles, and Atlanta but also in more traditional urban metropolitan areas such as Chicago, San Francisco, and Seattle.[21]

HOW SUBURBIA EVOLVED

The ultimate issue determining the geography of growth is preference. For at least four decades the portion of the population that prefers to live in a big city has consistently been in the 10 to 20 percent range, while roughly 50 percent or more opt for suburbs or exurbs. The rest generally opt for the countryside. A 2008 study revealed that suburbanites displayed the highest degree of satisfaction with where they lived compared to those who lived in cities, small towns, and the countryside.[22]

This reality stands at odds with claims of a supposed "flight from suburbia" that researchers and much of the media have proclaimed periodically since at least the 1960s.[23] Those claims fly in the face of well over a century of evidence. As early as the 1870s cities from Philadelphia to Chicago were spreading out into the surrounding countryside. By the 1920s suburban growth was occurring at twice the rate as growth in cities both large and small.[24]

Initially physical and financial factors limited this expansion. Many early suburbs were built for the wealthy, who could afford carriages or expensive train fares. Most found the option of suburbia limited by walking distances, such as over the East River bridges, or by the unavailability of ferry service. But with inexpensive mass transit, and later with the automobile, the zone of suburbanization grew.[25]

In the postwar era the pace of suburbanization again accelerated, accounting for a remarkable 84 percent of the nation's population increase during the 1950s. In that decade the suburbs grew at six times the rate that cities did.[26] Once a nation of farms and cities, the United States transformed itself into a primarily suburban country. No longer confined to old towns or "streetcar suburbs" near the urban core, suburbanites increasingly lived in new, ever-more-spread-out developments such as Levittown, which arose in the late 1940s and early 1950s out on the Long Island flatlands. Mass-production suburbs like Levittown represented, as *Fortune* put it, an "industrial revolution" that provided an unprecedented opportunity for property ownership. Some of this expertise came directly out of the Second World War, where one of the Levitt brothers had developed production expertise as a Seabee, the fabled engineering service of the U.S. Navy.[27]

For returning GIs and ensuing generations, the suburb offered a chance for the reinvention of the individual. For middle-class ethnic minorities, coming from a culture where everyone knew everyone's business, this was a refreshing change, a chance to establish oneself anew.[28] By the 1960s more Americans lived in suburbs than in cities; by the 1990s a majority of Americans resided there.[29] Lower-density living has become the norm, and for the most part the trend has continued. In 1920, 20 percent of the population lived in America's thirty densest counties; today that has been reduced to about 11 percent.[30] Nor does this process appear to be reversing. Since 1950 the suburban share of the nation's total population has doubled to its current 50 percent mark.

In the 1990s, the gaps in growth between central city and suburb widened. During the first seven years of the new millennium, a period much dominated by discussions of an "urban renaissance," the suburbs—and even more so, the peripheral exurbs—enjoyed the lion's share of all population growth in metropolitan areas, accounting for upward of 80 percent of the total. The farthest-out exurbs experienced the fastest rise in overall population, benefiting most particularly from the migration to these communities from central counties.[31]

These numbers may actually understate the full extent of suburbanization. Most of the fastest-growing "cities" of the late 20th century—Atlanta, Orlando, Phoenix, Houston, Dallas, and Charlotte—primarily, as one analyst put it, have little relationship to the original urban core."[32]

THE LURE OF LOWER DENSITY

The shift to suburbia has its roots in two quintessential aspects of the American ethos: the desire for self-betterment, and what historian Leo Marx has called "an inchoate longing for a more 'natural' environment."[33] As Joel Garreau noted in his classic *Edge City*, "planners drool" over high-density development, but most residents in suburbia "hate a lot of this stuff." They might enjoy a town center, a *paseo*, or a walking district, but they usually resent the proliferation of high-rises or condo complexes. If they wanted to live in buildings of this type, after all, they would have stayed in the city.[34]

Surveys by the National Association of Realtors and the National Association of Home Builders find that some 83 percent of potential buyers prefer a single-family home. By a factor of three to one, potential home-buyers deem highway access more important than access to mass transit.[35] Nor do young buyers, in particular, seem anxious to downscale to somewhere denser and more urban; two-thirds of Gen X buyers, according to a 2004 survey, wanted large homes, compared to only 40 percent of baby boomers.[36]

None of this suggests that suburbia will remain unchanged. Innovations resulting from concerns over energy and the environment, changes in the economy, and new telecommunications technologies will all radically transform life on the periphery, perhaps even more than in the core. Over time, as population forces land prices to rise, the one- or two-acre lot may become less common, and some forms of midrange density, even in the exurbs, may become more prevalent. But the basic pattern of the future metropolis will be built upon a predominantly suburban matrix dominated by cars, road connections, and construction such as is familiar to the denizens of contemporary Los Angeles, Phoenix, and Houston.[37]

Since many suburbanites fear the negative aspects of urbanization, such as greater risks of crime, crowding, and increased traffic, rapid densification is unlikely.[38] Simply put, most suburbanites have little reason to favor radical changes in the densities of their communities. Critics sometimes suggest that this desire to preserve modest density stems from racist, elitist motives.[39] But opposition to development is equally commonplace in old city neighborhoods.

Once residents have settled into what they consider an attractive community, they usually develop a vested interest to protect it. Political orientation seems to have little effect. Some of the strongest anti-growth hotbeds in the nation are areas like Fairfax County, Virginia, with high concentrations of "progressive" well-educated people who might seem amenable to environmentally correct "smart growth"—advocating denser development along transit corridors.[40] As one planning director in a well-to-do suburban Maryland county put it, "Smart growth is something people want. They just don't want it in their own neighborhood."

Fred Hirsch, in *Social Limits to Growth*, attributes this preference to what he calls "the paradox of affluence." The idea of land as a "leisure" good, he says, once a luxury of the aristocracy, has become increasingly mainstream. This is particularly true for scenic land, with majestic mountain, ocean, riverfront, or lake backdrops. Opposition to densification and development in areas with such characteristics tends to be particularly heated in the Front Range of the Rockies, in the Hudson Valley, and on the California coast.[41]

Structural changes in the economy may reinforce this opposition. Today fewer local people own shops that directly benefit from increased population; many basic local needs are now met by giant retail chains, whose managers are tied to a corporate identity more than to a particular place. A skilled "knowledge worker" whose business is conducted electronically with national and global customers naturally has a less keen interest in local growth than did the traditional Main Street merchant, whose livelihood depended on the locality and who hence propelled local pro-development policies.

During the next three decades such social, technical, and economic factors will drive development farther out toward the periphery. The need to accommodate fifty or sixty million more suburbanites (as projected by current trends and preferences) is likely to result in developments that leapfrog each other, as one area after another becomes more restrictive toward development.[42] "Growth," notes one California research study, "is like toothpaste. Squeezed out of one location, it must go somewhere else."

Given the opposition to growth in settled areas, it will head farther out, often to poorer areas seeking economic stimulus or to places where local landowners can still dictate key planning decisions.[43] As they develop their own economies and amenities, these new areas may prove even more economically and socially disconnected from the center city than are traditional exurbs, which depend on proximity to urban employment centers; they may emerge, as one observer put it, as "suburbs of interstate highways."[44]

THE GARDEN CITIES

The suburbs of the future will be less reliant on cities and will provide more of their own jobs as well as cultural and religious institutions. They will be less like extensions of industrial age cities than like preindustrial villages, which supplied most of the employment, cultural, and social needs of their residents.

The earliest attempts to recreate the village model emerged from the notion of the "garden city," promulgated in the late 19th and early 20th centuries by the British visionary planner Ebenezer Howard, a full century before the rise of "new urbanism" and "smart growth."[45] Horrified by the disorder, disease, and crime of Britain's contemporary industrial metropolises, Howard advocated the creation of "garden cities" on suburban outskirts. Each self-contained town, with a population of roughly thirty thousand, would enjoy its own employment base. Neighborhoods of pleasant cottages would be surrounded by rural areas. "Town and country must be married," Howard preached, "and out of this joyous union will spring a new hope, a new life, a new civilization."[46]

Many of Britain's leading minds saw in this pattern of dispersion the logical solution to long-standing urban ills. Instead of "massing" people in town centers, the author H. G. Wells foresaw the "centrifugal possibilities" of a dispersed population. He predicted that eventually all of southern England would become the domain of London, while the vast landscape between Albany and Washington, D.C., would provide the geographic base for New York and Philadelphia.[47]

Howard's garden city model influenced American planners, as well as those in Germany, Australia, Japan, and elsewhere. Frederick Law Olmsted, best known for developing Central Park in New York, eventually came to see the suburb as "the most attractive, the most refined, the most soundly wholesome" way of life, and he eventually applied his genius to the development of new suburbs such as Riverside (outside Chicago) and Druid Hills (outside Atlanta).[48]

Architect Frank Lloyd Wright gave this notion a peculiarly American take, imagining a sprawling, decentralized metropolis. A suburb he designed, called Broadacre City, was to consist of single-family homes connected by highways. It would be an urban area of an entirely new kind—as he put it, both "everywhere and nowhere"—with its center not downtown but in the individual home. Wright's vision was radical for its time, in part because employment was then concentrated in urban cores and in large-scale industrial parks.

Wright's concept proved unworkable, but there continued to be new attempts to create communities that would accommodate the desire for both the single-family home and the automobile.[49] One of the earliest appeared in 1929 in Radburn, New Jersey. Described as "a town for the motor age," the community offered a wide range of residential units, with interior parklands and access to walkways. Car and pedestrian traffic were to be strictly separated, with houses grouped around cul-de-sacs with a small access road. Lewis Mumford descried Radburn as "the first major advance in city planning since Venice."[50]

The goal of Radburn was to create a secure and healthful environment for the residents. The town had extensive community recreation opportunities and sought to provide an ideal environment in which to raise children. Initially planned to house 25,000 people, Radburn's development sadly was derailed by the Great Depression, which drove the builder into bankruptcy. The city today houses only 3,100 residents.[51]

Early efforts to develop garden cities in America received a huge boost during the New Deal, which led to the construction of the first great master planned communities—Greenbelt, Maryland; Greenhills, Ohio (near Cincinnati); and Greendale, Wisconsin (outside Milwaukee). These communities, designed with offices, industrial facilities, parks, and playgrounds, provided for a diversity of housing units and income groups.

But these federal efforts eventually provoked strong opposition by builders and conservatives, who denounced them as "communist farms." Plans to build some three thousand more master planned towns were never realized. After the Second World War, many of the principles behind these New Deal towns were ignored amid the construction of massive conventional production suburbs.[52] In the ensuing decades these communities enjoyed only mixed success but remain testaments to the idea of an alternative suburban future.

In the early 1960s the notion of building garden cities regained currency, in large part as a means to remedy the segregation by both race and income that was then prevalent in the suburbs. The new villages, operating under federal "fair housing" laws, would welcome many kinds of residents. The new initiative, led by Robert Weaver, head of the Federal Housing Authority under President John F. Kennedy, met opposition both from conservative mortgage bankers and from liberal mayors, who feared the new towns would siphon off jobs and residents from the increasingly beleaguered inner cities.

Nevertheless, some federal funding was made available to private developers interested in developing "new towns." Visionary developers, some of whom looked to the New Deal towns for inspiration, seized the opportunity. Reston, founded outside Washington, D.C., in the early 1960s, reflected the vision of Robert E. Simon, whose father had been involved in building Radburn and who hired a member of Greenbelt's design team to help develop the model.

Simon's idea was to mix various kinds of housing—high rise, mid-rise, town house, and single family—to create a diverse community in which people could live and hopefully work for their entire lifetimes. At a time when other developers were content to mass-produce homes, he wanted to create something quite different from the Syosset, Long Island, suburb where he, as a young man, had moved with his wife, "a place where couples come, have children and leave as soon as the children have grown up."[53]

Meanwhile Columbia, Maryland, launched in 1963, was designed by its founder, James W. Rouse, as an antidote to suburban "sprawl," mixing housing, shopping, and jobs. Rouse envisioned that Columbia would provide "a sense of place at each level of community in which a person can feel a sense of belonging." Rouse's goal was to produce a community with the small-town feel of Easton, Maryland, where he had grown up.[54]

Although he identified himself as an enemy of sprawl, Rouse's vision was distinctly private and suburban, confirming his notion that private solutions could deal with urban problems. He understood that America's cities would continue to move outward; what he sought was a better, more humane way to accommodate that growth. In most aspects he succeeded. By the time the Rouse Company was acquired in 2005, the area he had developed had grown into more than nine villages and a town center. With a population of roughly 100,000, it has become a major job center with over 3,500 businesses and nearly 90,000 jobs.[55]

GEORGE MITCHELL AND THE WOODLANDS MODEL

George Mitchell, the founder of the Houston's the Woodlands, one of the most successful master planned communities, was as much a visionary as any community builder of the late 20th century. Originally an oil man, Mitchell had a clear idea of the community he wanted to create, and since he controlled the development himself for over thirty years, he was able to see it to fruition further than most visionaries.

Mitchell had an eye on profit, but whether in energy or in land development, he tended to look for the long term. He was the son of Greek immigrants; his father, who was barely literate in Greek and spoke very little English, changed the original family name, Pararskevopoulous. Despite his hardscrabble background, Mitchell attended Texas A&M University, received a degree in petroleum engineering, and went on to found his own successful energy company. In the 1960s he moved into real estate development as well, seeking a hedge against the cyclical nature of the oil business.

His biggest investment was in the heavily forested country north of Houston, amounting to some 27,000 acres. But his interest in the property was not only about money. Mitchell was greatly disheartened by the social and environmental failures of American cities. He had toured places like Watts and felt there must be a different, more humane, and more sustainable way of growing communities. His vision grew from a traditional suburban tract to a community that was not only environmentally attractive and commercially successful but also, reflecting the dreams of the 1930s New Dealers, available to a broad range of income groups. "I can't turn it around," Mitchell once said, "but I can set an example. Let the Woodlands be designed to show the country you can do it better."[56]

Over the ensuing thirty years Mitchell supervised the development of the Woodlands into a model of suburban place-making. The area, now home to more than 77,000 residents, is made up of several small communities, each with its own shopping area and town center. Local residents often cite this substantial preservation effort as one of the most appealing aspects of the Woodlands. Twenty-eight percent of the community is dedicated to nature, and there are 135 miles of hike and bike trails.

Mitchell gave up the reins in 1997, but he has remained a presence in the area, which continues to evolve as a living, breathing community with a powerful sense of its own identity. As Vicki Fullerton, a thirty-year resident, put it succinctly: "If you live here for a while, you don't think of yourself just as a resident of a part of Houston. You say you're from the Woodlands."[57]

BEYOND THE MEGALOPOLIS: "SMART SPRAWL"

Be they planned suburbs or more conventional developments, the future will belong those communities that are able to blend work, culture, and recreation with the type of housing preferred by most Americans—single-family homes. One writer, Wally Siembab, has dubbed the process of creating work environments on the periphery "smart sprawl," which essentially means finding sustainable ways to manage a somewhat dispersed environment.[58] This will require the use of fuel-efficient cars to reduce gas consumption and the dispersal of work closer to the communities where people live. Smart sprawl will also require the generous purchase of open space by public agencies, perhaps with support of private developers, in the areas between the continually leapfrogging communities.

Promoting smart sprawl is a far more reasonable way to meet our environmental needs than hoping to shift back to the mass-transit-based models of the industrial age; after all, barely 2 percent of the U.S. population uses mass transit on a daily basis. The automobile has left an indelible imprint on our society, and it meets the needs of our dispersed economy in ways that have been, and will continue to be, highly resistant to fundamental change.

Increased transit use—particularly on various kinds of rapid bus lines and shuttles—could play a more critical role, but the car, albeit smaller and much cleaner, seems likely to remain the dominant mode of transportation, especially in the multipolar metropolitan regions most likely to grow over the next few decades.

Within multipolar cities the differences in commute times between auto users and transit riders are particularly severe: the average Los Angeles transit commuter spends almost twice as long reaching his destination as does his counterpart in a car. It's no surprise, then, that new urbanist and smart growth advocates' attempts to design dense, transit-oriented development in Los Angeles have generally been less success-ful than hoped.[59]

This is not to say that transit cannot play a useful role in serving those who cannot or would rather not drive, perhaps in cost-efficient and flexible dedicated busways or in local shuttles within "villages." But absent a crippling fuel shortage or some other catastrophic event, we will probably never see widespread growth of the dense, transit-oriented communities envisioned by some urbanists.

Similarly, big-box retail centers and strip malls, natural products of auto culture, will continue to thrive. The former serves the interests of efficiency and scale for consumers of commodities, allowing them to purchase large goods that can practically be transported only by car. As for strip malls, they will continue to provide opportunities for the smaller, less-well-capitalized entrepreneur, who often cannot afford space in large-scale developments, which tend to have high rents and strict regulations concerning appearance and signage. "Brainwashing ourselves into believing that we can go back to a time before sprawl," urban critic Karrie Jacobs has said, is fundamentally doomed. Yearning for "the day when people took the train to work, Main Street was the primary shopping venue, and everything revolved around the central city" is nostalgia, not connected to practical reality.[60]

TOWARD GREENURBIA

To succeed over time, the emerging suburban archipelago will have to provide a successful social model and establish a more harmonious rela-tionship with the natural world. What I call "greenurbia" is a system that seeks a path to development that is not only sustainable environ-mentally but also meets the needs of diverse families and businesses.

Suburban development is often castigated as poor for the environ-ment, but research suggests that modest, low-density development can use less energy than denser urban forms. Although automobile commuting now consumes more energy resources than well-traveled traditional urban rail systems, the future generation of low-mileage cars may prove more efficient than underutilized rail systems in newer cities.[61]

Moreover, tall buildings may not be as green as some advocates suggest. Recent studies out of Australia show that town houses, small condos, and even single-family homes generate far less heat per capita than the supposedly environmentally superior residential towers, particularly when one takes into account the cost of heating common areas and the highly consumptive lifestyle of affluent urbanites (with their country homes, vacations, and frequent flying). In terms of energy conservation, the easiest and least expensive option may be to retrofit single-family houses and wood-shaded town houses.[62]

Two- or three-story houses often require only double-paned windows and natural shading to reduce their energy consumption; one Los Angeles study found that white roofs and shade trees can reduce suburban air-conditioning by 18 percent. Such structures are particularly ideal for using the heat- and water-saving elements of landscaping: after all, a nice maple can cool a two-story house more efficiently than it can a ten-story apartment.[63]

Best of all, focusing attention on low-density enclaves would bring change to where the action is and where it's likely to stay in the future. Pragmatically, the creation of an archipelago of villages may be the best way to reduce the harmful effects of growth. In such an archipelago one could limit long commutes by dispersing workplaces and using home-based employment—potentially promoting a wider but less intrusive impact of humans on the environment.

Man's relationship to nature does not have to be adversarial. Even during the past twenty years of rapid suburban development, for example, the nation's forest cover has actually increased, as less productive farm and pasture land has been taken out of production.[64] The residents of the new archipelago can promote "greening" through the acquisition of open space. Ultimately the goal would be to nurture communities that are separated from one another by belts of open recreational or agricultural land.[65]

Greenways that cut through existing and future residential areas could provide a break from landscape monotony, "lungs" for residents of the periphery, and ideal sites for the preservation of wildlife.[66] These open spaces could actually *lower* the costs of infrastructure development and serve as buffers against flooding.[67]

Importantly, some of these ideas have already been put into practice. At the Woodlands. George Mitchell had these thoughts very much in mind back in the early 1970s. The Woodlands name, suggests Mitchell's longtime aide Roger Galatas, was more than "just real estate hype." Mitchell commissioned plans that allowed the community to grow without destroying the forest lands and natural drainage. Notes longtime resident Vicki Fullerton, "There's a feeling of tranquility here. You don't get overwhelmed with the signs and billboards like in so many places. Instead, you see the tops of trees." [68]

SUBURBS AND THE SEARCH FOR COMMUNITY

One of the great urban legends of the 20th century—espoused by urbanists, planning professors, and pundits and portrayed in Hollywood movies—is that suburbanites are alienated, autonomous individuals, while city dwellers have a deep sense of belonging and connection to their neighborhoods. One new urbanist claims that "sprawl" undermines "the public realm" and that once suburbanites "leave the refuge of their homes" they "are reduced to motorists competing for asphalt."[69]

Conventional urban theory holds that suburbs kill any sense of community. Jane Jacobs, for example, believed that "suburbs must be a difficult place to raise children." But as one historian notes, had Jacobs paid as much attention to suburbs as she did to her beloved Greenwich

Village, she would have discovered that they possess their own considerable appeal, particularly for people with children.[70] "If suburban life is undesirable," noted Herbert Gans in 1969, "the suburbanites themselves seem blissfully unaware of it."

On virtually every measurement—from jobs and environment to families—suburban residents express a stronger sense of identity and civic involvement with their communities than do those living in cities. One recent study found that density does not, as is often assumed, increase social contact between neighbors or raise overall social involvement. For every 10 percent reduction in density, the chances of people talking to their neighbors increases by 10 percent, and their likelihood of belonging to a local club by 15 percent.[71]

These assertions have been supported by other studies. A *Los Angeles Times* survey, for example, found "high levels of satisfaction throughout suburbia, and the degree of contentment increased every step from the city of Los Angeles."[72] Another study, conducted in the Miami Valley area around Dayton, Ohio, revealed a wide gap in the level of satisfaction between suburbanites and city dwellers. As the *Dayton Daily News* commented: "City and suburban residents in the Miami Valley feel so differently about some aspects of their quality of life it's hard to believe they live in the same region. On some issues, such as neighborhood safety and quality of housing, dissatisfaction in the city runs 10 times that of outer ring suburbanites."[73]

These preferences have helped make suburbanization the predominant trend in virtually every region of the country. Even in Portland, Oregon, a city renowned for its urban-oriented policy, barely 10 percent of all population growth between 2000 and 2008 took place in the urban core while the vast majority occurred in suburbs, particularly in the outer fringes. Job growth and office occupancy have also been heavily weighted to the suburbs. Ironically, one contributing factor has been the demands of urbanites themselves, who want to preserve historic structures and maintain relatively modest densities in their neighborhoods.[74]

THE SUBURBS OF THE FUTURE

In a dramatic change, the new suburbs will be far more diverse ethnically than those of the past. With considerable justification, social critics in the 1950s reviled suburbia for being "a crushing mass of uniformity" in housing, roads, streets, and class of people: a "treeless communal waste."[75] In 1970 nearly 95 percent of suburbanites were white. Journalist William Whyte thought suburbia represented not an extension of the metropolis but its negation, "the anti-city." "In some suburbs," he complained, "[you] may hardly see a Negro, a poor person, or, for that matter, anyone over fifty."[76]

But suburbia's future would be unrecognizable to Whyte. Many of present buyers come from immigrant communities; this group will continue to swell the pool of 25-to-34-year-olds, the critical mass of potential of first-time home-buyers. While the Census Bureau once predicted that this group would shrink by 700,000 between 1990 and 2000, immigrants helped push this age cohort up by over four million.[77]

Whatever disdain some urban dwellers may feel toward the suburbs of their childhood, recent immigrants do not appear to widely share their attitude. Immigrants, particularly Latinos, overwhelmingly favor single-family residences and therefore often seek homes on the suburban periphery. One reason may well be that the two primary immigrant groups, Latinos and Asians, are far more likely to live in married households with children than are other Americans.[78]

As a result, while immigrants were once largely associated with cities, today more live in the suburbs than in urban centers, particularly in the fast-growing Sunbelt. This pattern is most prevalent among the longest-established immigrants and in metropolitan areas that have become immigrant meccas only in the last few decades. In Greater Washington, D.C., the Northeast's most dynamic region in economic and demographic terms, 87 percent of foreign migrants live in the suburbs, while less than 13 percent live in the district, according to a 2001 Brookings Institution study.[79]

Nationwide, over 27 percent of suburbanites are minorities, but by 2050 immigrants, their children, and native-born minorities will become a dominant force in shaping suburbia. In fast-growing Gwinett County outside Atlanta minorities made up less than 10 percent of the population in 1980; by 2006 the county was on the verge of becoming "majority minority." Perhaps most revealing, this diversity is itself diverse, including not only African-Americans but also Latinos and Asians. Suburban counties such as Fort Bend, Texas, and Walnut, in the San Gabriel Valley east of Los Angeles, already have among the most diverse populations in the nation.[80]

Over time suburbs may well develop some of the problems long associated with inner cities. Although suburban income, particularly in older parts of the country, has actually risen compared to that of inner cities, the ranks of the poor have also increased. Poverty, although far less prevalent on a per capita basis in suburbia, has grown, along with the influx of immigrants and of low-wage jobs. This is particularly true in some of the older "first suburbs" like Bergen County, New Jersey, and the San Gabriel Valley, a trend that is likely to continue.[81]

But though poverty may increase, so will the benefits of greater ethnic diversity. Increasingly, the most lavish Latino shopping areas, the best ethnic restaurants, the biggest Hindu and Buddhist temples, and the largest African-American churches will be located not in the urban "glamour zone" or in the hardscrabble inner city but in areas that were once considered the ultimate in "white bread" homogeneity.

Sugarland, outside Houston, may appear to the visitor to be a typical suburban landscape—until you encounter a massive Hindu temple, made up of stones carved and transported from India. Local strip malls are home to sari shops and stores selling Indian sweets, as well as Vietnamese noodle houses and family-run Mexican restaurants. The San Fernando and San Gabriel valleys reflect a similar riot of ethnic diversity, with various Asian, Latino, and Middle Eastern populations living cheek to jowl or, given the huge role of the automobile, bumper to bumper.

To California developers like Dr. Alethea Hsu, the suburban future is not "future slums" and abandoned malls but "multicultural shopping centers" focused both on immigrants and on their children. As long as these newcomers, both affluent and working class, continue to save and work hard, they are likely to thrive through the recession and beyond. "We are leased up, and we think the supply of shopping still is not enough," Hsu told me in early 2009. "We are ready to go Saturday and feel great trust in the future." At a time when most mainstream American retailers are hiding under their desks, such sentiments are illustrative of the renewal taking place on the metropolitan periphery.

Ultimately the diverse suburb constitutes a development far more important than shopping, temples, or mosque. It is a revolution in the nature of our most critical geography. "If a multiethnic society is working out in America," suggests demographer James Allen, "it will be worked out in [these] places. . . . The future of America is in the suburbs."[82]

THE MULTIGENERATIONAL SUBURB

Families have long clustered in suburbs, and they seem likely to continue to do so. In virtually every region families with children are far more likely to live in suburbs than in cities, particularly more affluent, middle-class, educated families. These patterns hold up even around the most attractive urban areas, such as Seattle, where the percentage of children is much higher in the farther-out suburbs.[83]

In the 21st century the suburbs will be home to Americans with more of a range of lifestyles, including singles, nontraditional families, and empty nesters. All these groups are often said to be moving from suburbs back to the inner city. But evidence from the 2000 census shows that the number of "nonfamily" households—that is, singles or unmarried people living together, as well as married couples without children—grew far more rapidly in the suburbs than in the cities. In fact, largely due to the growth of singles and aging parents, there are now more "nonfamilies" in the suburbs than there are traditional families.[84]

Aging empty nesters will play a critical role in future suburbia. The baby boom generation far outnumbers its successor, Generation X, by roughly 76 million to 41 million. By 2030, due largely to the boomers, more than one in five Americans will be over sixty-five. "Downshifting boomers," as demographer Bill Frey calls them—people who are still working but are trying to cut down their hours—will make choices on where to live that will be critical for new residential and commercial development.[85]

Many anecdotal accounts suggest that this population is poised for a large-scale "back to the city" movement. Headlines like "Baby Boomers Are Leaving the Suburbs and Moving to Pedestrian-friendly Cities" and "Adult Builders Target Urban Locales" have become commonplace in the media. The Economist suggests that "more Americans . . . [are] abandoning their love affair with far flung suburbs and shopping malls," while another report enthused that "[fifty-plus] empty nesters are abandoning sprawling suburbs for pedestrian-friendly cities."[86]

Yet generally speaking, the greater one's age over thirty-five, the greater the chance of living in a suburb or exurb. Far more seniors, in fact, migrate from city to suburb than the other way around. A small minority of relatively wealthy older suburbanites do buy second homes in the city, but overall the flow goes heavily the other way. The boomers' tendency to "age in place," at least until they become too old to care for themselves, also reflects a reluctance to give up a place, particularly for something smaller and more expensive. "Suburbanites," summarizes economist Gary Engelhardt, "like the suburbs."[87]

In the coming decades most boomers will likely "age in place." According to Sandra Rosenbloom, a University of Arizona professor of urban planning and gerontology, roughly three-quarters of retirees in the first bloc of boomers appear to be sticking pretty close to the suburbs, where the vast majority reside. Those who do migrate, her studies suggests, tend to head farther out into the suburban periphery, not back toward the old downtown. Most continue to rely on their cars rather than on public transit.[88]

"Everybody in this business wants to talk about the odd person who moves downtown, but it's basically a 'man bites dog' story," Rosenbloom observes. "Most people retire in place. When they move, they don't move downtown, they move to the fringes."[89]

THE ECONOMIC IMPERATIVE

"At the outset of the Cold War," writes historian Margaret Pugh O'Mara, "the notion that more Americans might work in the suburbs than in the city would have seemed somewhat unbelievable." But in the future increased suburban economic power relative to that of central cities will further disperse living patterns.[90]

In 2000, in the largest one hundred metro areas, only 22 percent of people worked within three miles of the city center; but today in Chicago, Atlanta, and Detroit, more than 60 percent of all regional employment extends more than ten miles from the core.[91] Perhaps most important, this trend extends to the science- and information-based industries that are likely to drive much of our future growth and wealth creation.

The history of high-tech development—including the location of headquarters—has been a tale of suburban growth originating in Silicon Valley, Orange County, and the San Fernando Valley and extending to the outer rings of Boston, Dallas, and other technology hubs. The "surbanization" of both residences and "leading industries," notes historian Manuel Castells, suggest that "the suburban landscape will be increasingly the predominant spatial form of American cities."[92]

Despite the assertion that skilled professionals cluster in dense urban centers, the largest reservoirs of college-educated workers are actually found in suburbs. In 2003, for example, only two of the top ten counties in percentage of college-educated adults were urban, while the rest were suburban or exurban. These educated suburbanites tend be precisely the kind of parents heavily focused their children's education, which draws them to suburban towns with superior public schools. Despite some success with urban public education, graduation rates in cities remained nearly 20 percent below those of surrounding suburbs.[93]

This shift to the periphery extends well beyond a few key high-end growth sectors. In 1969 only 11 percent of the nation's largest companies were headquartered in the suburbs; a quarter-century later roughly half had migrated to major cities' outskirts.[94] In the 1980s even thriving urban cores like Atlanta and Manhattan possessed less office space than their surrounding suburbs.[95] During the 1990s this preference for suburbs extended to an even wider range of firms, including those with 2,500 employees and more.[96]

One of the traditional cornerstones of urban economies has been producer service, covering such things as advertising, engineering, and architectural service. But even this sector has been de-concentrating for decades, for example, in Atlanta. It is taking place not only in relatively new boomtowns but in older, more traditional areas such as Boston. In the first years of the new millennium the hedge fund industry, the fastest growth sector within the financial services industry, concentrated in the posh Connecticut suburb of Greenwich.[97]

If anything, work will continue to disperse over the next few decades, even within the suburban context. We may well be moving toward what Rob Lang at the Brookings Institution calls "edgeless cities"—collections of businesses located in random office complexes, strip centers, shopping malls, and increasingly, people's homes.[98] In the business service field—financial planning, insurance, consulting, graphic arts—microenterprises will depend less on daily access to large customers and more on the Internet and on clients scattered across the breadth of the expanding metropolis and beyond it.

When one's residential community is closer to one's work in a suburban office park than it is to a traditional downtown, the very notion of a convenient place to live is upended, and the historical relationship between core and periphery is forever altered. Downtowns will remain important, but mainly in symbolic terms, as regional meeting places or cultural centers. America's economic geography has changed.

REINVENTING THE OLD SUBURBIA

The future suburbs that face the biggest challenges may well be those built without a coordinated plan or a strong economic base. Unlike the Woodlands or Valencia, these areas never had a strong employment center or were built adjacent to industries that have now declined. Many were constructed primarily as residential areas and only later, and often haphazardly, became centers for retail and business.

Such organic growth often has its advantages (as in Houston) by allowing for rapid innovation and for immigrant and small businesses to expand at low cost. But these traditional bedroom communities are also susceptible to dramatic plunges in property prices, as occurred after 2007. This problem has led many critics to see these areas as the "frontier of decline."[99]

In the coming decade these communities will reinvent themselves in ways that will sustain their economic and social viability. Particularly well positioned will be those that were once proud and independent farming towns.

Fullerton, located some twenty-two miles south of Los Angeles in Orange County, thrived as an agricultural community until the 1950s, when mass suburbanization enveloped it. "When the malls were built, our downtown died," recalls Robert Zur Schmeide, Fullerton's executive director for redevelopment and economic development. "The area was filled with pawn shops and buildings unable to meet earthquake codes."[100]

But in the 1990s Fullerton restored its old central district, preserving over seventy historic buildings, including its hundred-year-old Mission Revival train depot. By the 2000s the downtown emerged not only as the acknowledged social and cultural center for the city's 126,000 residents but as a magnet for people from surrounding communities.

In the coming decade this development around a pre-existing town center will form the key organizing principle for many older suburban communities. It threatens little in the way of existing suburban tastes and provides a critical sense of place for a community amid a vast, ever-expanding metropolitan area. "Our downtown is what keeps us together," observes Christine Jeffries, president of the Development Partnership in Naperville, a small suburban community east of Chicago. "All of us feel we are at home here. It gives us an identity."[101]

A FUTURE FOR NOWHERE

Much of suburbia has developed without any significant traditional core. These are the places that are most commonly lambasted as being utterly without value—what James Howard Kunstler described as "the geography of nowhere"—and likely doomed to extinction.[102] Large-scale vacancies in traditional malls, critical elements in many suburbs, have been building for over a decade and shot up dramatically after the 2007 real estate crash.[103]

But what some see as dystopian, others see as a great opportunity. Rick Caruso, a brash L.A.-based developer, has made a small fortune building a future for nowhere. He has taken the suburban mall—the bête noire of urbanists—and turned it into a "lifestyle center" that provides a focal point for its community that, for the most part, has never had one.

The traditional mall's function as a retail center, Caruso understands, has been undermined by competition from big-box stores—stand-alone centers built around a Wal-Mart, Target, or Costco—and by Internet marketing.[104] What these suburban communities need, he believes, are gathering places, places that provide opportunities for walking, and venues for the spontaneous social interaction long associated with urban centers.[105]

Shifting tastes, particularly among affluent consumers, underpin the need for neo-downtowns. Retailers, Caruso suggests, should understand the negative consequences of severing themselves from their surrounding communities. If retail districts become interchangeable, a given community has little reason to tie its sense of identity to that marketplace. A newer, splashier, more cost-effective place just down the road can easily wipe out your market.

"The discussion of retail in America is really about community," Caruso notes. "Lots of communities want to preserve something of Main Street and to keep the organic retailers who grew up in the area and are one of a kind. I think it works best in the long run. The key for a developer is how to keep both that feeling and the newer developments. You want to be seen as part of the future of the community."

Caruso's "lifestyle centers" provide, if not exactly a downtown, at least a simulacrum of one. He has built his centers in the Los Angeles suburb of Calabasas and in Thousand Oaks, and similar ones can be seen in Pleasant Hill (in the San Francisco Bay area) and in Schaumburg (outside Chicago).

These new suburban hubs, suggests Caruso, refocus on the commercial district's place-making role. At the Calabasas Commons small open spaces constructed between the stores provide extensive and attractive walkways. Parking is depressed below the development. It all provides the illusion that the center is less a brand-new mall than a somewhat sanitized version of a well-preserved central district in a small European town.

Caruso has tried to convert the Commons into a community center, with streets, ample places to sit, and many sidewalk cafés. Designed to perform the civic functions of a traditional Main Street, it provides space for community celebrations for everything from Thanksgiving to Hanukkah.

On a typical weekend at the Calabasas Commons, families gather, singles meet for coffee, and teenagers line up at bookstores and at the movies. The streets of the Commons, and other such centers, often have more life than can be found in many downtown districts.

The "lifestyle center" is just one adaptive approach to the evolving suburban landscape. One San Francisco–based analyst, Mark Borsuk, promotes the development of themed residential developments, wellness centers, continuing education centers, and pet necropolises. Another option will be the creation of ethnic-themed centers that reflect the suburbs' growing diversity. A glimpse can be seen at Plaza Mexico, in the south L.A. suburb of Lynwood, or even more dramatically at La Gran Plaza, the recently opened 1.1 million-square-foot retail center in Fort Worth, Texas.

In 2005 Los Angeles–area Latino retail specialist José de Jesus Legaspi helped take over a failing old mall on the outskirts of the Texas city and redid the facades along the lines of a northern Mexican town. He and his partners built family-oriented amusements like a mariachi stage and other communal facilities but also have started selling homes around it, essentially creating a residential market.

Such malls do not constitute villages in the traditional sense, and they are still private spaces. But increasingly such blurred spaces—what California architect John Kaliski has termed "hybrid suburbs"—will evolve along with the suburban communities that serve as their homes. Such developments have taken hold in Canoga Park (in the suburban San Fernando Valley), around Denver's Front Range, in the sprawling suburbs around Washington, D.C., and in Dallas and Chicago.[106]

EVERYPLACE A CITY

The increasing emphasis on the social and economic aspects of development suggests a suburb that, far from dying, will become more dominant, albeit in a new form. Over the past half century suburbs have taken on characteristics of cities, enough that one historian asserts that they have evolved into "a new and influential kind of urbanism."[107] The periphery, which originated in response to dysfunction in the urban core, will increasingly provide the critical elements that are the heritage of the traditional city, such as community, identity, and a "sacred space."

In a historical context today's suburban "sprawl" may be compared to Deadwood. That rough-and-ready mining town on the Dakota frontier was developed quickly for the narrow purpose of being close to a vein of gold. But over time many such towns developed respectable shopping streets, theaters, and other community institutions.

Similarly, today's suburban areas over time can take on the characteristics of cities. Redevelopment efforts, notes Chicago-area developer David Fanagel, are ever more common in scores of suburban towns, particularly around older midwestern and northeastern cities. "All these villages are looking at their downtowns to create an identity and get away from the cookie-cutter look," Fanagel suggests. "You are trying to create a little piece of Chicago's North Side."[108]

One critical aspect of "suburban urbanism" will be the development of "sacred places," centers of culture, the arts, and spirituality. Churches, an important part of America's village life from earliest times, proliferate in the suburbs. The diversity of this spiritual development is often unappreciated. Much is made of the expansion of evangelical megachurches, which one critic has described as "a Disneyesque utopian vision with a Christian spin."[109] But the reality is far more protean, and important. Churches are disappearing from many cities, but new ones are flourishing in suburbs, creating schools, holding fairs, and providing services to families and to the elderly. They are not only Christian churches, black and white, but synagogues, Hindu temples, and mosques.[110]

Even less recognized has been the growth of cultural institutions in suburban areas. For decades suburbs have been dismissed as "stupefied," culturally barren wastelands.[111] But today the rapid dispersion of people and talent is expanding the realm and reach of culture beyond anything seen in the past.[112] A total of 335 regional theaters able to stage Broadway plays—up 8 percent since 2000—are bringing high-level entertainment into previously obscure areas. The new $100 million, 2,000-seat Strathmore concert hall in northern Bethesda will serve as a second home of the Baltimore Symphony Orchestra, which has been struggling to find subscribers for its downtown venue.[113]

In Greater Chicago arts-related jobs on the periphery have not only been growing faster than in the core city but now account for the majority of such positions in the region.[114] Neal Cuthbert, arts program manager for the Minneapolis-based McKnight Foundation, says a "quiet arts revolution" is taking place in his region's hinterland; he points to major arts developments in Anoka, Hopkins, and Minnetonka as well as a new $7.2 million arts project in suburban Bloomington, home to the massive Mall of America.[115]

Many suburban political and economic leaders, Cuthbert notes, see cultural development as key to creating civic focus in the periphery. Most importantly these projects are not Disneyland attractions for visitors but places of civic engagement for locals. "There's a rush of amenity raising in suburbia," he says. "They are trying to find an identity for themselves."[116]

"This place used to be a place people went to sleep," says Patricia Jones, president of the Arts Alliance, a group that helps raise funds for the sprawling $63 million Civic Arts Plaza in the Los Angeles suburb of Thousand Oaks. "Now it's a place where people live, work, and find their entertainment. It's a totally different environment. It's not boring anymore."[117]

A NEW WAY TO LIVE

The transformation of suburbia is part of a wider evolution of American geography and lifestyles. Suburban development, conceived in the heat of the industrial revolution, initially engendered an extreme separation between home and work, offering what one Long Island developer describes as "the means of withdrawing from the labor and anxiety of commerce to the quiet of their families."[118]

In the future, as suburbs develop along more of a village model, they will help break down the commuter culture that has been so oppressive a part of the postwar era. Already suburbs old and new have strong town centers, such as Bellevue, Washington; Reston; the Woodlands; and Irvine, California, where between 40 and 50 percent of local residents work close to their homes. In more conventional suburbs this proportion can be less than one in five.[119]

To be sure, this development will be subject to serious constraints, in large part due to the growth of two-career families and the reluctance of managers to allow workers to work in satellite offices closer to home or even at home.[120] But advances in telecommunications will drive massive changes in the way we live and work, particularly in the suburbs. Shifts to the periphery have always been conditioned by changes in mobility, first by commuter rail, later by cars, and now by the Internet. David Bombach, president of Saratoga Homes in suburban Chicago, sees great parallels between the car and the Internet: "The automobile got it going, and I think the Internet's merely going to accelerate it, a catalyst to keep it going. So [growth is going to] the smaller communities on the fringes. I think it's something we won't see go back the other way."[121]

The process will become inexorable. Between 1990 and 2000 the number of Americans working at home full time increased by 23 percent to over four million. An additional twenty million—more than 10 percent of American adults—work at home part time. According to the firm Work Design Collaborative, roughly 17 percent of the total workforce works at home two days a week or more, up from 11 percent in 2004.[122]

One effect of the mobility change will be to make dispersion more feasible. The ability to work full time or part time from home, notes one planning expert, expands metropolitan "commuter sheds" to areas well outside their traditional limits. In exchange for a rural or exurban lifestyle, this new commuter—who may go in to "work" only one or two days a week—will endure the periodic extralong trip to the office.[123]

The shift toward cyberspace may increase the demand for living space, long an attraction of dispersed living. The "extra room" necessary for a home business is far more likely to be found in a suburban setting than in a dense urban one. Indeed, some new suburban developments, such as Ladera Ranch in southern Orange County, California, have incorporated such mixed usage into their floor plans, with separate entrances for business clients.

This new model of dispersed living could shatter the traditional bedroom suburb. "The biggest jolt the industrial revolution administered to the Western family," suggests historian Peter Stearns, "was the progressive removal of work from the home."[124] The emerging archipelago of postindustrial villages could restore that balance between workplace and family.

In the future distinctions between social and professional life, between community and work, may fade.[125] The new way of life will have enormous appeal. Future generations of Americans will live in suburbs because they represent the best, most practical choice for raising their families and enjoying the benefits of community. For this reason suburbs will remain "where the action is" in the coming decades, as America tries to accommodate an additional hundred million people.

CHAPTER FOUR: THE RESURGENT HEARTLAND

I n the rolling countryside of eastern Nebraska, amid spreading cornfields and cattle ranches, lies the small town of Aurora. With its neat town square and redbrick civic buildings, it is a snapshot from the bucolic past of the American Heartland—the vast, sparsely populated expanse that constitutes most of the nation's landmass. But Aurora also offers a preview of how a significant number of Americans may live in the coming decades.

In the first half of the 21st century, as the nation moves from 300 to 400 million people, Aurora and other places in the Heartland can provide a critical outlet for the country's restless energies and entrepreneurial passions. The region may even reprise its role in America's evolution and in the shaping of our national identity.

This renewed promise is manifest in towns like Aurora, whose population has been expanding since the 1960s and is on target to grow from 4,500 to 5,000 over the current decade.[1] Unlike many rural communities, it has not experienced a chronic decline, due mainly to expanding telecommunications operations. Its redbrick buildings on tree-lined streets around the main square are in good repair, and the local shops, if not luxurious by city standards, conduct a healthy local business.

"A lot of people are coming to us and turning away from India," long-term resident Gary Warren suggests. "There is a strong work ethic and it's very constant. We are not dying here, we are building. . . . We think this town has a great future." [2]

Warren operates Hamilton Communications, which employs 250 workers in Aurora and another 350 spread across Nebraska. His firm provides telecommunications solutions software, call centers, and other services for firms around the country. Hamilton is not the only telecommunications-based business in town. Low electrical costs, access to the interstate highway to Omaha, and excellent high-speed telecommunications make the town a desirable location for several such businesses; so too does a reliable, literate, and highly trainable workforce. Residents of the Great Plains are products of a culture that values basic skills and reliability. And their communities offer lower costs for both living and doing business.

Warren and other local entrepreneurs see in such telecommunications businesses a way to recapture some of the jobs that, since the late 1990s, have been moving to India. "We're seeing a shift now," Warren explains. "The offshore thing is slowing down. People are figuring out they need domestic knowledge and that flat, neutral American accent."

But it's not just onshore services that drive the local economy. New ethanol facilities, a seed research facility, and a burgeoning group of small technology companies are also contributing to the town's growth. Unemployment in the Great Plains has remained low, even during the recession that began in 2007; for much of the decade the biggest problem facing many businesses has been finding enough workers. "Our biggest concern now is building houses for people," Warren says. "There is no sense of dying here. Aurora is all about the future."

BEYOND THE "BUFFALO COMMONS"

What is happening in Aurora, and in many other parts of the American Heartland, contradicts much of the conventional wisdom about the vast region between the Rocky Mountains and the Mississippi. Often the media portray the Great Plains as a kind of Mad Max environment—a postmodern, desiccated, lost world of emptying towns, meth labs, and militant Native Americans about to reclaim a place best left to the forces of nature.

Typical of these dismal portraits was a 2007 *New York Times* article that described North Dakota as "Not Far From Forsaken." The piece painted a portrait of "irresistible decline": dying villages, aging populations, a place to visit now before it all blows away.[3] Other journalists have suggested that the shrinking population of the Heartland might be not altogether a bad thing; as one writer put it, "there are more Indians and bison on the Plains than at any time since the late 1870s."[4]

Some policymakers see the area's debilitating dependence on federal subsidies and decreasing population as reasons to hasten the decline. In a call for a reversal of two centuries of national policy that promoted growth in the Great Plains, two New Jersey academics, Frank J. Popper and Deborah Popper, have proposed that Washington accelerate the depopulation of the Plains and create "the ultimate national park." Their suggestion is that the government return the land and communities to a "buffalo commons."

The Poppers' prescription is breathtaking in its boldness: empty large parts of the Plains and populate the area with herds of buffalo. In the early years of the new millennium that idea gained currency among environmentalists and reporters, many of whom cited the area's ongoing population decline.[5] The Poppers argue:

We believe that over the next generation the Plains will, as a result of the largest, longest-running agricultural and environmental miscalculation in American history, become almost totally depopulated. At that point, a new use for the region will emerge, one that is in fact so old that it predates the American presence. We are suggesting that the region be returned to its original pre-white state, that it be, in effect, de-privatized.[6]

But in the next few decades, this Heartland-as-park concept is likely to feel as anachronistic as the pre-Columbian past it seeks to evoke. Restoring the natural environment where possible is no doubt a worthy idea, but many places in this broad swath are hardly at death's door and have been, and are likely to continue, rebounding in jobs, population, and income. Even as many smaller communities continued to depopulate, Fargo, North Dakota, for example, grew by more than 20 percent between 1990 and 2000. This pattern continued throughout the decade; scores of other Heartland towns and cities, such as Sioux Falls, Des Moines, and Bismarck all grew well faster than the national average through 2008.[7]

This development holds considerable promise. As long as the Heartland (and the inner cities) lag behind, the nation's productive capacity will remain far below its potential. But the Heartland, with the preponderance of the nation's land and natural resources, arguably represents the great opportunity region for 21st-century America.

To seize this opportunity, Americans need to see the Heartland as far more than a rural or agricultural zone. Although food production will remain a critical component of its economy, high-technology services, communications, energy production, manufacturing, and warehouses will serve as the critical levers for new employment and wealth creation.

The emerging Heartland revival represents the completion of the aspirational cycle that started with the historic movement west, then focused on the burgeoning cities in the late 19th century, and finally spread to the suburbs and exurbs. As urbanized regions become even more crowded and expensive, and as new technologies emerge, more and more Americans will find their best future in the wide open spaces that, even in 2050, will still exist across the continent.

THE IMPORTANCE OF LAND

When it comes to the Heartland, the trends that will define the future are rooted in the past. Even in the 21st century the Heartland will still have a critical component of its historic strength: its vast and rich natural environment. Among the great industrial and developing countries, America has the greatest expanse of arable land and number of resources. On a per capita basis, its endowment is far richer than that of its prime competitors, including the European Community, India, China, or Japan. As Arnold Henry Guyot, a Swiss-American geologist and geographer, observed in 1849, "the extent of spaces" available in the United States provided resources that a crowded "exhausted Europe" would not have at its disposal.[8]

This advantage is not likely to diminish in the coming decades. Although the past thirty years have seen some loss of farmland, the amount of land that actually grows harvested crops has remained stable. Clearly some prime farmland close to metropolitan centers is threatened and perhaps should be protected; but the notion, popularized by environmental and "smart growth" advocates, that the United States is running out of productive farmland or open space, due to urban sprawl, seems fanciful at best.[9]

Today only 10 percent of people in rural areas live on farms, and only 14 percent of the rural workforce is employed in farming.[10] Yet the farm sector will remain a crucial part of the Heartland economy. The U.S. farm sector provides abundant output with just a small fraction of the domestic labor force, leveraging technology to considerable advantage. The American economy today benefits from relatively low-cost food, the average consumer spending only about 10 percent of disposable income on food.

But in an increasingly competitive environment that is no longer limited to traditional exporters such as Australia, Canada, and Argentina, American agriculture will have to evolve considerably. Countries now making significant investments in agriculture also include Brazil, Russia, Ukraine, and Kazakhstan. In the 21st century American agriculture will have to move toward high-value products, like wine, specialty crops, livestock, and organics.

Early signs of this transition can be seen across the agricultural horizon. For years the number of farms has been gradually decreasing, in part due to demand for the land for tourism, recreation, and housing development.[11] But this trend has started to reverse: between 2002 and 2009 the number of farms increased by 4 percent. Although large farms predominate, accounting for 75 percent of production, ever more of these smaller farms appear to be finding an expanding market. Many utilize the Internet to follow market trends and keep in touch with customers.[12]

The growing popularity of organic products has opened new market opportunities for producers, and organic farming is now one of the fastest-growing segments of U.S. agriculture. During the 1990s retail sales grew 20 percent or more annually. Organic products are available in nearly 20,000 natural foods stores and are sold in 73 percent of all conventional grocery stores.[13] By 2002, when the USDA implemented national organic standards, certified organic farmland had doubled, and it doubled again between 2002 and 2005. Organic livestock sectors have grown even faster.[14]

This phenomenon has tremendous long-term potential for American farmers. The global market for organic food and beverages was worth $22.75 billion in 2007, after more than doubling in five years, according to market research firm Euromonitor International. The United States accounted for about 45 percent of that total.[15] Farmers' markets, especially popular among organic producers, have multiplied over the last decade. Organic farmers are finding ways to capture a larger segment of the consumer food dollar through on-farm processing, producer marketing cooperatives, and direct marketing.

At the same time, community-supported agriculture—in which farmers sell directly to individual or groups of consumers on a regular basis—has emerged as a new model of food production, sales, and distribution, aimed at heightening both the quality of food and the quality of care given the land, plants, and animals. This increasingly common part of American agriculture allows small-scale commercial farmers and gardeners to gain access to successful small-scale markets. "Community-supported" farms use a system of weekly delivery or pickup of vegetables, flowers, fruits, herbs, and even milk or meat products. It keeps more food dollars in the local community and contributes to the maintenance and establishment of regional food production.

The rise of smaller-scale agriculture, more specialized and more closely linked to urban consumers, offers a glimpse into an emerging future for the Heartland. No longer isolated by distance, the Heartland can become integrated into the larger economy in more direct ways than ever before. By the mid-21st century the Heartland could become not a relic of American history, but a vital part of accommodating a population of over four hundred million.

ENERGY FUTURES

The vastness of the American continent provides the United States with a unique opportunity to meet the future energy challenges. In fundamental terms, we will have to shift to new fuels. It won't be the first time the country made a transition to greater self-sufficiency. During the

Second World War farmers responded to incentives to create fats and oils that were indispensable for making war materials like explosives, tin plate, paints, and soaps.[16]

The shift to alternative fuels should be encouraged, for many reasons. Over time biofuels will create new jobs, increase commodity prices and farm income, improve the country's balance of trade, and reduce our dependence on imported fuel and chemicals. These products will likely expand well beyond corn-based ethanol and toward other, perhaps more sustainable nonfood fuels based on wood and agricultural waste in addition to switchgrass. Equally important, a strong domestic energy industry would allow the country as a whole to slow down, or even reverse, the flow of capital to often hostile oil-rich states in the Middle East and elsewhere.[17]

The Heartland is well positioned also to play a greatly expanded role in the development and implementation of new energy solutions through the production of biofuels, many of them not taken from food-stocks.[18] Many states in the Heartland—the Dakotas, Wyoming, and Montana—contain significant conventional fossil fuel resources. In many places, contrary to claims about "peak oil" that hold that the world is about to run out of fossil fuels, higher energy prices have stimulated new production of oil and lower-carbon natural gas, in the Great Plains and the Intermountain West.[19]

This new wave of exploration is often being led not by major oil companies, but by independent "wildcat" operators. Although these entrepreneurs sell to the majors, they are often locally based and enrich small cities, such as Midland, Texas; Casper, Wyoming; and Williston, North Dakota. Thanks to this renewed production, per capita income in these states has risen since 2000, with energy-rich Wyoming, Montana, North Dakota, New Mexico, and West Virginia ranking in the top five states in terms of income growth.[20]

Over time some significant potential energy gains will come from wind. The Great Plains have been referred to as "the Saudi Arabia of wind"; North Dakota alone could eventually provide enough wind power, by some estimates, to supply 20 percent of the nation's electrical needs. The Plains region from Texas through Montana and Minnesota also possesses enormous potential wind resources, which could power the country if the capacity of the transmission lines is greatly enhanced.

If taken seriously, wind power could provide opportunities for economic growth and development in some of the country's traditionally poorest regions. On the hardscrabble Rosebud Sioux reservation in South Dakota, new turbines are bringing electrical power to local residents; expansion could end up supplying electrical power to metropolitan regions. "When those blades went up," said one Sioux, Robert Gough, "our hearts went up with it."[21]

THE STILL OPEN COUNTRY

The production of fuel, fiber, and food is only one role that the Heartland will play in the America of 2050. As population growth continues to pressure the major urbanized regions, the country's physical vastness, especially in its once-inaccessible regions, will take on greater importance. Already as farms consolidate or are abandoned, once-remote Montana, New Mexico, and Wyoming have experienced an inexorable urbanization. The Rocky Mountains and the Appalachians, which are not ideal for mass agriculture or for mining, will become increasingly attractive not only as tourist locations but as places of resettlement for restless urban and suburban populations.[22]

The long-term success of these regions will depend on their ability to develop beyond a purely amenity-based economy, which generally produces lower-wage opportunities for local residents. Here technological advances in telecommunications and transportation may prove vital to break down the traditional intellectual and cultural isolation that has kept nonmetropolitan areas backward and unattractive to skilled, educated workers.

More than anything, the Internet has diminished the metropolis's historic near-monopoly of information. What Karl Marx called "the idiocy of rural life" no longer applies.[23] A Heartland-based farmer, securities dealer, machine shop worker, or software writer enjoys virtually the same access to the latest market and technical information as someone located in midtown Manhattan or Silicon Valley.

This access, both tangible and digital, could allow individuals and businesses to reap the American Heartland's underutilized, largely untapped assets: low housing costs, a relatively good business climate, quality schools, a reasonably educated and productive workforce, and land availability. This urbanizing tendency may even help preserve the natural environment, as people are far more likely to protect a region where exploitation of the resource base is not the sole basis of the economy.

REPRISING THE HISTORIC ROLE OF THE HEARTLAND

The Heartland could once again have a critical influence on our national identity and serve as a powerful outlet for the entrepreneurial energies of both immigrants and current urban dwellers.

From the earliest days of the Republic the rural countryside played a central role in shaping a unique American identity. During the Revolution land bounties along the western frontier were a major inducement to enlist and re-enlist Continental soldiers. Visionaries such as Thomas Jefferson saw the production of foodstuffs as the ideal occupation for the new country's energies; he viewed democracy as best suited for agrarian communities, comparing "the mobs of great cities" to "sores" on the body of the Republic.[24]

Even the urbane Benjamin Franklin, a strong advocate of manufacturing, saw the land and its produce as the key to the new country's greatness. "The business of America is agriculture," he proclaimed in 1780s. "For one Artisan or Merchant, I suppose, we have at least a hundred Farmers, by the most part Cultivators of their own fertile Lands."[25]

Although farming dominated rural growth, it also created a thriving, sprawling network of towns and small cities. On his visit to America in the early 1830s, Alexis de Tocqueville was struck by the country's decentralized nature. "The intelligence and the power are dispersed abroad," he wrote, "and instead of radiating from a point, they cross each other in every direction."[26]

The settlement of the Heartland is a critical narrative of American history. It is a centuries-long story of great sacrifice and great cruelty, particularly in its deleterious effects on indigenous peoples. Nonetheless the great westward migration and settlement, particularly in the Great Plains, should not be seen as a massive miscalculation but rather as an impressive entrepreneurial and social achievement, perhaps the nation's greatest.

The movement west, like the formation of the great cities, was a critical component of America's aspirational ethic. With its wide expanses, early America offered a welcome refuge for Europeans who sought freedom from the shackles of a still-entrenched feudal culture. A persistent agricultural surplus and a general labor shortage meant that even in colonial times European peasants who migrated to America could enjoy freedom from starvation, as well as higher wages, lower mortality rates, and greater opportunities to own land.

Such ambitions were unleashed with particular ferocity in the decades that followed independence. As the nation stretched westward, land sales expanded dramatically, from 1.3 million acres in 1815 to 12 million four decades later.[27] Much of the risk was taken by individual families. In what the historians Charles Beard and Mary Beard described as an era of "agricultural imperialism," many of the most energetic and ambitious young people from the eastern seaboard headed to the frontier. Between 1810 and 1860 the mainly agricultural region west of the Appalachians enjoyed enormous population growth, from roughly 15 percent of the national total to over 47 percent.[28]

This period saw the emergence of great Heartland cities such as Cincinnati, St. Louis, Chicago, and Kansas City, whose economies depended on servicing the needs of farmers and marketing their huge agriculture surplus. Mass production of animal products was undertaken on a hitherto unimagined scale. Soon dubbed Porkopolis, Cincinnati's enormous slaughterhouses dropped "rivers of blood" into Deer Creek and from there into the Ohio.[29]

THE ENTREPRENEURIAL TRADITION

For much of the 19th century American farming was primarily small scale and family run.[30] They were generally more oriented toward property, innovation, and profit than their counterparts in Europe, since European farming families tended to be more tied to a specific place in ways that transcended the search for profit.

The emphasis on profit helped drive rapid technological innovation, particularly in the "free" states of the North.[31] De Tocqueville made this connection as well, noting that the American agriculturalist was by nature a restless person, whose ambitions led him to apply "industrial pursuits" for improving his land or, in a way almost unthinkable in Europe, to sell his farm and move on to other businesses or other lands. "Almost all the farmers of the United States," he wrote, "combine some trade with agriculture; most of them make agriculture itself a trade."[32]

The passage of the Homestead Act in 1862 opened to settlement a vast new portion of the American land base, from the western edges of the Midwest to the Rockies. In 1860 there were two million farms in the United States; in 1910 there were more than six million.[33] Nowhere were the changes more dramatic than in the Great Plains where, starting in the 1880s, sprawling new farms added to the nation's enormous productive capacity. Like the earlier Heartland settlers, those who braved the harsh conditions of Plains were highly entrepreneurial and risk-taking by nature. Many were new not only to the land but to the country itself. In 1890 some 43 percent of all North Dakotans were foreigners.[34] These new residents were highly innovative, constantly on the lookout for new methods of animal husbandry, planting, and marketing.

INDUSTRIALIZATION AND THE ROOTS OF HEARTLAND DECLINE

In the 1820s federal officials expected the settlement of the frontier to take five hundred years, but the process was actually so rapid it created unforeseen problems. In the late 19th century America's new farmlands surpassed the total growing areas of Germany and France combined. Between 1860 and 1910 the annual output of wheat grew from 173 million tons to 700 million, one-sixth of the world's total.[35] But this productivity, on which much of the country's prosperity depended, also turned into a curse. The ever-expanding surplus of agricultural goods often faced opposition from European farmers and competition from emerging land-rich countries like Canada, Australia, and Argentina.[36] Low prices, as well as often difficult natural conditions, drove many off the land and into bankruptcy.[37]

In some senses the American farmer was his own worst enemy. Between 1840 and 1900 the man-hours needed to produce wheat and corn were cut in half. But this remarkable boost in productivity did not find equally expanding markets. Except in a few periods, such as during the First World War, production routinely outstripped demand. Agriculture, once seen as a stable occupation, became progressively more subject to "boom and bust" patterns.[38]

The legacy of this "too much mistake," as historian Ellwyn Robinson called it—too many small towns, too much production, too many governments—still troubles the Heartland today.[39] Farmers' ability to control their destinies gradually eroded. By the 1920s the "too much" phenomenon was creating environmental problems. Across large swaths of the Central Plains, some of which may not have been suited to intensive agriculture, drought conditions created great clouds of moving soil. The "dust bowl" bankrupted thousands of farmers. Whole populations migrated to California and other far western states.

The solutions that arose—subsidies and price supports—saved some farms, but often at the cost of dampening the entrepreneurial spirit of farmers and townspeople. Perhaps the most wrenching changes were incentives to limit, instead of expand, production. "Instead of Teddy Roosevelt's exhortations toward a more strenuous effort lest the United States lose its world standing," observes historian Donald Worster, "conservationists in the 1930s frequently maintained that it was too much strenuousness, not too little, that put the country on its back."[40]

After the Depression the agricultural industry, stabilized and newly wedded to sounder conservation techniques, became even more productive than it had been in the past, while using far less land. But despite this explosive growth in productivity, rural America became less and less important to the national scheme. By the late 1890s agricultural exports as a percentage of total U.S. exports had already begun to drop, replaced first by manufacturing and later by service exports. America remains the world's largest exporter of many commodities, including wheat, but it represents a shrinking component of overall exports.[41]

The number of American farms was falling, just as the average acreage was rising. Despite the massive subsidies, rural poverty persisted, as government support focused on the largest farmers. By 2000 in the Mississippi Delta, the top 1 percent of farmers received 26 percent of the federal subsidies, while the bottom 80 percent garnered only 9 percent. A similar if less extreme pattern can be seen in many midwestern and Great Plains states, and in Texas.

The whole policy, suggests Indiana senator Richard Lugar, himself a family farmer, has been "ineffective" in reviving the Heartland economy. Instead it has led to a "ritual of overproduction" and ever-increasing "consolidation of farm ownership." Over the years what the *Wall Street Journal* denounced as a "farm state pig out" has done little to help rural communities retain residents, attract newcomers, or diversify their economies.[42]

This dependence on subsidies led to an erosion of the entrepreneurial, self-reliant ethos of the region's farmers and townspeople. As the number of farms declined, many towns emptied out, losing their young and ambitious to the cities and suburbs. In some small towns the problems were made worse by an aging leadership resistant to new ideas. "Some rural areas prefer a slow death to having to change," one North Dakota businessman complained to me over a beer back around 2000. "You wonder if you can raise a family in a place that seems about to die."[43]

SPRAWL BEYOND SPRAWL

At this very time, however, a new demographic trend was building throughout the Heartland. As early as the 1970s demographers began to notice a slowdown—and in some places a reversal—of the long-standing pattern of out-migration from rural areas.

This rebound was an extension of the national outward movement to suburbs and exurbs. Over the past three decades the most rapid growth in rural America has taken place in the peripheries of major metropolitan areas. The desire for a more rural lifestyle, ironically, has transformed many once rustic areas into extensions of the suburbs. Between the 1970s and 2004 some four hundred former rural areas grew by 50 percent and are now home to over 70 million people.[44]

In his prescient 1978 book *The New Heartland,* author John Herbers recognized that the movement first to suburbs, then to the exurbs on the suburban fringes, represented something other than a "return to the land." Traditional "boundaries" between rural and urban, small town and city, were breaking down into something new, "mostly a movement of a prosperous, adventurous middle class superimposed over small towns and countryside."[45]

This trend appears to have accelerated during subsequent decades. Since 2000, according to the most recent census information, more than 2.7 million Americans have moved out of the largest cities. Although the smallest communities under 50,000 continue to lose population, and much of the migration went to small and midsize locations, a significant portion went to places with between 50,000 and 500,000 residents.[46]

These changes, which represent a relatively small percentage of the overall population, nonetheless mark a significant reversal in the relentless migration of large populations into the very largest urban centers. Demographer Wendell Cox has described this process as "sprawl beyond sprawl."

In some areas this development will take place at the far fringes of great metropolitan areas, creating small agricultural hamlets. In the northern reaches of Dallas and outside Decatur, Georgia, for example, suburban communities were embedded within protected agricultural areas. In the Decatur project sixty-seven units are sited on eight acres, while the surrounding twelve acres are left for agriculture and woodlands. Gardens produce fresh produce for the residents and for local markets.

These new developments will create a new kind of rural-urban community that might appeal to people who wish to live on the fringe but still need access to the city. Residents will be able to engage in small-scale agriculture and consume food that is locally produced. As new urbanist architect Andres Duany says half-jokingly, "Agriculture is the new golf." For empty nesters, notes one developer, it's a perfect opportunity to "enjoy the burbs and live green."[47]

This trend is expected to grow, suggests demographer Cox. If it does, then in coming decades we may see something akin to the network of vital smaller communities that characterized America in the 19th century.

THE RISE OF URBALISM

In the coming decades growth in the Heartland is likely to be concentrated in specific places, as it has always been in the arid West, where the need to bring in water supplies forced the development of relatively small areas amid wide open spaces.[48] In the 21st century this clustering will be driven by the need to concentrate critical infrastructure such as high-speed telecommunications, airports, and cultural institutions and, for an aging population, health care and cultural facilities. As Fargo, Sioux Falls, and Des Moines grow, smaller communities close to these hubs will also expand, while those farther away from roads, airports, and natural attractions will continue to diminish.

The emergence of what might be called "urbalism" is already visible. Demographer Richard Rathge states that since 1950s the overall population of the Great Plains has more than doubled. In the 1990s the Great Plains population as a whole grew by 6.7 million people, or 17 percent, but 85 percent of the growth took place in metropolitan areas, which account for 71 percent of the entire Great Plains population. In contrast, the 358 rural counties in the region, which account for only 4 percent of the population base, grew by only 5 percent or 82,721 people.

For the most part, this growth is occurring in formerly agriculturally oriented small cities. Fargo and Sioux Falls grew up during the period of rural expansion in the late 19th century, then generally declined or plateaued in the mid-20th century. In the coming decades these areas will enjoy lower housing and energy costs, excellent public schools, good local universities, and other quality-of-life attractions for middle-class families. The most successful small cities will be those adept at exploiting these benefits to lure high-end business and professional service firms, information companies, and diversified, innovative small manufacturers.[49]

Even as many of the smaller towns shrink, and some marginal farmland is returned to nature's domain, these cities are attracting returning residents and newcomers, who see opportunities both to build a business and enjoy a more bucolic, low-key lifestyle.[50] Many of these communities are college towns, such as Ames, Iowa, and Grand Forks, North Dakota; the schools provide both an economic base and a source of new talent.

But the key driver of this growth is the technology that allows people to locate where they wish. "Both individuals and corporations are beginning to define the meaning of space as opposed to being defined by that space," suggests Ryan Mathews, a futurist who runs Black Monk Consulting in Eastpointe, Michigan. "You used to build cars in Detroit because that's where the rail lines met, where you had access to massive supplies of coal and steel. So people would go to the city for that job. Now we're not so dependent on infrastructure or we're redefining what it means—now it's high-speed lines and satellite links—so we're moving beyond the industrial model, with economic activity diffusing from great population centers."[51]

Smaller, historically rural communities outside the Plains will also undergo this change. Particularly well positioned will be areas like Washington's bucolic Wenatchee Valley, which lies across the Cascades from the Puget Sound. With a population of 60,000, Wenatchee's agriculture-based economy has declined. But by 2000 it was attracting high-tech talent and professionals from the Seattle area who were drawn to its bucolic setting and sunnier weather.

The area invested in high-speed Internet and, using its clean and relatively inexpensive hydro-electricity as a lure, attracted numerous technology firms, including Yahoo! and numerous start-ups.[52] Even the agricultural economy has revived—specialty apples have replaced commodity products, and wine production has exploded. The renewed prosperity can be seen all over the area but particularly in the old downtown.

CAFFEINATING THE CAPPUCCINO ECONOMY

Similar growth can be expected in highly attractive resort areas like the Rapid City–Black Hills region of South Dakota and St. George, Utah. The new telecommunications technologies could help many of these "cappuccino communities" evolve well beyond sites for tourism and second homes. Some resort areas that are not too expensive have already developed sophisticated technology and high-end, service-based economies.[53]

This focus on productive business will become especially critical for resortlike areas. As the 2007 real estate crash made clear, an economy based purely on speculation and second homes has limited stability. Nowhere is the impact clearer than in Bend, a scenic town of 75,000 located amid volcanic peaks in the center of Oregon. Highly attractive to migrants from California, the city saw a huge spike in housing prices as speculators from the Golden State invested in homes while others bought second residences there. In 2008, notes real estate appraiser Steve Pistole, prices were rising 2 percent *a month*, while those in Portland were rising "only" 8 percent a year.[54]

This surge in home prices created a kind of false economy. Many of the new residents paid for housing with income they had earned elsewhere; once fairly modest in its restaurant offerings, Bend now saw chefs from San Francisco opening high-end, trendy restaurants. Once the housing bubble imploded, this market tumbled. Construction and tourism jobs, the engines of growth, evaporated, raising local unemployment by 2009 to over 15 percent.[55]

In the future, communities like Bend will come back to life, not because of second-home buyers or speculators but by capitalizing on the natural attraction it holds for talented individuals. Already some newcomers have founded significant tech firms such as Bend Research, Micro-Semi, and G5 Search Marketing.

Bend is also home to many smaller-scale entrepreneurs, like thirty-eight-year-old Michael Taus, who has set up small tech businesses in his residence. A recent arrival from Los Angeles, Taus made it big as one of the founders of Rent.com, which was sold to eBay in 2005. After living in Bend for only a few months, he launched his own start-up and consulted for other local firms. Taus believes that others of his generation will want to establish businesses in central Oregon, lured by both its lifestyle and its affordability. Some of the new business may be in software, Taus says, but others could sprout in specialty agriculture, wood products, and other industries. "People are here for a reason," he says earnestly. "There's a good amount of talent, and you can get more here. There's a great potential. We just have to get down to business."[56]

OPTING FOR "THE BOONDOCKS"

In the coming decades the collective impact of another hundred million Americans on costs and congestion in big cities and along the coasts will drive more and more people into the Heartland. Compared to most metropolitan areas, costs in the Heartland have generally remained remarkably reasonable, a trend that should continue.[57] As a rule, rural residents spend less of their income on housing than do residents in metropolitan areas, even though rural incomes tend to be lower. In 2003, even before the peak of the latest housing boom, roughly 15 percent of all metropolitan households spent over half their income on housing, while only 10 percent of those in nonmetro areas carried this same level of burden.[58]

Quality-of-life considerations could play a decisive role in attracting newcomers to the region, even young families, a demographic that has hitherto been leaving the region. Another pivotal group, baby boomers, may now be considering an "equity migration" from the coasts. Both kinds of households could enjoy significant capital gains and reduce debts, while still engaging in economic activities made possible by the Internet.

According to the 2000 census, boomers particularly favor high-amenity locations in the Rockies, the Upper Great Lakes, the Ozarks, and the rural Northeast. Rather than head to the expensive and congested Sunbelt areas, many are choosing a more diverse array of rural destinations.[59]

For much of our history, going back to the Jeffersonian era, Americans have expressed a desire for a low-key, small-town lifestyle. They still do today. Recent surveys reveal that as many as one out of three U.S. adults would prefer to live in a rural area, compared to some 20 percent who actually do live there. Another poll, conducted in 2008 by the Pew Research Center, found that a majority of Americans would actually prefer to live in rural areas or small towns, more than twice as many as opted for urban or suburban areas. More Americans, it appears, yearn to live in the countryside, not the city.[60]

Most Americans believe that rural areas epitomize traditional values of family, religion, and self-sufficiency and that they are more attractive, friendlier, and safer, particularly for children. These perceptions, interestingly enough, are also held by the majority of suburbanites and an only slightly larger proportion of rural residents. However exaggerated this image may be, it suggests that there is a large, mostly untapped population that would consider a move to a smaller community in the Heartland.[61]

One large segment of rural newcomers may be returnees: people who left the Plains or other rural areas as they entered adulthood, but are inclined to return if opportunities were sufficient. Many natives of the Dakotas, for example, see themselves as enjoying a good quality of life, which is not just a reason to stay but also a reason to return.[62]

"We now can work in a challenging industry but live in a place we want to live," suggests Vern Dosch, a Bismarck native and president of National Information Systems Cooperatives, a software firm employing some 250 people in his home city. "We can send our kids to a public school where 98 percent of the kids graduate and 95 percent go to college. You don't worry about crime, and a long commute just isn't in the vocabulary."[63]

RETURN OF THE IMMIGRANTS

Since the mid-20th century the Heartland has been widely seen as homogeneous and somewhat unaffected by, even resistant to, the country's broader demographic changes. But in more recent times, these areas have witnessed a new wave of immigrants, who now constitute a large part of the population in many Heartland areas. During the 1990s Iowa, North and South Dakota, and Kentucky experienced among the fastest growth in immigration. Immigrants, like many other newcomers, may be attracted by lower housing costs, new job opportunities, and a perceived better environment to raise children. Asian and Latino immigrants have turned some rural places, like Finney County, Kansas, into "majority, minority" counties.[64]

A Hispanic migration has taken place in rural communities that had previously been experiencing considerable depopulation. In fact, Hispanics—not only migrant workers but those employed in manufacturing and construction—accounted for one-quarter of the nation's rural population growth in the 1990s. Much of this growth took place across the Sunbelt, but it also extended to the Great Plains, which had not seen much immigration since the 1920s.

In many Heartland towns, such as Lexington, Nebraska, immigrants originally came to work in local factories, such as meat-packing plants, and in construction, but they ended up putting down roots. In 1990 only 329 Hispanics lived in Lexington, located in the south-central part of the state; today they account for a majority of the town's 10,000 residents.

Immigration is both reviving Heartland towns and providing major challenges, typical historically of areas with sudden increases in newcomers, including upsurges in crime and suddenly crowded schools. But from an economic point of view, immigrants have transformed dying places into enlivened ones. Where small stores had once been languishing, there are now Latino markets and restaurants. Rural Wal-Marts offer yucca roots, tomatillos, and tripe. Communities like Lexington that were otherwise losing families, jobs, and workers now feel tensions but also a sense of a future. "I can remember when every house on the street was for sale except ours and our neighbor's," recalls Barry McFarland, a local resident, reflecting on how much has changed due to the newcomers.[65]

The migration is not composed solely of immigrants working in poultry and other food-processing facilities. In some states the movement of educated immigrant and minority professionals has started to balance out the long-term loss of native-born youth. Although still predominantly white, the Heartland is becoming more diverse, and it is beginning to share in the demographic vitality hitherto associated with more urbanized areas.[66]

ECONOMIC DE-CLUSTERING

These demographic events—immigration, and migration from the metropolitan regions—are mirrored in the Heartland economy. "Whether people follow jobs or jobs follow people is the subject of much debate," Harvard's Nancy McArdle has said, "but over the long run, they move together."[67] Along with the demographic dispersion that has marked the last half century, employment has been deconcentrating. In contrast to the old industrial paradigm, where jobs clustered in the densest areas, economic growth now tends to move toward the less dense areas. The driving force is the "de-clustering" of industries from their traditional urban centers, such as California's Silicon Valley and New York City's financial sector, to less-dense, less-expensive areas like Sioux Falls, Des Moines, and Fargo.

The evidence for the de-clustering of industries, and of jobs in general, remains powerful. Between 1961 and 1996 the percentage of American jobs located in the densest areas declined from 84 to 66 percent. Although the most remote areas did not have the strongest growth, the less-dense areas experienced far higher growth than those close to the urban core.[68] Overall, between 2000 and 2007, job growth rates in smaller communities were better than three times those of core cities, although less than those of suburban areas.[69] Economic contractions may slow the process, but future expansions seem likely to accelerate it.

De-clustering may be headed even farther out. Many areas in the periphery are already creating jobs much faster than the biggest cities. This is true not only for amenity-rich areas such as St. George, Rapid City, and Wenatchee but also for more traditional Sioux Falls and Fargo.[70] Occasional "clusters" of enterprises in the Heartland, for example, include software in Fargo, insurance in Des Moines, and electronics manufacturing in Boise.

ECONOMIC PROSPECTS IN RURAL AMERICA

Equally critical to the growth of jobs will be the ability of Heartland economies to gain in high-wage sectors like business services, finance, logistics, and advanced manufacturing. Although rural areas overall have lagged in these arenas, technology and business service growth has clearly been shifting to smaller cities like Des Moines and Boise.[71]

The strongest boomtowns are precisely where population growth has been strongest, such as rural parts of the Intermountain West. But the overall shift of job growth to the farther periphery suggests a broader opportunity. Over the past three decades the Heartland's strongest gains have been in manufacturing and wholesale trade, which between 1970 and 2000 expanded more rapidly in rural places than in cities. Large metropolitan areas have dominated service sector exports, but in tangible goods the globally competitive economy seems to be shifting to the far periphery.[72]

The Heartland's strongest economic growth took place, once again, either in "amenity regions" or in reviving rural centers such as Fargo, Sioux Falls, and Dubuque. These areas have benefited from industrial shifts that began in the late 20th century and appear to be gaining 21st-century momentum with the movement of manufacturers from traditional centers to lower-cost, more business-friendly areas.[73]

Manufacturing's role in promoting job and income growth is often understated. Although manufacturing employment overall has dropped, the percentage of higher-wage, skilled industrial jobs has been climbing over the last two decades. Much of this growth has been concentrated in formerly rural regions in the West and South as well as in small towns.[74]

Dubuque, for one, has seen a revival of a previously moribund manufacturing base. Its turnaround has been the product of a pro-business climate, a strong commitment by local educational institutions to supply industry with skilled workers, and regional traditions of hard work and manual labor. By the mid-2000s Dubuque was enjoying the fastest job-growth rate of any city in the Midwest, with steadily low unemployment and rising wages.[75]

Although economic reverses due to the current global recession could hamper such growth, over time Heartland communities will be able to attract and retain manufacturing industries because of their attitude toward industry, which differs from that found in larger metropolitan areas. "We've gone with the basics; we've tried to stay good at things that matter, including things like manufacturing and agriculture," Rick Dickinson, director of the Greater Dubuque Development Association, explains. "We look at attracting people who might have a reason to be here. Everyone talks about doing the glitzy stuff, but we think this is a model for Middle America."[76]

James Schrempf, plant manager at the local John Deere facility, gives much of the credit to local educational and political institutions, which have worked hard to train, attract, and retain skilled workers. With a perspective that is rare in today's America, Dubuque revels in its traditional manufacturing culture. Some twenty six thousand people attended the plant's recent sixtieth anniversary celebration. "The big advantage we have here is that this is a great community that supports what we do," Schrempf explains. "This is a place people want to be."

Such changes could accelerate elsewhere in the Heartland. Meanwhile in Dubuque economic growth has brought a revival of the town's old central core. Dubuque's story suggests that towns once written off as dead can come back, if they offer not only economic opportunities but also the lifestyle advantages that are increasingly difficult to secure in ever-more-crowded metropolitan areas. Even as many of the smallest communities lose population, other regions are revitalizing in ways that show how the country can grow comfortably in the next decades.

Sam McMahon, the son of a factory worker, remembers leaving Dubuque in the early 1990s. It was, he recalled, "a tough place to be" after his father lost his job and, as he put it, "the future was bleak." Seeking a better opportunity, he moved to Milwaukee.

But by 2007 things had changed. McMahon has moved back to Dubuque to work as a production manager at a local metal-fabrication plant. "I didn't think I'd move back here at age thirty-two," he says, "but you really get the sense the place is getting back. . . . We're getting to the next level."[77]

THE RISE OF THE BRAIN BELT

As industrial work becomes more productive and less job generating, the Heartland economy will depend more on the migration of information-sector workers and industries. One significant trend will be the rise of what New England researcher Amy Zuckerman has called "hidden tech": growing concentrations of tech workers in various non-metropolitan regions from Wenatchee, Washington, to the Pioneer and Happy valleys of western Massachusetts.[78]

These areas, she points out, have experienced among the strongest increases in educated residents. Many newcomers are home-based entrepreneurs connected directly or indirectly to the information economy, as investors, graphic artists, writers, software designers, and engineering professionals. As Scott Cooper, Hewlett-Packard's manager for technology policy, told Zuckerman in 2002, "The old terms of quantification don't work. What matters is that instead of people moving to Silicon Valley, they're moving to lifestyle places like the Happy Valley. They're redefining the notion that you need a cluster of tech companies to attract tech employees. With the Internet, you can grab staffing and ideas from all over the world."[79]

We can expect the rise of "hidden tech" to continue, as well as the expansion of tech-oriented companies into Heartland regions. Although rural America is often perceived as lacking in educated workers, in reality, nonmetropolitan New England, the Great Plains, and even parts of the Sierras can be characterized as having a skill "surplus."[80]

The core of this surplus is highly educated young people. Students in Nebraska, the Dakotas, Montana, and Idaho tend to perform better in school than those in more metropolitan ones (as measured by graduation rates, college attendance, or enrollment in upper-level science and education programs). As a result the Heartland has an opportunity to serve as a veritable "brain belt" for the 21st century. Historically, many of these young people, once they gain skills, leave or are inadequately employed if they choose to stay.[81] But in large part due to advances in communications, many of these workers are now being redeployed. Between 1990 and 2000 the percentage of counties with a "skills surplus," according to researcher Sean Moore, actually dropped more dramatically in rural areas than in metropolitan locations—likely because information, business services, and other technology-related business have shifted location to the far periphery.[82]

One harbinger of the future is Renaissance Learning, a leading educational software company that has chosen to base itself in Wisconsin Rapids, a small city of 17,500 in central Wisconsin. The company, a leading provider of reading software for K-12 students, employs over 700 people, and its software products are used in approximately 50,000 classrooms across North America.

Central Wisconsin, once dependent on agriculture and paper manufacturing, has diversified its industrial base into software and specialized services. Farming, particularly cranberries, and some specialized paper operations are still important, but much of the new growth has been fueled by a quiet in-migration of skilled professionals.

Wisconsin Rapids has a small-town feeling, with a broad river and wooded countryside, the firm's technical director Mark Swanson notes; that appeals to many technical workers. "We don't have any trouble recruiting people here," he says. "A lot of people are willing to move from California or the East after chasing the silicon dream. Now they get into their thirties, have families, and they want to live someplace that's good to live."[83]

THE ONSHORE REVOLUTION

Technology jobs started moving to the Heartland after the dot-com bust. While employment dropped in the San Francisco Bay area, Boston, and even Minneapolis, it grew in Fargo, Sioux Falls, Des Moines, and even smaller Heartland towns.[84] As the tech economy expanded in the mid-2000s, growth rates in many small communities remained considerably strong. Although rural states and communities have been hit by the recession that began in 2007, on average they have maintained their job levels more than the more populated areas and have suffered far lower unemployment.[85]

The rise in housing costs after 2000 helps account for the shift in talent. The movement out of California has been particularly marked. By 2003 roughly half of the 973,000 tech workers employed there had left either the industry or the state. Similarly, congested, high-cost northern Virginia has been loosing jobs to southwestern Virginia.[86]

This movement to the interior has generally been overlooked, while national interest has focused on the shift of American office and technical jobs offshore, which by some estimates is expected to reach 3.3 million positions by 2015.[87] Lower costs have been often cited as the primary reason for moving jobs offshore, but relocation to the Heartland brings many of the same benefits.

Over time the movement of technology to the Heartland could slow the movement of call and technology support centers to India and other offshore locales. Companies that have moved their telecommunications operations to the Heartland include major corporations like Dell,

1-800-Flowers, and Choice (owner of the Comfort Inn, Quality, US Bank, and Clarion chains).[88]

At the same time homegrown firms have proliferated, such as Rural Sourcing (based in Arkansas), Cross USA (based in Eagan, Minnesota), and SEI Technology (in Oak Brook, Illinois).[89] These firms report that onshoring has advantages: a greater receptiveness by customers, who prefer to conduct business with English-dominant workers, and a greater perceived security for sensitive personal information. A gradual decline in the quality of workers in overseas call and service centers, due to increased competition and a scarcity of qualified workers, including in India, may contribute to the future growth of onshoring.[90]

BOISE: A NEW MODEL SILICON VALLEY?

One place where all these trends have come together is Boise, a city where tech growth continued even during the harsh dot-com recession of the early 2000s. Software entrepreneur Jason Crawforth, previously based in Silicon Valley, believes that companies operating in Boise have a leg up on competitors operating in California and other high-cost environments. Boise's modest prices—housing costs are one-fourth those in the Bay Area—makes it far easier for him to keep employees and offer them a better quality of life, while paying them perhaps 30 percent less than he would in Silicon Valley.

"There's no doubt that cost of living is about eighty percent of why I'm here," explains Crawforth, a tall, thirty-six-year-old redhead, whose firm last year enjoyed almost $10 million in revenues. "The other twenty percent is the people and the culture. I like the consistency. I have almost no turnover, and people love the opportunity to be here."

Customers, he says, particularly businesses, who want help on software don't like to deal with geographically distant people from a different culture. Indian call works might suffice, he thinks, for someone with a credit card question or a basic rote technology issue, but for a business wondering how best to use a server or a network, a native English-speaking person is infinitely preferable.

"That is what makes this such a great place to do home shoring," Crawforth, who grew up in the Boise area, suggests. "People here are competent, speak well, and tend to be patient and have a good attitude."

If headquartering in Boise has any problems, he says, it's the challenge of convincing people elsewhere that you can run a serious company from a small, somewhat isolated spot hundreds of miles from the nearest big city (Portland, Oregon). "When I go to a customer sometimes and say I am from Idaho, they still wonder if I am selling potatoes," he admits. "But then they see what we can do, and that's that."[91]

THE NEW HEARTLAND BOOMTOWN

Perhaps no city better epitomizes the dynamic of the emerging "brain belt" than Fargo, North Dakota. A decade ago it seemed a hopeless backwater and, after the release of the movie with its name, something of a national joke. A proposal in the 1990s to change the state's name to "Dakota" brought even more scorn; one writer noted that "North Dakotans possess a sublime talent for talking to the brink of death just about any subject that pertains to North Dakota."[92]

But by then Fargo's sad-sack reputation was already changing. Ironically, a central character in the turnaround was one of the prospective name changers, Doug Burgum. A local boy originally from nearby Arthur, Burgum moved back home from Chicago to join a fledgling local start-up called Great Plains Software. Soon afterward he saw great potential in the area's considerable engineering expertise from North Dakota State University and from its large, and expanding, specialty farm equipment industry. "My business strategy is to be close to the source of supply; it's like being near fertile land or a raw material," Burgum, dressed casually in jeans and a down vest, explains. "North Dakota gave us access to the raw material of college students, and distance in this business was not a factor."

By leveraging some farmland, and with help from family members, he bought the company. In the next fifteen years Great Plains became a force in the information business. In 2001 it was acquired by Microsoft. By 2007 the company employed roughly one thousand people in its sprawling, wooded complex on the outskirts of Fargo, and it plays a critical role in the overall strategy of the world's dominant software company.

The success of Great Plains Software sparked other start-ups, in fields that range from biotechnology to wireless networking to radio frequency identification systems. Today North Dakota has one of the highest rates of high-tech start-ups in the nation, and the Fargo area is the undisputed epicenter. By the early 2000s the area was luring businesses from the coasts.

This growth has created some remarkable changes in Fargo. The influx of well-paid, educated professionals has transformed the once-desolate downtown, which even locals considered "sleazy." It now has numerous coffee shops, ethnic restaurants, and high-class dining establishments, all frequented by a thirtysomething clientele who would not look out of place in West Hollywood, Dupont Circle, or Portland's Pearl district.

The place also has a first-class boutique hotel, the Donaldson, founded by Carole Burgum, Doug's ex-wife. Rooms are decorated with artwork by local artists, and the hotel has become a source of pride for North Dakotans who have never stayed there but show it off to visitors. "People thought I should be put in a padded cell for doing this," the tall, blond mother of three jokes. "But I wanted everything to be done by local yokels. I didn't want it to be trendy. It's what a bunch of small-town people who live in a town that's not so bad do. This shows who we are."[93]

Like her ex-husband, she's stopped talking about changing the state's name. Things have gotten too good—and the future too alluring—for that kind of thing.

THE FUTURE HEARTLAND: THE NEW SMALL CITY

In the first decades of the 20th century, rural America seemed to have entered in a long-term decline. Frederick Law Olmsted, who dedicated much of his life to preserving the natural environment, described his own hometown in rural Connecticut as a place of dilapidated churches, closed mills, and abandoned old taverns. Cities, he argued, offered the "poorest working girl" more opportunities for stimulation, culture, and education than even "people with the greatest wealth" in country could enjoy. [94]

But in the 21st century a very different prospect has emerged in the American countryside. Fargo, Dubuque, Iowa City, Sioux Falls, and Boise are already experiencing strong revivals: growing populations, more jobs, restored downtowns, and new cultural and retail venues. In so doing they are reprising the once-vibrant network of small towns that existed in the 19th century.[95]

In the coming decades such vital places will seem less exceptional. Other smaller towns, particularly those close to the emerging hubs, could also rebound.[96] But this revival, akin to the old small towns in terms of vitality, will be different in significant ways. For one thing, most centers will not depend primarily on servicing surrounding farms. Instead, they will be part of the emerging urban archipelago that will characterize mid-21st-century America.

The economic basis of this growth will differ by community. Some will thrive by the production of energy or specialized manufactured products. Others will serve as magnets for tourists, hunters, bird-watchers, arts festivals, and pageants.[97] Small rural college towns may serve as refuges for empty nesters relocating—or returning—from the congested, expensive coasts.

THE "EXPANSIVE CHARACTER OF AMERICAN LIFE"

As the United States adds another hundred million people, it makes little sense to try to freeze nonmetropolitan America into a demographic and economic still life. More than any other region, the Heartland can provide an outlet for our expanded population and provide businesses with new locales to produce globally competitive goods and services.

Equally critical, the Heartland will reconnect America with its own historic strengths as a great, largely open, continental nation, a place of aspiration that can accommodate future growth. This opportunity has always differentiated us from our European and Asian competitors, and it will continue to do so in the future. The Heartland reinforces our national character, what Frederick Jackson Turner called "that restless, nervous energy; that dominant individualism, working for good or evil . . . that buoyancy and exuberance which comes with freedom."[98] As the population expands to four hundred million people, Americans will need to tap that spirit more than ever.

The Heartland offers the country an outlet for the entrepreneurial and creative skills of its rising population. It will offer millions the chance to enjoy more spacious, less congested, and more healthful lives than can be found or easily afforded in the largest cities. No longer geographically isolated or cut off from vital information, the Heartland is one of America's critical assets as it prepares to accommodate the next hundred million.

CHAPTER FIVE:
POST-ETHNIC AMERICA

Al Colbert grew up in the East Texas town of Beaumont, in a community that was predominantly black but controlled largely by whites. It was in Beaumont that oil was first discovered in Texas, at Spindletop, the gusher that launched the great Texas oil boom. Beaumont was a southern, conservative kind of place, more Louisiana backwoods than modern Texas. "It was a place where people knew who they were, and knew their limits," he recalled over a soda many years later.[1]

A promising young student, Colbert, like many African-Americans from the South, attended a historically black college. In 1995, during his senior year at Houston's Texas Southern University, he and his cousin, Ja Ja Ball, a TSU senior studying business, hatched a plan to make some money during the January-to-mid-April tax season. They rented an inexpensive storefront in a low-income neighborhood and offered tax-preparation services, specializing in electronic filing and quick refunds. The Colbert/Ball Tax Service handled 270 tax returns the first year. Sensing an opportunity, the two Beaumont natives kept the fledgling company going after graduation.

The goal, recalls Colbert, now in his mid-thirties, was to become "the black H&R Block. We knew that market and felt it would be the right one for us to serve." The business quickly took off, doubling the number of returns it prepared the next year and increasing to 1,800 in 1997. By then the company's main office was in the Astrodome area, with two satellite offices in the city, still catering to a largely black clientele. "It's easier to start with people who you know," says Colbert, the company's chief executive. "These are people who stuck with you in the beginning—they are the base."

But Colbert and Ball soon realized that Houston's burgeoning Hispanic population might be another reservoir of unmet demand, growing far faster than either the African-American or the Anglo market segments. Although they had little firsthand experience with Hispanics, they began targeting them and found a receptive market of working-class people, often self-employed, making $35,000 to $50,000 a year, just the sort of clients Colbert/Ball was seeking.

By 2008 Hispanics accounted for more than 30 percent of Colbert/Ball's business, which had spread far beyond Houston. The company had franchised its operation and grown to two hundred affiliates in twenty-three states that prepared more than 35,000 returns annually. "Who would have thought of a black business growing in the Hispanic market?" Colbert says. "But in free enterprise you don't worry about the color of your customers. You take advantage of opportunities."

To be sure, Colbert enjoys his adopted hometown's diversity and its staggering array of restaurants, cultural offerings, and shops. But above all, when he considers that diversity, he sees more customers. They may not look just like him, but he senses that, like him, they seek a future in an immigrant-dominated city of promise. "The key to success is finding an underserved market, and if you look beyond your own, you will see plenty of people in need of service," he observes. "You don't care if the client is black or white, you just go to the people who can get you the revenues."

THE CRITICAL ROLE OF IMMIGRATION

Although race will remain an issue in the next decades, Al Colbert's success reflects a powerful component of America's strength in the 21st century: its ability to transcend even the most entrenched racial barriers. The election of President Barack Obama made it clear that America is evolving toward what historian David Hollinger calls a "post-ethnic" society, marked by new "solidarities of wide scope that incorporate people with different ethnic and racial backgrounds."[2]

In the next decades the fate of western countries may well depend on their ability to make social and economic room for people whose origins lie outside Europe. The United States, Canada, Australia, Britain, Germany, and France produce insufficient new children of European descent to prevent them from becoming granny nation-states by 2050.[3] Other societies, particularly in Asia, seem resistant to the very notion of widespread immigration.

But only successful immigration can provide the markets, the manpower, and perhaps most important, the youthful energy to keep western societies vital and growing. The most dynamic, bustling sections of American cities—the revived communities along the number 7 train line in Queens, Houston's Harwin Corridor, and Los Angeles's San Gabriel Valley—often are dominated by immigrant enterprise.

Without these newcomers many cities would never have rebounded from the catastrophic population losses of the 1970s, when millions fled the older inner cities for the suburbs and new Sunbelt boomtowns.[4] Over the past few decades Cleveland, Pittsburgh, and Cincinnati, all of which have failed to attract immigrants, have suffered severe population declines.[5]

Even smaller towns have been enlivened by immigrants, where refugees often have an even greater impact than in the biggest cities. In the 1990s Bosnians and Russians newly arrived in Utica, New York, sparked growth and jobs in that stagnating community, which had lost half its population in the previous three decades and much of its economic dynamism. Brought into town by federal humanitarian agencies, the Bosnian newcomers came to escape the wartime chaos of their native land.

By 2006 some seven thousand Bosnians had settled in Utica, where they make up roughly 10 percent of the population. They brought with them, as city leaders acknowledge, the critical values of hard work and sacrifice. They see even a hardscrabble upstate New York town as full of opportunities. "Here in America you have many chances, you can do whatever you want," says Sulejman Latic, who opened a karate club in the town.

The local Muslim community, after renting a space, constructed their own mosque. But it seems to have caused little stir among the local citizens, who generally see the Bosnians as contributors to a civic revival. "How long before they become Americanized?" asked the head of the local chamber of commerce. "Right now all we know is we love them, and we want more."[6]

AMERICA'S UNIQUENESS

This is where America's future diverges most clearly from that of its competitors, both the older advanced nations and the newly emergent powers. Over the past few decades Iran, Egypt, Turkey, Russia, Indonesia, and the nations of the former Soviet Union and the former Yugoslavia have constricted their concept of national identity. In Malaysia, Nigeria, India, and even the province of Quebec preferential policies have been devised to blunt successful minorities. Because of these restrictive policies, which in some places are accompanied by lethal threats, Jews, Armenians, Coptic Christians, and diaspora Chinese have often been forced to find homes in more welcoming places.[7]

In recent decades Europe has received as many immigrants as the United States, but it has proven far less able to absorb them. The roughly twenty million Muslims who live in Europe have tended to remain segregated from the rest of society and economically marginalized.

Remarkably, as late as the 1990s, some American scholars still believed that the "exclusionary ghetto" did not exist in Europe, even when its existence was apparent even to a casual visitor.[8] The economic segregation of immigrants within Europe may further widen the gap between the American and European experiences. In European countries immigrants can receive welfare more easily than join the workforce, and their job prospects are confined by education levels that lag behind those of immigrants in the United States, Canada, and Australia.[9]

In Europe, notably in France, unemployment among immigrants—particularly those from Muslim countries—is often at least twice that of the native born; in Britain as well Muslims are far more likely to be out of the workforce than either Christians or Hindus. But in the United States immigrant workers with lower educations actually tend to be working more than their nonimmigrant counterparts. Overall, immigrants from Mexico had generally lower unemployment than white and other workers, at least until 2007; then with the housing-led recession their unemployment rate began to rise, since so many were involved in construction and manufacturing. Once the economy recovers, the historical pattern should reassert itself.[10]

Similarly, while European societies have become more diverse statistically, immigrants are often separate from the dominant culture. For example, in Britain in 2001 up to 40 percent of the Islamic population believed that terrorist attacks on both Americans and their fellow Britons were justified;[11] meanwhile 95 percent of white Britons say they have exclusively white friends.[12] In comparison, only 25 percent of whites in twenty-nine metropolitan areas reported having no interracial friendships at all. This measure of racial isolation ranged from a low of 8 percent in Los Angeles to a high of 55 percent in Bismarck,

North Dakota.[13] Overall, the integrative process in the United States, which over the past century has experienced the largest mass migration in history,[14] generally has proved more successful than that of Europe.

The contrast is particularly telling when it comes to Muslim immigrants. In the United States most Muslims are comfortably middle class, with income and education levels above the national average. They are more likely to be satisfied with the state of the country, their own community, and their prospects for success than are other Americans—even in the face of the reaction to 9/11.

More important, more than half of Muslims—many of them immigrants—identify themselves as Americans first, a far higher percentage than in the various countries of western Europe. This alienation may be a legacy of the European colonial experience, but it can also be seen in Denmark and Sweden, which had little earlier contact with the Muslim world.[15]

In contrast, American Muslims seem to be integrating with remarkably rapidity. More than four in five are registered to vote, a sure sign of civic involvement. Almost three quarters, according to a Pew study, say they have never been discriminated against. "You can keep the flavor of your ethnicity," remarked one University of Chicago Pakistani doctorate student in Islamic studies, "but you are expected to become an American."[16]

AMERICA, THE MULTIETHNIC SPONGE

The belief that America's national identity transcends race or religion, and the country's general receptivity to immigration, is a critical difference between it and other advanced countries in Europe and East Asia. In 2005 the United States swore in more new citizens than the next *nine* countries put together. The trend accelerated after the terrorist attacks of 2001, reflecting concerns among immigrants about a potential tightening of immigration policies. Worried about a possible crackdown, many immigrants who were anxious to remain in the country took this step.[17]

More than half of all skilled immigrants in the world come to this one country. Skilled workers form a larger share of immigrants only in Australia and Canada, which have much smaller populations; there they also play a similarly outsized role.[18]

Significantly, even with its slow-growing population, Europe continues to be a major source of American immigrants, particularly skilled workers.[19] By 2004 some 400,000 European Union science and technology graduates were residing in the United States. Barely one in seven, according to a recent European Commission poll, intends to return. "The U.S. is a sponge that's happy to soak up talent from across the globe," observes one Irish scientist.[20] During the 1990s European immigration to the United States grew by some 16 percent; during that period the total number of European-born Americans increased by roughly 700,000.[21] In the late 1990s European immigrants constituted over one in four New York immigrants; the former Soviet Union edged out the Dominican Republic as the single largest source of newcomers to the city.[22]

But by far the majority of the nation's immigrants, both undocumented and legal, come from developing countries: China, India, Mexico, the Philippines, and the Middle East. Since roughly four in five immigrants come from nonwhite countries, by the early 2000s the majority of new workers were nonwhite. By 2039, due largely to immigrants and their offspring, the majority of working-age Americans will be "minorities."[23] Over the coming decade these immigrants will radically transform the American economy.

Even if immigration slows down dramatically, particularly with a weak economy, these groups will grow in significance as we approach midcentury. In 2000 one in five American children were already the progeny of immigrants; by 2015 they will make up as much as one-third of American kids.[24] Most demographers agree that sometime around 2050, if not sooner, non-Hispanic whites will be in the minority. Even if immigration were to slow dramatically, due to harsher economic conditions, America's racial and ethnic die is already cast.[25]

THE FADING COLOR LINE

W. E. B. DuBois predicted in the early 20th century that "the problem of the twentieth century is the problem of the color line." And in many ways the prediction was accurate, with the rise of National Socialism, and the emergence of civil rights struggles in the United States, South Africa, Australia, and elsewhere. Eight decades later, in 1992, the late great African-American scholar John Hope Franklin could "venture to state categorically that the problem of the 21st century will be the problem of the color line."[26]

But recent history suggests that America, as it becomes more diverse, is actually becoming more adept at integrating its diverse populations. Class differences may grow, but race is likely to decline as the primary source of American social ills. Black immigrants from Africa, for example, have established themselves in many American communities, from Houston and Chicago to the two coasts. Some, such as Nigerians, enjoy higher-than-average educations, in Houston surpassing both whites and Asians. "If you see the average Nigerian family, everyone has a college degree these days," notes Foluke Udeh, a physical therapist at Herman-Texas Medical Center. "But a post-graduate degree, that's like pride for the family."[27]

Given the success and integration of African and Muslim immigrants, Franklin's fears about a continued racial divide in America may have been overstated.[28] The divide on which many academics, journalists, and intellectuals have predominantly focused is the one between African-Americans and whites, arguably the most enduring of racial chasms. But much of the progress that has been made—by not only African-Americans and whites but an increasingly diverse populace—takes place not on campuses, in newspapers, or at conferences but in the everyday realm of neighborhoods, parks, schools, churches, and perhaps most important, commerce.

This grassroots integration is what Sergio Munoz, a Mexican journalist and longtime Los Angeles resident, has called the "the multiculturalism of the streets."[29] It is not the same as the more political variety taught in ethnic studies programs or embraced by governments when they impose racial quotas, set up "official" Islamic councils, or even consider the application of Koran-based shariah law for their Muslim citizens (as has been discussed in both Canada and the United Kingdom).[30]

It is also very different from the French model of enforced secularism that denies ethnicity and bans the personal expression of differences, such as the wearing of crosses, *kippot*, or head scarves. Europe's imposed secularism—and general aversion to religion—may itself encourage separatism in a way that diverges from America's combination of "separation of church and state" and its widespread spiritualism.[31]

Largely ignored by academics and government are the practical reasons to integrate cultures. In Atlanta and Houston, southern cities with long histories of discrimination against African-Americans,[32] economic leaders eventually recognized that preserving institutionalized racism would be bad for business. Recalls the Reverend Bill Lawson, a major Houston civil rights leader and pastor emeritus at Wheeler Avenue Baptist Church, "It was not a moral issue, it was an economic issue. Leaders recognized the downside of national publicity at a time they wanted to start the [federally funded] space program."[33]

By 2005 Atlanta and Dallas, as well as Houston, were seen as among the best places for black businesses and families.[34] The remarkable progress made on race, even in the Deep South, has charted the path for immigrant communities, including Mexican-Americans and Chinese-Americans, who have also faced discrimination. More important, the road to economic success, unobstructed by institutionalized racism, will be even more open for their children.

THREE UNSPOKEN PRINCIPLES

Though the United States has made progress on racial acceptance, the confluence between certain ethnicities and higher rates of poverty is persistent. Massive immigration has brought large numbers of poorly educated and non-English speaking newcomers to New York and Los Angeles, driving down per capita income rates. Although immigrants often increase their wages over time, the influx of more arrivals tends to keep wages for Latinos consistently below native levels and likely depresses wages for the least skilled natives.[35]

Pockets of poverty and social segregation exist within virtually all immigrant groups, often leading to higher crime rates. Many first-generation Chinese, one of the nation's most successful ethnic populations, still cluster in historic enclaves, where they work at low wages and operate small businesses with little immediate hope of upward mobility. Criminal gangs are often a potent force in these neighborhoods.[36]

Immigrants by their very nature are a work in progress. Over time, except in periods of rapid economic contraction, the average immigrant income grows, and the percentage of children who finish high school or enter college rises (in some groups more decisively than in others). Rates of home ownership also rise with time, reaching native levels after about three decades. Between 1994 and 2006, despite a massive influx of newcomers, the poverty rate among Hispanics dropped from over 30 percent to near 20 percent.[37]

These realities can be seen in Houston, Miami, Los Angeles, New York, and the suburbs that are emerging as the great immigrant portals. Often the political nor the cultural arguments about immigration are remote from immigrants' everyday lives. Concepts such as "ethnic solidarity," "people of color," and "cultural community" generally mean less than principles such as "Does this sell?" "What's my market?" and ultimately "How do I fit in?"

Immigrant commerce manifests most visibly in the proliferation of small stores, restaurants, food-processing businesses, garment factories, and trucking lines, as well as in high-tech and financial services. Immigrants are more likely to start a new business than native-born Americans. The number of self-employed immigrants has grown even in New York City, where the number of self-employed among the native-born has dropped.[38]

Immigrant motivations pair well with entrepreneurship. Most immigrants come to America, and have for generations, for pragmatic reasons: to find a better life for themselves and their families. The Russian-born novelist Gary Shtyengart, recalling his own high school days as an immigrant in New York, wrote in a 2003 essay: "To this day, immigrants come to America because the elites of their native countries are committed to keeping the middle class small and stunted, since banana-republic crony capitalism can only exist in a country with a vast, impoverished labor pool. . . . Work hard, please your parents, make a killing—these were the three unspoken principles of Stuyvesant High School."[39]

As Shteyngart's success suggests, most immigrants do not come to America to recreate the conditions they left back in their ancestral homelands. They come to reinvent themselves, in the process reaffirming the essential uniqueness of America and adding a new distinctiveness to it.

AMERICA'S RACIAL EVOLUTION

Since the early years of European settlement, America's evolution has been a process of continuing reinvention. The idea of what constitutes an American has changed dramatically and now includes groups—racial minorities among them—that were beyond consideration by earlier generations.

A population that placed great "pride of origin" in its British roots, Alexis de Tocqueville noted, feared close contact with other ethnic groups, even white ones. Non-Britons generally were excluded from the upper reaches of society. In the 1840s, as immigrants arrived from Catholic Ireland, Germany, and Scandinavia in great numbers, these worries deepened. The Native American Party, or Know-nothings, declared in the 1850s that America faced "an imminent peril from the rapid and enormous increase of the body of residents of foreign birth, imbued with foreign feelings, and of an ignorant and immoral character."[40]

By 1860 two-thirds of newcomers were either German or Irish and easily outnumbered immigrants coming from Great Britain. The shift happened so quickly that by the time of the Civil War the African-American population had a higher percentage of native-born Americans than did the white population. Fully one-quarter of the Union troops who served in the Civil War were foreign born, including Irish who shouted Gaelic war cries as they entered battle.[41]

Many immigrants soon found ways to enter the mainstream economy. By mid-19th century ethnic businessmen in New York—Irish, German, and Jewish—were reaching the upper echelons of the merchant and manufacturing business community. Although some opposed this early, street-wise commercial mixing, notes historian Sven Beckert, among most Americans "the ethnic diversity of merchants as well as industrial[ists] was a point of pride, not contention."[42]

Between 1840 and 1914 twenty-four million immigrants entered the country. By 1920 almost half of all residents of Boston, New York, Chicago, Detroit, and Cleveland were immigrants; when the offspring of immigrants was included, they accounted for as much as three-quarters of city dwellers.

But the newest immigrants differed significantly from the previous wave. Immigration from Russia, Poland, and Italy surpassed the mid-19th-century waves from Ireland, Scandinavia, and Germany. America underwent a dramatic ethnic transformation and experienced the highest-percentage immigrant population in its history. One-fifth of the population of the northeastern states was now foreign born, and overall, half of the country's urban dwellers were immigrants. In contrast, the native white stock remained predominantly rural or lived in small towns.[43]

Many leading social scientists and intellectuals found this transformation profoundly disturbing.[44] The immigrant communities that they saw in the cities were very different from the fundamentally Anglo-Saxon-led nation that had emerged as a world power.[45] Others inhaled the sights, smells, and sounds of the immigrant street and identified them as sources of social decay and disunion. Writing in 1890, the political scientist Richard Mayo Smith warned that the new immigrants were inimical to "social habits which are distinctly American." Germans, he said, were far too oriented toward state intervention in the economy; Hungarians and Poles were anarchistically inclined "elements of violence and disorder." Italians were prone to "seeking vengeance for personal wrongs with a stiletto."[46]

Beneath the pretense of superiority lay the fear that the newcomers might succeed too well. Henry James wrote menacingly of "the Hebrew conquest of New York" and the "inward assimilation of our heritage and point of view." Henry Adams worried that the "old stock" might not be able to compete with the newcomer who, he wrote, "had a keener instinct, an intenser energy, and a freer hand than . . . [the] American of Americans with Heaven only knows how many Puritans and Patriots behind him."[47]

These fears would lead to a wide-ranging restriction of immigration in 1924. (Policies would not again be liberalized until the 1960s.) Meanwhile in the West successful anti-immigrant drives had limited or banned immigration from China, Japan, and other Asian countries. Fear of cheap labor and of determined enterprise, combined with concerns about cultural incompatibility, drove this movement, which was also directed against another key western immigrant group: Mexicans.[48]

Resistance to Asian immigrants has a long history on the West Coast. As southerners had once feared race-mixing with African-Americans, westerners palpably feared the same with Asians.[49] Some Californians regarded the Chinese and Japanese newcomers' strong sense of cultural identity as particularly threatening. The African, noted one writer, posed less of problem, since he had at least been "robbed of his idols" and "obliged to hear the Gospels or nothing"; the Asian, however, often remained stubbornly tied to his own ancient beliefs.[50]

Latino immigration, predominantly from Mexico, posed a different challenge. The Americans who took control of the southwestern United States assumed sovereignty over an already-existing Spanish-Mexican culture. Although some Latino upper classes were incorporated by marriage or financial ties into the new Anglo establishment, most Latinos in the Southwest remained a marginalized population.

In the chaos following the 1910 Mexican Revolution, a new and massive movement emerged south of the border, and by the 1920s some one million newcomers had crossed into the United States. This new population raised serious concerns in the Southwest, especially in Los Angeles. Worries were voiced about the "Mexican problem" and about whether what one nativist called "moral morons of the most hopeless type" could ever possibly assimilate into the broader society.[51]

MESTIZO MECCAS

The immigration wave that began in the late 20th century and contin-ues today has been massive. From ten million in 1970, the foreign-born population rose to close to forty million in 2004.[52] Unsurprisingly, like the influx of a century ago, this rise has raised concerns among native-born Americans about the immigrants' compatibility with the existing culture, even though most objective evidence suggests such concerns are exaggerated.[53]

The great political scientist Samuel Huntington, the classics scholar Victor Davis Hanson, and more controversial political figures like Pat Buchanan have helped revive the very concerns about national iden-tity that animated immigration critics a century ago. Hanson raises the prospect that large numbers of undereducated Latino workers will cre-ate a "social calamity" in his native California, which he fears will even-tually become what he calls "Mexifornia."[54] Buchanan, for his part, ties the tide of nonwhite immigration to a bleaker global vision:

> The prognosis is grim. Between 2000 & 2050, world population will grow to over 9 billion people, but this 50 percent increase in global population will come entirely in Asia, Africa, & Latin America, as 100 million people of European stock vanish from the Earth. But the immigration tsunami rolling over America is not coming from "all the races of Europe." The largest population transfer in history is coming from all the races of Asia, Africa, and Latin America, and they are not "melting and reforming."[55]

Geography plays a role in these fears. Unlike European and Asian immigrants, Mexicans migrants cross a land border, and most enter a region that, in the distant past, was part of their own homeland.

Huntington suggests "the migrant tide" (as he calls it) will promote "revanchist sentiments" supportive of reattaching the southwestern United States to Mexico."[56]

In reality, the evidence is thin that Mexican-Americans, particularly those in the second generation, have separatist notions. And as 21st-century America becomes ever more diverse, groups will have an even greater need to stress elements of commonality. One in three Latino immigrants describes themselves primarily as American, but that rises to 85 percent in the first native-born generation and 97 percent in the generation after that.[57] Latinos also represent a growing portion of the U.S. military—hardly a sign of disaffection from the national culture.[58]

Many recent arrivals do retain a primary loyalty to another country and culture, and many plan to return, but this has always been the case with newcomers. British immigrants frequently considered "home" to be not in America but across the Atlantic; Britons resisted naturalization more than immigrants from less "related" countries did, and many hoped to return. As one British immigrant says in John E. H. Skinner's 1866 book *After the Storm*, "Give me England for spending money and this country for making it."[59]

Over time most British immigrants, and even more so their children, fully integrated into the American culture. Similarly, the Catholic immigrants, whose loyalty was so suspect to 19th-century nativists, evolved into an integral part of the American scene, even outperforming established Protestant communities in terms of education, upward mobility, and income.[60]

By the 1990s many once-fiercely held distinctions among ethnic groups had faded. Fewer than one-quarter of American children today can be called "purebred" WASPs; most people with English heritage have one parent of different origin. The number of Americans identified as Irish, German, or English has continued to drop, even as the nation's population has grown.[61] Poles, Italians, Greeks, and Jews have been intermarrying at rates of 50 percent or more.[62]

This social integration parallels success in the economic arena. Initially virtually all immigrant groups, particularly in cities, cluster in ethnic enclaves, places where they work together to find their way in the new country.[63] The early-20th-century American city functioned, in some senses, as an archipelago of self-sufficient and unique ethnic enclaves.

Within these neighborhoods immigrant businesses thrived by providing basic services, such as banks, insurance agents, funeral homes, and grocery stores. Some of these businesses arose because the mainstream community had failed to identify opportunities in these markets or had consciously decided to exclude them.[64]

Faced with this isolation, immigrants tried to improve their status by concentrating on an economic specialty—Jews in the garment industry, Chinese laundries, Greek diners, and Italian greengrocers, barbershops, and fish stores. Because their owners and workers initially arrived without families to support, these businesses accumulated capital quickly. Later, as immigrants married, they benefited from the fact that their households were roughly twice as likely as native-born ones to have more than one wage earner.[65]

Some of the financial institutions where these newcomers placed their capital—and from which they could borrow—grew into major companies. A. P. Giannini's Bank of Italy in San Francisco, for example, eventually became Bank of America, one of the nation's largest financial institutions. Other ethnic businesses drew on ways of doing business brought from abroad. Jewish immigrants from eastern Europe came with tailoring skills that proved critical in the garment trade.

All this took place in a matter of only a few decades. Virtually all the founding generation of the film industry—Samuel Goldwyn, Louis B. Mayer, Harry Cohn, Jesse Lasky, Adolph Zukor—had their roots in the Jewish enclave economy in the eastern cities. Irving Howe notes that the immigrant need to find an unoccupied or underserved niche shaped these often "vulgar, crude and overbearing" men. That they became founders of the nation's premier cultural industry, Howe noted, "was something of a miracle and something of a joke."[66]

FROM CHINATOWN TO SILICON VALLEY

America's future ethnic evolution is likely to follow a similar course. Asian immigrants, particularly Chinese, also concentrated in ethnic enclaves; for many of them, the prototypical Chinatown was both a ghetto and a refuge. But in the 21st century Asians, like the Jews and Italians before them, have concentrated in specific niches and expanded outside the boundaries of historic ghettos.

Asian Indians, who arrived in large numbers starting in the 1970s, specialized in hotels and motels across the country. Koreans opened up greengroceries in New York and Los Angeles. Vietnamese became well known for nail parlors, and Cambodians for owning doughnut stores. Overall Asian enterprises expanded roughly twice the national average through the first years of the new century.[67]

Perhaps most remarkable has been the movement of Asians into the technology industry. Between 1990 and 2005 immigrants, mostly from the Chinese diaspora or from India, started one of every four U.S. venture-backed public companies. In California they account for a majority of such firms, particularly in technology.[68] Today many regions at the center of the high-tech economy—Silicon Valley, Orange County, and parts of suburban Seattle come to mind—have become heavily Asian-American.[69]

Although many of these companies are small, a significant number have also become sizable; the founders of Sun Microsystems, Yahoo!, AST Research, and Solectron include at least one person of Asian descent, mostly immigrants.[70] Their experience as new immigrants, suggests John Tu, the president and cofounder of Orange County–based Kingston Technologies, the world's largest independent producer of computer memory, has forced them to think differently. Like their Jewish counterparts in the early 20th century, many found that their prospects in bigger, established companies were limited by their lack of facility in English and by their deferential habits brought over from Asia. But the experience of immigration also helped them succeed to an extent few ever expected. As Tu reflects, "The key thing is, being an immigrant makes you flexible . . . IBM, Apple, and Compaq were inflexible. They told the memory customers take it or leave it. We thought about the customer and the relationship with the employees. I guess we didn't know any better."[71]

ETHNIC SUCCESSION IN THE NEW MECCAS

Latinos have also made considerable strides into the mainstream culture, although mainly outside the technology field. Usually arriving with less education and fewer useful global connections than their Asian counterparts, Latino immigrants have moved increasingly into the mainstream economy and, in part due to their numbers, made a profound impact on the overall economies of many cities.

At the same time the modern American business culture has had an impact on a large wave of immigration that has mostly come from developing countries. After a period of living in Houston, notes sociologist Arnoldo de Leon, most Latinos are "seduced" by its prevailing atmosphere of "capitalism, modern consumer culture, schooling, and faith in democratic processes." Even the most militant ethnic activist, he suggests, is "as acculturated as any advocate of assimilation might envisage."[72] Los Angeles, by far the largest Latino immigrant destination, suggests author Carlos Monsivais, has replaced Mexico as "the new Mecca" of Mexican life, turning "the land of gringos" into "the land of gringos and relatives."[73]

Given the scale of current immigration, these newcomers will continue to reshape the face of American business, creating new businesses at a rate far above the national average. Some of the country's highest rates of entrepreneurship are found among immigrants from the Middle East, the countries of the former Soviet Union, Cuba, and Korea. These businesses can be found in a broad array of industries, including food and retailing as well as manufacturing and technology.[74]

In the first generation many of these ethnic enterprises may seem "cannibalistic" toward each other, but out of this struggle the strongest survive, then turn their attention to the larger economy around them. They have played a critical role in improving local economies, particularly in urban centers. According to a recent report by Harvard's Michael Porter, they are one of the few sources of positive job growth for such immigrant-rich cities as Jersey City, New Jersey, and Long Beach, California.[75]

In many ways what we are witnessing—and will continue to witness—is ethnic succession. Immigrants in the rural South and the Great Plains have replaced older generations of native-born workers in industries such as carpets, furniture, and food processing. Over time some of these workers, or their children, are likely to rise as leaders in these fields.[76]

It is not necessarily a matter of one group pushing out another. In southern California Japanese-Americans once dominated the landscaping industry, but by the 1980s most children of Japanese gardeners were too well educated to accept such hard manual work and preferred professional jobs.[77] Hispanics now dominate L.A.'s gardening industry both as workers, and increasingly, as owners.

Javier Reyes, who came to southern California from Zacatecas, Mexico, in 1988, learned the basics from Japanese landscapers. "They were very into quality. Whatever the job needed, you did it," he recalled. Later he worked for Williams Brothers, an Anglo-owned landscaping firm, where he learned about bidding for jobs and dealing with employees.

At Williams, Reyes became the first Latino manager, aided by his ability to communicate with the largely Latino workforce. In 1986, along with an investor, he founded Villa Park Landscape Company and has since grown it into a $16 million-a-year business with four hundred employees: "I came up the hard way and didn't take anything for granted. It helps—you can learn from other people and still relate to the work because you did it yourself. The hard part is to get to this point. You progress in this country by being willing to do what others don't want to do anymore."[78]

CROSSOVER RETAILING: YOU ARE WHAT YOU EAT

In the future new Americans, nonwhites, and the "blended" population will reshape the commercial landscape in radical ways. Taken together, purchases by African-Americans, Asians, and native Americans, according to the Selig Center for Economic Growth at the University of Georgia, have exploded, moving far more rapidly than the national average. Combined with Latinos, these minorities could account for over $2.5 trillion by 2010, close to one in every four dollars in total U.S. consumer spending.[79]

Perhaps nothing better illustrates these changes—and their impact on daily life—than the shifts in that most basic of industries, food. In the old paradigm ethnic groups, like Italians, cooked their traditional foods, such as pizza, first for their own compatriots; then in a generation or two, they marketed to the mainstream population. At the same time immigrants, and particularly their children, acclimated to "American fare" like McDonald's.

Today the shift from niche to mainstream is progressing ever more rapidly. In Houston, once dominated by southern cooking, nearly one in three restaurants serves Mexican or Asian cuisine. Together they account for more establishments than hamburger, barbecue, and Italian restaurants put together.[80] Nationwide, as pizza, hamburger, and "traditional" fast food restaurants have stagnated, new chains that sell quick, inexpensive Mexican or Asian food have flourished.[81]

Meanwhile new ethnic markets around the country attract a wide array of customers. A Fiesta market in Dallas may cater primarily to Hispanic customers, but it will also draw Asians, Middle Easterners, and African-Americans. The traditional Chinese vegetable bok choy has become the most lucrative vegetable crop in Los Angeles, driven by demand by supermarkets within and without the region. Even major commodity food companies like General Mills and Kraft now market Chinese and Mexican foods, both in the United States and in China.[82]

AN "EVERYONE" MARKET

Over three decades ago the Cárdenas family started selling and slaughtering pigs raised on their two-acre farm near Corona, California. Jesus and his wife, Luz, quickly realized that the market for fresh-killed food was expanding. By 2008 the company had grown to a business with over $300 million in sales. In his plush corporate office José, one of the four sons who now directs the business, recalls, "We'd shoot the hogs through the head and sell them off the truck. . . . We'd sell the meat to people who liked it fresh. It was Filipinos, Chinese, Koreans, and Hispanics . . . we'd sell to anyone."[83]

Their first store, predominantly a *carneceria*, or meat shop, took advantage of the soaring Latino population in Ontario, a burgeoning city east of Los Angeles. Most were located in the expanding area of Latino settlement from San Bernardino and Riverside counties down to the Coachella Valley near Palm Springs. Other Mexican-owned markets—such as Vallarta—expanded into other parts of California and into neighboring states.

Yet the Cárdenases were not satisfied with just owning supermarkets that catered to Mexican and other Latino immigrants. In 2008 they started to produce packaged Mexican food, including some developed from their mother Luz's recipes, to distribute through such mainstream chains as Costco. Mexican food, notes Jesus Cárdenas, is no longer a niche but increasingly a mass market product: "When you look at this business, eighty percent of our customers are Anglos. Mexican food has been accepted. Our food doesn't have a Mexican market anymore, it has an everyone market. It's a crossover product now."[84]

"AMERICANS ARE GETTING MORE CHINESE"

In the past, according to historian Donna Gabaccia, Chinese cuisine has been difficult to mass-market, compared to other ethnic foods. Although individually owned Chinese restaurants were among the first to bring fast-order and takeout to the marketplace, she notes, the complexity of preparing Chinese food at home made it less susceptible to standardization and duplication. For the most part the nation's 39,000 full-service Chinese restaurants remained very much mom-and-pop affairs.[85]

But in recent years entrepreneurs have begun to capitalize on Asian food's growing popularity. Perhaps the most ubiquitous has been Panda Express, a California-based chain that hopes to become the Starbucks or McDonald's of Chinese food. Panda Express's story shows how "the multiculturalism of the streets" shifts the culture through the marketplace.

Founders Peggy and Andrew Cherng grew up in Guangzhou, Hong Kong, and Taiwan, then came to Kansas to study mathematics before settling down in southern California's San Gabriel Valley. In 1973 they opened their first restaurant in Pasadena, which then had only a small Asian population. One day the developer of the Glendale Galleria ate at their restaurant and asked them to consider building a fast-serve

restaurant inside the new mall. That gave them the idea of mass marketing. "We realized there was a business that could be had outside
the Asian community," Andrew Cherng recalled at his headquarters in
Monterey Park. "We kind of followed the business where it led us."[86]

Where it led, in 1982, was to the founding of Panda Express,
designed to mass-produce Chinese food the way McDonald's sells ham-
burgers and, more recently, Starbucks sells coffee. By 2007 the chain
had roughly a thousand restaurants.[87] "The whole idea is to do it fast,"
Andrew says, "and do it right."

Panda Express is not quite McDonald's or Starbucks, but it has
established itself as the leader in mass-produced Chinese food. Cherng's
goal, immodestly, is to build ten thousand stores "in my lifetime. It's just
twenty percent growth for the next twenty years. For every hamburger
place, I want at least one Panda Express."

The biggest challenge, he believes, has been to build up his firm
with primarily non-Asian personnel and cooks. Many of the trainees,
in fact, initially learn about the company in Spanish, since they don't
speak English either. "The key is people, to get non-Chinese to work
and cook like Chinese," he suggests. "It's all part of this process. Americans are becoming more Chinese, and the Chinese are becoming the
mainstream."

THE NEW GEOGRAPHY OF DIVERSITY

The location of these businesses on the geographic fringes of Los
Angeles reflects a major shift in immigration patterns. Although immigrants continue to play a vital role in major cities—without them, most
cities would have shrunk in population—and nonwhites now constitute
a majority of urban dwellers, minority populations are also moving to
the periphery, creating an expansive new geography of diversity.[88]

In the past ethnic immigrants often tried to speed the acculturation of their children, but due to discrimination, they had to do so within the safe confines of their enclaves.[89] But after World War II Mexican-American veterans returning home no longer saw their insular neighborhood as the only place to live. Like their Anglo counterparts, they looked to the more bucolic suburban areas for a new life and better conditions.[90]

Other groups followed the same pattern. Not only were many immigrants moving from the cities to the suburbs, but by 2007 nearly two in five migrated *directly* there. In metropolitan areas, too, immigrants have moved from denser cores to outlying areas, such as Queens and New Jersey in the New York area, and the San Fernando and San Gabriel valleys outside central Los Angeles.[91]

In the first decade of the 21st century, immigrants were choosing to live in single-family homes and settle in suburbs at rates roughly equivalent to the native born. Most did so on the fringes of the immigrant-rich "gateway regions" such as New York, Los Angeles, Miami, and Chicago. In some cities rising housing costs accelerated the exodus of ethnic populations from cities. Urbanist E. Michael Jones has argued that some city governments' promotion of "gentrification," pricing African-Americans, white ethnic communities, and immigrants out of neighborhoods they once dominated, sometimes evolves into a form of "ethnic cleansing."[92]

The search for reasonably priced housing, and the desire for more space and better access to employment, have all helped shift the locus of ethnic diversity farther out to the periphery. By 2008, more Latinos lived outside Chicago than in the city itself. In greater Washington, D.C., 87 percent of immigrants live in the suburbs, almost half of them outside the Beltway; California's Santa Clara County now has a far higher proportion of immigrants than more traditionally cosmopolitan San Francisco.[93]

CROSSOVER SUBURBS

This shift in immigrant destinations is likely to move well beyond the traditional "gateway regions." As major metropolitan areas become still more expensive, due to gentrification and growth restrictions,[94] immigrants will be forced to settle ever farther from the city center.

Beginning in the 1990s, immigrants rapidly moved into regions once considered inhospitable to newcomers, particularly nonwhites: exurbs, the Southeast, and the Great Plains.[95] As less-accessible areas develop their infrastructure, immigrants will find it easier to settle in Bridgewater, New Jersey (an hour from New York), Sugarland (in the outer reaches of Houston), and even in Fargo, North Dakota.

Remarkably, suburbs—once derided for their uniformity and homogeneity—are becoming the new melting pots of American society.[96] Along with immigrants, African-Americans have moved to the suburbs in huge numbers: between 1970 and 2009, the proportion of African-Americans living in the periphery grew from less than one-sixth to 40 percent.[97]

In the coming decades suburbs, exurbs, and smaller communities will produce a social economy more ethnically blended than that of the dense, urban settlements that predominated at the turn of the 20th century. Nonurban areas tend to be car-dominated and sprawling, changing the very nature of day-to-day contact. "Turf" between ethnic groups, common historically in dense urban areas, is far harder to establish and mark in suburbs. Suburbs, notes one researcher, "hold the potential to provide more opportunities for interaction among different groups and can give rise to a much more integrated, rather than 'balkanized' relationship among groups."[98]

For newcomers and their children, suburbs will offer an experience profoundly different from the typical urbanization of the past. Nor will suburbs even be uniformly heterogenic. In the coming century these outlying areas will epitomize American diversity, just as the major cities once did. Already the most diverse three- and four-way cities—places where the population is divided between three or four major ethnic groups—are located in such suburban locales as California's Orange County, the San Gabriel Valley, and along the southwestern rim of Los Angeles County. And this is not merely a Californian phenomenon: Aurora (outside Denver), Bellevue (the Seattle suburb), and Blaine (outside Minneapolis) are becoming ever more diverse even as the nearby city centers become less so.[99]

As kids grow up in ethnically and racially mixed suburbs, they experience diversity at both school and the mall. This hybridity will be further reflected by more mixed-race households. By 2000 well over half of mixed-race households were in the suburbs, a percentage that was growing.[100]

As for those immigrants who still live in the cities, they too represent a new evolution of the old paradigm. In New York, Los Angeles, San Francisco, Miami, and Houston, immigrants, and more important their offspring, are the vanguard of street-side realities. The food, the music, even the look of these cities reflect, rather than a single cultural influence, a plethora of them, and residents, particularly the young, dabble freely in the variety.

THE ENDURING DOMINANCE OF ENGLISH

The process of integration is evident in the continued dominance of the English language, even in immigrant-heavy communities. Some contend that Latinos moving into the Southwest, returning to areas "once theirs," will create an essentially bilingual society. Despite such fears of an emerging Babel, Latinos and Asians in America are ever more likely to speak English. Ninety percent of Latino high school graduates prefer English over Spanish; in the late 1990s the proportion of U.S. residents over the age of five who did not speak English was roughly one-quarter that of a century earlier.

Among Hispanics in California, 90 percent of children of first-generation immigrants speak fluent English; in the second generation, half no longer speak Spanish. Only 7 percent of the children of immigrants speak Spanish as a primary language.[101] Of those who pay attention to politics, only a small minority look at it through Spanish-language media; roughly two-thirds follow the English-language news.[102]

In the ratings of radio stations in Los Angeles, long-dominant Spanish-language stations are losing out to rock-oriented formats that appeal to Latino youths. Similarly, Spanish-language theaters have been going out of business all over southern California, primarily because youthful moviegoers prefer English. "Right now everyone is discovering the importance of using Spanish," notes Patricia Suarez, head of a California advertising firm, "[but] we're seeing Latinos become the backbone of the English-language audience."[103]

Perhaps most revealing may be the names that Latino parents now give their offspring. The once-popular name José has been losing popularity, while Anglo names are gaining, noted a 2009 Pew Hispanic Center study. This process will intensify. In places where bilingual education is still embraced, the Spanish-dominant first generation is becoming a smaller percentage of the Latino population; American-born Hispanics account for 60 percent of all the U.S. Latino growth. By 2040 the second generation is expected to double, while the third generation, the vast majority of whom don't speak Spanish at all, will expand threefold. If immigration from Mexico slows, as may occur given its slowing birthrate, the process may accelerate, as the English-speaking second, third, and even fourth generations of Latinos expand.[104] "The big picture," notes sociologist Richard Alba, "is that bilingualism is very hard to maintain in the U.S., and by the third generation it is extraordinarily difficult to maintain. This is because English is so dominant and so highly rewarded."[105]

THE HYBRID CULTURE

In the coming decades the millennial generation—those born between 1982 and 2004—will drive the trend toward "hybridization" among both minorities and Anglos. Today's young Americans are the most multi-racial group in modern American history. Major attitude shifts have taken place concerning interracial contact, even at an intimate level. In 1987 slightly less than half of Americans approved of dating between black and whites. By 2007, according to the Pew Center, 83 percent approved. Such changes are most evident among the millennial genera-tion, the very people who will make up the majority of adults in 2050; 94 percent of them approve of such matches.

This shift to mixed race has been building for years and grows sig-nificantly among people under eighteen and, geographically, in Hawaii, California, Alaska, Oklahoma, and the New York area. In California between 1980 and 1997 one of every seven babies born had parents of different races. Nationwide the 2000 census counted 3.1 million inter-racial couples, or about 6 percent of married couples. That year for the first time the census allowed respondents to identify themselves as being two or more races, a category that now includes 7.3 million Americans, or about 3 percent of the population.

This number seems certain to swell dramatically. Between 2000 and 2007 the number of people declaring a mixed-race heritage jumped by 33 percent to over 5.2 million. They tend to be a young group; over two-fifths of mixed-race Americans are under eighteen years of age. In the coming decades this group will play an ever greater role in soci-ety. Indeed, according to sociologists at UC Irvine, by 2050 mixed-race people could account for one in five Americans. The very notion of race may become more fluid as it becomes obvious from DNA testing that people's racial or ethnic origins are far more diverse than usually imagined.[106]

During the 1990s interracial marriages between black and whites, once very rare, increased seven times as rapidly as marriages overall. Intermarriages between native-born Hispanics and Asians with other groups covered upward of 30 percent in the first native-born generation and over 57 percent in the next. Famous people of mixed heritage such as Barack Obama, Derek Jeter, Tiger Woods, and Mariah Carey are no longer rarities but role models.[107]

THE FLUID IDENTITY

This new 21st-century reality is already in full bloom on American streets and in the marketplace. Not content to hew to a single cultural or racial identity, the new generation will help erase the formerly unbreachable divide that has marked—and marred—race relations in America from its earliest days.

This generation casually presumes cultural diversity as a normal aspect of daily life; in their highly fluid marketplace young people adopt, exchange, and shed cultural identities as simply and efficiently as if they were eBay transactions. "The whole idea of ethnic marketing will change and have to focus on cross-ethnic pollination and lifestyle issues," observes ethnic marketing expert Thomas Tseng.[108]

Tseng, who grew up in the Los Angeles suburb of Alhambra, believes we will see not so much the Latinization of American culture as its reinvention, incorporating (as it has done in the past) the new generation's outlooks. Immigrant-run businesses are already influencing the culture, creating fads in everything from fashion to frozen yogurt.[109]

The youth scene, Tseng says, now includes clubs where remixes and songs from different cultures bring a new resonance to the concept of integration. The mash-up creators themselves are increasingly diverse. In northern California the underground DJ scene has long been dominated by Filipino "turntablists," who spin hip-hop beats to enthusiastic throngs of clubgoers of every nationality and color.

NEW AMERICANS, NEW AMERICAN CULTURE

In 2050 our children will inherit an America whose outlines are being developed today in suburban strip malls as well as on city streets. With tens of millions of Asians, Hispanics, and Middle Easterners, America will be a post-ethnic mélange of cultures, foods, and words.

To be sure, race and class will remain connected: poverty among African-Americans well exceeds that of Anglos and even of some recently arrived ethnic groups.[110] But by 2050 long-held notions that to be black in America "is to be branded for failure"—or any such stereotype—will seem absurd in a nation where many achievers are people of nonwhite descent.[111]

In a positive, critical source of continuity with the past, the newcomers will profoundly desire to integrate into the wider American identity. At the turn of the 20th century H. G. Wells, visiting the squalid immigrant sections of New York, was startled by the energy of the newcomers and the sight of a little immigrant boy saluting the American flag. The immigrants, he wrote, "come ready to love and worship. . . . They give themselves . . . They want to give."[112]

By embracing, and being embraced by, immigrants, America follows the path of history's most successful civilizations. The notion that race and ethnic origin are less important than achievement was important, for example, to Alexander the Great, who envisioned a multiracial empire sharing a common bond of Hellenistic ideals.[113] Ancient Roman civilization, which started in a tribal city-state, gradually opened citizenship to all Italians, and eventually, in the 3rd century, Roman citizenship was made available to free men throughout the "multinationed" empire;

less than half the Senate came from Italy. "Rome," wrote Aristides in the 2nd century, "is a citadel which has all the peoples of the earth as its villagers."[114]

The multiethnicity of the American republic, open to all, has been far from perfect, yet its essential strength should not to be underestimated. The Swedish sociologist Gunnar Myrdal observed in 1944 that even long-persecuted African-Americans maintained a remarkably strong allegiance to American "creed." As the African-American statesman Ralph Bunche wrote in the 1940s, "Every man, white black, red or yellow, knows that this is 'the land of the free,' the 'land of opportunity,' 'the cradle of liberty,' the 'home of democracy,' that the American flag symbolizes 'the equality of all men.'"[115]

For much of American history, this faith has all too often been experienced in its breach. But the trajectory of the country's evolution is clear. The same nation that in 1928 rejected Al Smith as too Irish Catholic to be president eventually elected John Kennedy.[116] By the end of the 20th century candidates of Greek, Jewish, and Italian backgrounds could run for office without their ethnicity being a serious impediment; in 2008 an African-American, of mixed-race parentage, achieved the highest office in the land.

In the business world "American" companies will increasingly be not simply white ones; even such icons as Hartford Financial Group, Ethan Allen Interiors, and Coca-Cola have had ethnic CEOs, reflecting the rise of a more diverse generation of business leaders. This diversity will allow Americans to tap the global market, and culture, in ways simply impossible in the past.[117] America, wrote Walt Whitman, is "not merely a nation, but a teeming Nation of nations."[118] The United States of the mid-21st century will increasingly reflect that description and aspiration.

CHAPTER SIX: THE 21ST-CENTURY COMMUNITY

Ellen Moncure and Joe Wong met and fell in love while living in the same dorm at the College of William and Mary. After graduation they got married and, in 1999, moved to Washington, D.C., where they worked and lived among mostly single and childless people. Like many in their late twenties, the couple eventually wanted something other than exciting careers and late-night outings with friends. "D.C. was terrific," Moncure recalled over lunch near her lower Manhattan office. "It was an extension of college. But after a while, you want to get to a different place."

The place Ellen and Joe were looking for was not just a physical location, but a sense of community, a neighborhood to raise the children they were planning to have. Although they considered some of New York's suburbs, ultimately they chose the Ditmas Park neighborhood of Brooklyn, a mixture of Victorian homes and modest apartments where Joe had grown up in the 1980s.

At first it seemed a risky choice. While Joe was living there as an adolescent, the neighborhood had become crime-infested. The older families were moving out, and newer ones were not replacing them. But Joe's mom still lived there, and they liked the idea of having her nearby when they had children.

But when their firstborn came on to the scene, the absence of other families in the neighborhood frustrated the young couple. Even with Joe's mother around, they felt isolated. "I didn't have any peers in the neighborhood with small children," Ellen recalls, "and my friends were all single or nowhere near having children. Having a child at the age of 27 is unheard of in this city, and I felt very alone! I started going to Park Slope (stroller central) to be around moms and babies and one day met a mom . . . who lived in our neighborhood. We got to be friends and thought—why can't we do this in our neighborhood?"[1]

So in 2003 they revived an old organization, the Flatbush Family Network, and established a Web site to serve as a sounding board and communication platform for area families. Since then the network, which Ellen manages, has grown from 10 families to more than 750.

The site now has numerous links, and members use it to exchange information on local parks and restaurants, to set up play dates, and to exchange recipes or the latest on local developments from new apartments to road closures. Paralleling this digital progress, other signs of an increased presence of the middle class are appearing, such as child-friendly restaurants and shops along once-decayed Cortelyou Road.[2]

More important, some of the local elementary schools have improved markedly, with an increase in parental involvement and new facilities. Even in hard economic times the area has become a beacon to New York families, as well as to singles, who are seeking a community where they can put down long-term roots.

The digital network plays an important part in this resurgence, as technology both replaces and supplements the traditional community adhesives of schools, churches, synagogues and clubs. In a neighborhood that, by some measurements, is the most ethnically diverse in the nation,[3] institutions that focus on nurturing a sense of community can be critical. As Ellen explains, "The churches and synagogues are part of the network we reach out to, but it's all part of a broader effort to make this a more family-friendly neighborhood. Without the network, without the friends and the connection, we'd never stay. . . . There's an attempt in this neighborhood to break down the city feel and to see this more as a kind of a small town. It may be in the city, but it's a community unto itself, a place where you can stay and raise your children."

THE NEW NEIGHBORHOOD NETWORK

The renewal of neighborhoods like Ditmas Park suggests that family and community are likely to remain central forces in the next few decades. Rather than "pigeon-hole ourselves into separate worlds of interests," as one futurist predicted in 2006, social networking and instant messaging are actually bringing Americans closer together, facilitating such interactions as helping children with homework, or coping with illness and other life changes.[4]

The Flatbush Family Network, like Peachhead, a popular parent-oriented network in southern California, underscores a remarkable shift in social priorities back to family and community. So do networks in lower-income areas like Newark, New Jersey, where a neighborhood-based network of Family Success Centers (Newarkfamilysuccess.org) provides peer counseling on family issues. Many of the workers there are parents from the neighborhood, trained by a long-standing non-profit agency.[5]

Other groups work as agents of family and community activism. Perhaps most important, these community networks connect people who might want company to, say, make their daily exercise at the park seem a bit safer or less lonely.[6] Two researchers who studied networks in a certain suburb described them as "[an] opportunity for neighborhood interaction that is ultimately responsible for increased community involvement, in the forms of social ties and increased public participation."

Digital networks perform some of the functions that urbanist Jane Jacobs's "eyes on the street" did in the old, cohesive city neighborhood.

Information about the arrival of a promising new store or restaurant, or the unwelcome appearance of a possible child-molester, travels through these community networks much as it did when mothers spoke over the washing, men went to the pool hall or Kiwanis, or kids hung out at the corner candy store.[7]

NOMADS NO MORE

Perhaps nothing will be more surprising about the 21st century than its settledness. For over a generation we have believed that American "spatial mobility" would continue and feed an inexorable trend towards childlessness and anomie.[8] This vision of social disintegration was perhaps best epitomized in Vance Packard's 1972 best-seller, *A Nation of Strangers*, with its vision of America as "a society coming apart at the seams."[9]

In 2000 Harvard's Robert Putnam made much the same point, although in somewhat less hyperbolic terms. In his landmark *Bowling Alone*, Putnam wrote that a "civic malaise" was gripping the country, as evidenced by the marked weakening of traditional civic organizations and all sorts of voluntary associations. His was a vision of a society whose central core was being undermined by everything from suburbanization to changing sexual mores to "the growth of mobility."[10]

In fact, Americans are becoming not more nomadic but less so, as our population ages and as urban amenities become accessible in more locales. As recently as the 1970s one in five Americans moved annually; in 2004 that number was 14 percent, the lowest rate since 1950. In 2008 barely one in ten moved, a fraction of the rate that occurred in the tumultuous 1960s. Workers are increasingly unwilling to move even for a promotion, due to family and other concerns. The 2007 economic turndown accelerated this process, but the pattern appears likely to persist even in good times.[11]

Among those who own homes, the stay-at-home trend is particularly marked, reaching the lowest levels. The economic downturn, as demographers Bill Frey and Wendell Cox have observed, dried up opportunities to sell houses and find new employment, thereby bolstering this trend. Mobility continued, but at a slower pace. Similarly, a weak economy may slow birthrates, as families postpone having additional children and young couples delay marriage and child-raising.[12]

But whatever the state of the economy, the trend toward more stable, less mobile families is likely to continue. Most people who do move, as a 2008 Pew study reveals, go to areas where they have relatives. Family, as one Pew researcher notes, "trumps money when people make decisions about where to live."

"A FUNNY THING HAPPENED ON THE WAY TO SPINSTERHOOD"

The desire for stability and cohesion may be more prevalent today than ever, according to the social historian Stephanie Coontz. Americans are more likely to be in regular contact with their parents. Some 90 percent consider their parental relations close, and far more children are likely to live with at least one parent now than they were as recently as the 1940s. Due to drops in death rates, a couple is more likely to celebrate their fortieth wedding anniversary than at any time in history.[13]

Overall, the 21st century is likely to confirm not the demise of the family, but its adaptability and vitality. Marriage, notes sociologist Andrew Cherlin, has not lost its allure, although more people may delay tying the knot. Overall, Cherlin notes, 80 or 90 percent of Americans eventually get married, often after a period of cohabitation. "Americans still strongly value marriage," he says. "What's different is that marriage used to be the first step into adulthood. Now it's often the last."[14]

There have been some changes in who gets married. As recently as two decades ago, successful career women were less likely than other women to marry. But today a single thirty-year-old woman with a graduate degree has about a 75 percent chance of getting married; one with less education has about a 66 percent chance. Overall, reports the Center for Economic and Policy Research, women in their late twenties and early thirties who are in the top 10 percent earning bracket are just as likely to be married as other women who work full time.[15]

The renewed emphasis on family has surprised many in the media, academe, and the political world, whose assumptions about the future in the 1980s were quite different. *Newsweek* famously claimed in 1986 that a white college-educated single woman at thirty would have only a 20 percent chance of getting married. In reality, wrote an editor at the magazine some twenty years later, her chance was at least twice that. Of the eleven women in the original story who could be located, eight had married and several had had children. As *Newsweek* editor Dan McGinn quipped, "A funny thing happened on the way to spinsterhood."

Much the same pattern can be seen in childrearing. Younger women today may be less likely to have children, but many more older women are giving birth; since 1982 the number of those over thirty-five who give birth has more than tripled. This trend has accelerated and will continue to do so given advances in natal science, including the use of donor eggs. In the coming decades new fertility technologies are likely to increase the number of individual children born as well as multiple births. This suggests a tremendous upcoming boost to U.S. fertility rates. Denmark, where the use of new fertility techniques is more commonplace, has already seen such a boost.[16]

"NOT ONE AMERICAN FAMILY LEFT"

The American family is resurging—albeit in an altered form—for many reasons, including large-scale immigration, a greater geographic spread, higher degrees of religiosity, and greater community involvement.[17] But whatever its causes, few pundits predicted this development or included it in their projections for the future.

As birthrates declined in the 1970s, commentators widely predicted that families would become increasingly threatened and even irrelevant. Baby boomers had far fewer offspring than their 1950s-generation predecessors, and nearly twice as many of the women born in the late 1950s went childless entirely.[18] In 1977 "communitarian" advocate and sociologist Amitai Etzioni went so far as to suggest that conceivably by the 1990s "not one American family would be left."[19]

Thereafter alarm about the family did not diminish. Shortly before her death Jane Jacobs, who understood the central role of family in society, pronounced the institution to be in "grave trouble." She compared the rise of nonfamily households of unrelated individuals—including roommates, unmarried couples, singles, and the elderly—to social conditions during the "disorder of the Dark Age after western Rome's collapse."[20]

Conservative observers such as Francis Fukuyama, author of the influential 1992 book *The End of History*, expressed similar sentiments. The "much despised suburban family of the 1950s," he suggested, at least provided "the locus of a certain moral life" that now may be in danger of being lost.[21] Much the same point has been made by right-wing pundits such as William Bennett, who indentified various "social pathologies"—many centered around the family—as "quantifying" America's overall decline.[22]

At the same time many liberal "family advocates" argue that, on average, American children live under harsher conditions than their less numerous counterparts in Europe, because of the larger welfare states in Europe, and because of the presence of large nonwhite and immigrant population in the United States. The notion that our nation cannot take care of its future generations contributes to the widespread sense of familial decline—even as we continue to have more children.[23]

THE FLIGHT OF THE EMPTY NESTERS

Perceiving the purported decline of family, some have seen opportunities for profit there, and clues to the long-term future of housing, retail, and community. Business recruiters, city planners, and urban developers have focused their attention on the growing ranks of the unattached: the "young and restless," the "creative class," and the so-called yuspie (the young urban single professional). These advocates suggest that companies and cities, if they wish to inhabit the top tiers of the economic food chain, should seek to capture this segment, described by one as "the dream demographic."[24]

Barely one in five households—but more than one-third of the total population—consists of a married couple with children living at home; this reality that has led marketers and trend watchers to shift their focus from families to the autonomous individual. Some have celebrated the retreat from family life as reason to promote the idea that people will live in dense urban places, rather than in conventional suburbs, which are deemed "out of sync with today's culture."[25]

These new urbanites, as the hype goes, will include legions of baby boomers who have already raised children. These empty nesters are expected to give up their dull family existence and rediscover the allure of a fast-paced, defiantly "youthful" lifestyle, appealing to what luxury homebuilder Robert Toll calls a "more hip and happening" generation of seniors.[26]

This notion is supported by those who believe the family—even extended—will remain the central unit of society. Author Barbara DeFoe Whitehead calls it "a cultural devaluation of child-rearing."[27] Some political progressives in both the United States and Europe see "the slimmer family"—smaller, less strongly bonded—as the key to a "new political culture" (so called by scholar Terry Nichols Clark) that deemphasizes the role of parents in childrearing. Some celebrate this culture of "individuation" for producing a greater tolerance for alterna-tive lifestyles. In their view, a decline in the importance of family would be liberating and an overall positive for society.[28]

The antinatalist implications of this view receive considerable vali-dation from some environmentalists. The green-oriented scholar Robert Short thinks keeping down "galloping population growth in highly consumptive, greenhouse-producing nations" is a good thing and that efforts to increase fertility, such as in vitro fertilization, should be dis-couraged as environmentally unfriendly.[29]

A VALUES RE-REVOLUTION?

Whatever the state of the family, we are likely to see a continued emphasis on childbearing and relations between related persons, but well beyond the narrow nuclear family as defined in the 1950s. For one thing, only a small percentage of adult Americans plan *not* to have children. Among those over forty who, for one reason or another, did not have children, more than three-quarters in 2003 regretted the fact, a considerably higher proportion than in surveys back in 1990.[30]

It turns out that the new generations of Americans are as family ori-ented, and perhaps more so, than earlier ones. Perhaps it is because close to half come from divorced homes, but opinion surveys indicate that Generation Xers—those born between 1968 and 1979—place con-siderably higher value on family, and less on work, than their boomer counterparts. Women from that age cohort actually are having more children than their boomer predecessors and, particularly the college educated, appear to be working somewhat less.[31]

This family-friendly shift is likely to continue in the coming decades. As Morley Winograd and Michael Hais suggest in *Millennial Makeover*, the rising "millennial" or "echo boom" generation—those born after 1983—is not only twice as numerous as Generation X but has markedly lower rates of teen pregnancy, abortion, and juvenile crime. This is surely due in part to increased use of birth control, but it may reflect other changing values as well. Millennials tend to have more favorable relations with their parents: half stay in daily touch, and almost all in weekly contact.[32]

The attitudes of these young people will shape our approach to family well into the mid-2000s. Three-quarters of 13-to-24-year-olds, according to one 2007 survey, consider time spent with family the greatest source of their own happiness, rating it even higher than time spent with friends or a significant other. More than 80 percent think getting married will make them happy, and some 77 percent say they definitely or probably will want children, while less than 12 percent say they likely will not.[33]

Finally, economic factors may contribute to a familial resurgence. Higher college debts, high home prices, and a less-than-vibrant job market all could have the effect of extending virtual adolescence, in which children maintain strong ties of dependence into adulthood. Although these conditions may increase support for more governmental assistance, young people are equally likely to cling to the one group of people who, irrespective of political shifts, can be counted on: the family.[34]

THE RETURN OF THE FLEXIBLE FAMILY

The resurgence of the family paradigm does *not* suggest a return to the culturally conservative values of the postwar era. The families of the 21st century, rather than looking like those of the 1950s, will recall the more flexible and diverse families of the 19th century. Unlike the typically "nuclear" families of the 20th century, earlier generations of American families tended to be more ad hoc or, as we would say today, "blended," with uncles, aunts, grandparents, stepparents, and domestic employees.[35]

Two critical forces in American history—the frontier experience and immigration—shaped the American family. Life in the newly opened lands of the West, suggested turn-of-the-century historian Frederick Jackson Turner, fostered "a kind of primitive organization based on family," with far less concern for conventions of either organized religion or government. The new opportunities on the frontier, as historians Charles and Mary Beard noted, "made girls more defiant of parental authority and more determined to exercise their own pleasure both in choice of work and husbands."[36]

The frontier experience often disrupted early American families. Young people in huge numbers deserted New England and other coastal states. As a consequence, parents, aware that their children might not be around to support them in their old age, simply had fewer of them. Between 1830 and 1890 birthrates plummeted by nearly 50 percent, even as death rates fell dramatically, as also happened at the close of the 20th century.

Immigrant families, crowded into the rapidly expanding cities, weathered tremendous stress. Caught between traditional values and the realities of city streets, children rebelled against their parents. This was true even among groups renowned for their strong family ties; for example, Jewish immigrants from eastern Europe accounted for almost a third of those brought to Manhattan's "children's court" in 1906.[37]

Throughout the late 19th century the family grew more flexible from hard necessity. Parents, particularly working-class males, often died early from harsh working conditions. Many poor Irish immigrant laborers, notes historian William V. Shannon, died in their thirties out of "nothing more identifiable than a nameless weariness." Families soldiered on, helped by relatives and neighbors, and by children who peddled papers, ran errands, and rummaged in junkyards.[38]

Over time the industrial system undermined extended, flexible families. Work once done at home—sewing garments, running a family farm, or living above a family shop—shifted to factory, which separated adults from their children, who spent their days either in school or on the streets.[39] This gap between work and home accelerated the development of an individualist culture. The Jazz Age of the 1920s challenged conventions about sex, family, and marriage, and the process of ever-greater individualism would be constrained only by the Depression and World War II.[40]

After the war there was a deep-seated longing to return to a perceived set of "family values." But the new family that emerged was different from its antecedents. The postwar suburban idyll signaled the primacy of a new "nuclear" family and consolidated the separation of work from household. The rising middle class of the 1950s certainly enjoyed a higher standard of living than preceding generations but at a considerable social cost. The new denizens of mass suburbia, suggested historian Lewis Mumford, lived an increasingly "encapsulated life." He contrasted this isolation to the richer communal life enjoyed in traditional cities and villages.[41]

BEYOND *OZZIE AND HARRIET*

The 1950s, notes social historian Stephanie Coontz, represented something of an historical anomaly, with extremely high birthrates, few divorces, remarkable social stability, and a preponderance of intact nuclear families. Mom, Dad, and two young kids as a stand-alone, all-inclusive unit came to be epitomized by the television show *The Adventures of Ozzie and Harriet*, which ran between 1952 and 1966. The centrality of family life and Nelson family "adventures," such as they were, were so celebrated that Ozzie famously did not even appear to go off to work but inexplicably hung around the house in a cardigan.

(In the following years the real Nelson family was revealed to be completely dysfunctional and came to represent critiques of the decade.)

The 1950s family phenomenon was short-lived, Coontz notes. The age of marriage, which dropped in the 1950s, has now risen up roughly to that of the late 19th century. In this sense the 1950s represented a "very deviant decade." Now families headed by a single parent are a significant proportion; their re-emergence appears to be a return to the old norm in which relatives and stepparents played a major role. The web of relationships—not completely captured in census data—often extends beyond the geography of a household.[42]

Now that a majority of married women work and have their children at a later age, childrearing roles extend beyond the biological parents and are often shared by divorced parents, their new spouses, and other family members who, although not living with the children, are still deeply involved. Grandparents and other relatives help provide care for roughly half of all preschoolers, something that has not changed significantly over time and is unlikely to do so in the future. This is even true in the Obama White House, where Marian Robinson, the First Lady's mother, has moved in to help raise the couple's two children.[43]

Other family units follow unconventional forms: groups of genetically unrelated people live together in everything from nursing homes to urban neighborhoods. In 2005 gay or lesbian partners formed as many as 800,000 households, a 20 percent increase from 2000. Roughly one in five were also raising children, including some 65,000 adoptees.[44] Families, notes Dr. Pat Voydanoff, are less confined to one physical location, or to direct bloodlines, but serve more as a "psychological unit."[45]

New technologies are also reshaping the family. Today, in the age of computers and cell phones, children who leave home are no longer "gone." They send text messages, maintain blogs, and write e-mails to keep parents informed of their activities.[46]

These social changes may baffle ideologues of the right and the left more than they do the bulk of Americans. As social historian Alan Wolfe's studies on suburbanites suggest, most families are no longer strictly traditionalist. The largest number, he suspects, are "realists" who, "instead of glorifying gay marriages or stepfamilies as a move away from oppression of the nuclear family . . . acknowledge that changes have taken place in the family, and one simply has to adjust to them." If American does "swing back" to a more family oriented society, Wolfe notes, "it will be with a difference."[47]

American families, then, are not going out of fashion, but the shape of family life will continue to evolve. Anyone looking into the future of the country without considering the protean nature of this most basic institution will miss a great and critical force.

POSTPONING THE ROAD TRIP

High costs are going to prolong parental involvement in their children's lives. The burgeoning costs of education and other young-adult needs will extend the timeline of parental responsibility well beyond the traditional spans. As parents struggle to keep their twentysomething children afloat, they may have to postpone a lifestyle free of familial entanglements.

Instead of taking early retirement, boomer and Gen-X parents may be forced actually to delay their retirements.[48] Americans already have the oldest male retirement age of any advanced country besides Japan. That age is likely to increase over time. Between 1998 and 2004 the percentage of Americans who did not plan to retire until after age 65 increased from 36 percent to 57 percent; as many as three-quarters expect to work for pay after retirement, reversing a long-term trend toward earlier and more complete retirements.

To be sure, the trend toward delaying retirement also reflects improved health and the need for personal fulfillment. But for many it will be driven by necessity: the need to help children far longer than expected. One-quarter of Generation Xers, for example, still receive financial help from their parents, as do nearly a third of those under 25. More numbers of people between 24 and 35 are living with their parents, a choice that is likely to become more common where home prices remain high. The recession may accelerate this "back to home" migration and keep it in place for many years.

As a result, older Americans will remain a far more active force in the economy—and in their children's lives—than was the case a generation ago. Most plan to stay near where they currently live, rating proximity to family members as a major factor in their decision. Contrary to the celebration of "independence" created by marketers and advocates of the "slimmer" family, most Americans are as concerned with passing on an inheritance to their children as their parents were.[49]

THE RETURN OF THE MULTIGENERATIONAL HOUSEHOLD

As people live longer and produce offspring later, family ties are strengthening. Many commentators have viewed this national aging negatively, as a great burden to the young and middle-aged. But as author Marc Freedman points out, an active older generation could be a tremendous source of assets—in the financial sense—and serve as emotional bulwarks as well. In a society where people commonly live well into their seventies and eighties, he correctly suggests that "the long gray wave" could be as much an "opportunity as a crisis to be solved."[50]

In this scenario grandparents—as well as other childless relatives—play a larger role in family life, both as financial supporters and as sources of reliable child care. As caregivers age, in turn, they will require help for themselves. This period of providing assistance to aging parents has lengthened considerably. In 1900 it averaged nine years; in the early decades of the 21st century it can extend as long as two decades.

Since the 1960s observers have widely believed that we would, in Mumford's phrase, "hive off" the generations from each other. Mumford rightly decried this trend toward segregation by age, and the institutionalization of seniors, as both wasteful and a sadly premature form of "early euthanasia."

But the scenario may prove less inexorable than once imagined. One welcome change, already evolving, is the growth of multigenerational households. Institutionalized care for people over seventy-five, once seen as inevitable, has dropped since the mid-1980s, as more families hire part-time help or have the aging parents move in with them.

Today as many as six million grandparents live with their offspring, allowing, by one estimate, as many as half a million people to avoid nursing homes. Between 2000 and 2007, according to the Census Bureau, the number of people over sixty-five living with adult children increased by more than 50 percent. Ever more children and grandchildren serve as informal caregivers for their elderly relatives, while grandparents serve as mentors and watchful eyes over the young.

As healthy life spans lengthen, the opportunities for such multigenerational arrangements will expand, reversing the tendency to separate generations and reducing reliance on institutional care. One California builder reports that one-third of new homebuyers want a "granny flat," an addition to accommodate an aging parent. Roughly one-third of American homes have the potential to create such units. In the coming decades homes that can be adapted to the changing needs of families will become an increasingly desirable commodity.[51]

FAMILIES AND SUCCESSFUL COMMUNITIES

To those who associate singleness and independence with prosperity, this linkage of families to successful communities might seem anachronistic. But married people with children, far from being a burden on society, tend to be both successful and motivated—precisely the people who drive the national economy. They are twice as likely to be in the top 20 percent of income earners, according to the 2000 census, and their incomes have been rising considerably faster than the national average.

Nowhere has this trend been more evident than in African-American families. The controversial 1965 Moynihan report linked poverty among African-Americans to the decline of intact family units. Today more than half of black children live in households with a single mother, a number that has doubled since the 1960s, and they are much more likely to live in poverty than nonblacks. But among intact African-American families "the racial gap" diminishes markedly.

The confluence between upward mobility and strong family net-works remains extraordinary, not only among African-Americans but among all groups. Only 6 percent of married-couple families live in poverty, and most of them, like previous generations of newcomers, are likely to climb out of that state.[52]

These studies suggest that support for strong families must be at the heart of any socially sustainable future and the primary focus of our community efforts. Interventions later in life can help, of course, but the "early environment" at home—preferably with two involved parents—is the biggest predictor of children's future adjustment. Single-parent families, roughly one in five, appear most at risk. "Families," suggests Nobel Prize–winning economist James Heckman, "are the major source of inequality in American social and economic life."[53]

AT HOME IN THE ELECTRONIC COTTAGE

In the coming decade the expansion of broad-band communications and teleconferencing will provide unprecedented opportunities for families. Before the Industrial Revolution, the household was the center of economic life, since the family was integrated and intimately exposed to work life. For the better part of the 20th century, this form of economic integration suffered prolonged decline. But since the mid-1990s it has grown rapidly.

As technology improves and the unpredictable cost of energy discourages conventional commuting by car, the process is accelerating. By 2006 the size of the home-based workforce had doubled twice as quickly as in the previous decade. By 2015, suggests demographer Wendell Cox, more people will be working electronically at home full time than will be taking transit, making it the largest potential source of energy savings on transportation.

Even more Americans will work at home part of the time; in 2006 more than 28 million people did so, a 40 percent increase from just four years earlier. In the San Francisco Bay Area and Los Angeles, almost one in ten workers are part-time telecommuters. Home offices, particularly in upscale homes, have become a critical necessity, demanded more often than security systems. Some studies indicate that more than one-quarter of the American workforce could eventually participate full or part time in this new work pattern.[54]

This shift suggests a potential sea change in the way our families and communities will be structured. In preindustrial societies family members worked at home or walked to work. The industrial epoch changed all that; its need for mass standardization suggested the efficacy of office and factory. Karl Marx, the ultimate chronicler and prophet of the industrial age, saw that "agglomeration in one shop" was "necessary" for human progress.

A century later futurist Alvin Toffler foresaw that the rise of the "electronic cottage" would return work to the domicile. Toffler envisioned that his "Third Wave" society would break away from the "behavioral code" of "Second Wave" industrialism, where work and family were purposely segregated. As he put it, "social and technological forces are converging to change the locus of work" back to the home, neighborhood, and village.[55] The rapid rise of at-home work, both full and part time, creates new opportunities to close the space between productive work and family life.

These trends will continue as economic relations between firms become less constrained by distance. Information inputs can come from any source and any place. Some see the universities as the new "factories"—the centers of economic and social life—since they cluster many autonomous information providers. But Toffler rejects this idea as "little more than a professorial wish fulfillment fantasy." The true locus of postindustrial society, he notes, even for those who might be affiliated with larger organizations like universities, is "the home."[56]

Promoting home-based businesses, he suggests, may contribute more to the health of the family than following the moralistic blandishments of conservative "family values" activists to return to the strictly delineated gender roles of the 1950s. In a world with fewer permanent employees and longer work hours, working from home will help mothers to stay employed even while raising children, and aid a growing number of fathers that want to more actively participate in childrearing.[57] "If we really want to strengthen family and make the home the central institution again," says Toffler, "we must forget the peripheral issues, accept diversity, and return important tasks to the household."[58]

THE RISE OF FAMILY-FRIENDLY CITIES

Many contemporary real estate agencies, planners, and architects minimize or ignore the critical importance of families and the potential for home-based business.[59] But recruiters and developers in the nation's fastest-growing regions find that what lures skilled workers long term is not gourmet restaurants, street fairs, and trendy nightclubs but family-friendly communities not too distant from work, ample economic opportunities, and affordable housing. The nation's fastest-growing cities have been the ones that have managed to attract families, like Salt Lake City, Dallas, Austin, Houston, Raleigh-Durham, and Charlotte.[60]

"People who come here tend to be people who have had long commutes elsewhere and who have young children," notes Pat Riley, president of Allen Tate company, a large residential brokerage in Charlotte. "The kids are in elementary and secondary school with parents in their thirties and forties. They want to be somewhere where they don't miss their kids growing up because there's no time. Having children means a reality check about what's important."[61]

To be sure, the dichotomy between a "luxury" city and a family-oriented one need not be strict. Since the early 1990s Austin, Texas, one of the strongest economic performers, contains elements of both. It appeals to singles and to childless couples because of its strong music and arts scene, excellent restaurants, and college-town feel; yet its relatively low prices for single-family homes, particularly in the suburbs, attract couples with children as well.[62]

As a result, Austin offers the diverse options—in terms of age, life stage, and family status—of a future successful community. In some ways it resembles a luxury city, but it has also managed to hold on to its middle-aged population. Indeed, in sharp contrast to its high-tech rivals Boston and San Francisco, Austin draws a high proportion of educated people well into their thirties and forties.

"California might work well for the apartment-dwelling, single-guy lifestyle person, but when you get married, you can't afford Los Gatos [Silicon Valley]," says former Silicon Valley entrepreneur Mike Shultz, the CEO of Infoglide, a software firm headquartered on Austin's outer ring. "In Austin the same person can grow up, move into a reasonable house, and have a reasonable life."[63]

It has become increasingly clear: wherever families choose to settle generally will experience the strongest long-term job and population growth. This will be even more evident between 2010 and 2020, when the front edge of the millennial generation hits their thirties and early forties, and enters the prime years for starting families and settling down for the long run. In the future, the health of cities will prove likely more dependent on good schools and safe parks than art galleries, chic boutiques, and convention centers.

NEXT BIG TREND: THE THREE-GENERATION 'BURB

The most successful and socially sustainable community model for the 21st century will be one that allows diverse opportunities for a broad spectrum of people. As the population ages, options for older Americans do not have be substantially different or separate from those for singles, young families, single-parent families, and families that include young-adult "children" who live at home.

Rather than segregate themselves in adult communities, many aging but still-active adults may look for multigenerational settings close to their personal networks, offspring, churches, or clubs.[64] To accommodate seniors, successful communities will have to develop cultural amenities and an array of specialized stores and restaurants, while also offering a secure environment. So-called naturally occurring retirement communities are places that have, for one reason or another, attracted seniors organically; they help seniors with everything from grocery shopping to maintaining a home or to attending cultural events.[65]

Such communities could reverse the well-established movement of seniors to warm-weather states like Florida or Arizona. Some 90 percent of people over fifty, notes AARP, want to stay in or around their current locations rather than move anywhere. "They don't want to move to Florida, and they want to stay close to the kids," notes Washington-area developer Jeff Lee. "What they are looking for is a funky suburban development—funky but safe."[66]

All this suggests that the suburbs will increasingly become home to aging Americans. They did in the 1990s, and they are likely to continue, given retiring boomers' stated preferences. Overall, downshifting boomers seem to prefer what one critic calls "the bland American dream": according to one 2005 survey, barely 2 percent want to move to experience the "excitement" of a dense urban area. And like their younger counterparts, aging Americans remain tethered to their cars; less than 10 percent of seniors over sixty-five walk, bike, or take public transport as their primary means of getting around.[67]

Moreover boomers (and the next generation to retire, today's Xers, in around 2040) have generally wanted more space, not less. They are likely to want rooms set aside for visiting children and grandchildren, or a home office. If they eventually downsize, it will not likely be to something radically smaller, at least not until they are considerably aged.[68]

Communities that meet the desires of a huge aging population will find new uses for large sections of suburbs, as their demographics become more diverse. Something less conventionally suburban, but still only modestly dense, may emerge. As architect John Kaliski has pointed out, these new communities may be denser than conventional suburbs but will retain the low-key, secure ambience of peripheral communities. They will remain, as he suggests, "suburban, not neo-urban."[69]

In other words suburbs will evolve but remain themselves. The old "Ozzie and Harriet" model will likely be replaced by a more diverse, multigenerational model, but the essential values will stay the same. Notes Upland, California, community developer Randall Lewis, "Some of the basics of suburbs are there. Schools are important, but also people like the sense of place. But the basic amenities are children, grandchildren, where people go to church, where their work networks and friends are. Suburbia is going to be a melting pot, not just by race, but by ages and lifestyle."[70]

WHY RURAL VILLAGES AND SMALL TOWNS?

A significant portion of aging Americans are likely to live in smaller towns and villages.[71] One-tenth of Americans already live in smaller, rural areas, anchored by towns of less than 50,000; some of these towns are experiencing a strong in-migration of downshifting boomers. As the coastal areas become ever more crowded, with an estimated twenty-five million more people 2020, the reasons to move to smaller towns, whether in the Heartland or near more populated centers, will only multiply.[72]

By 2000 the migration of retirees and downshifting boomers to the Sunbelt metropolises of the Southwest and Florida had slowed.[73] Increasingly older Americans seem to prefer "amenity" regions—places close to national parks and scenic open space, such as Douglas County, Colorado, and certain counties in Idaho; the Berkshires of New England; and even parts of Alaska. Such counties, according to the U.S. Department of Agriculture, grew ten times faster than other rural counties.[74] In many of these counties' central towns, old Main Streets are being restored, and as downshifting seniors move in, this process should accelerate rapidly.[75]

This migration of older people will surely change small-town America in the mid-21st century. Among other things, it will bring skills, capital, and technological expertise to once-neglected places, as aging Americans retain an active lifestyle that often includes part-time work. Many college towns, which are particularly attractive to older residents, have seen this change.[76]

But the newcomers may bring other, less tangible assets to these communities. An urge for a sense of family and community traditionally ranks high as a reason that people move, or move back, to smaller towns.[77] They may well volunteer in their new communities, like the group of retired California police officers who branded themselves

"Cold Case Cowboys" help solve old homicides in their adopted rural community of Roseburg, Oregon. The desire to volunteer may motivate boomers to move into college towns: according to the corporation for national and community service, college towns are hot spots for volunteering, with high rankings in particular for Provo, Utah; Iowa City, Iowa; and Madison, Wisconsin.[78]

THE NEW LOCALISM

The growth of urban-style options—such as diverse restaurants, religious institutions, and cultural venues—in suburbs, exurbs, and even smaller towns suggest that Americans desire "a sense of place," or identification with their local community. Just as the family is gaining more coherence and staying power, so too are communities likely to express a more conscious sense of themselves.

To survive, thrive, and motivate allegiance in their inhabitants, communities will depend greatly on an ability to develop what the Jewish philosopher Martin Buber once called "a vocation of uniqueness."[79] This process might best be named the New Localism. The trend toward greater localization works on the premise that the longer people stay in their homes and communities, the more they identify with those places, and the less they see them as just transitory locations.

The New Localism will not replicate older forms of association. Bowling clubs and Boy Scout troops that were lost in the shift to a postindustrial society are not likely to be resurrected. Instead, we need to develop new institutions that make sense in the new demographic and geographic realities. There are already signs: after a generation-long decline, volunteerism has spiked among millennials and seems likely to surge among downshifting boomers. In 2008 some 61 million Americans volunteered, representing over a quarter of the population over sixteen.[80]

At the same time online social networks are gaining influence, both among young people and adults. They sometimes serve simply as cyber meeting places for friends and family, but they can also create community within a geographically specific location, as we saw in Ditmas Park.

These developments contradict the assertions by the architect Daniel Liebeskind and others that "public space is dead." To be sure, traditional town squares have declined over the past few decades, but something else has emerged that Florida architect Richard Reep calls a "countercyclical element in our cities."

As an example, Reep points to the proliferation of farmers' markets. In Maryland the number of farmers' markets has grown from twenty in 1991 to eighty-four in 2008. In 1977 California had four such markets; it now has over five hundred. An even more ambitious effort (discussed in chapter 4) is community-supported agriculture, in which local households contract directly with farmers, who produce and deliver fresh foods. CSA has blossomed in numerous states, including Minnesota, Oklahoma, and Wisconsin.[81]

In the Orlando area, where Reep lives, public space is very much alive and is assuming a new role in neighborhoods: weekend flea and farmers' markets are springing up in public nooks and crannies around the older, urban core and in the suburban public parks as well. "These markets are exciting because they are growing," notes Reep, "despite all the forces working against them: crime, internet commerce, and the accelerated kinetic lives we lead in this new millennium. People are finding something important at these small, crowded, open-air market stalls, and it isn't just good tomatoes."[82]

NEW FORMS OF COMMUNITY

Farmers' markets are just one way communities will continue to develop new forums for interaction, enlisting numerous different spaces—some private, some public—to serve distinct social purposes. A mall, a private ball field, or a "community" room in a private development may all become important locales in community life. Whether it is located in a traditional neighborhood or a gated community, in a planned development or a cluster that emerged organically, the critical issue is the quality and coherence of the social interactions that take place within it.[83]

Community in the 21st century will take many forms, some of which have been widely criticized as artificial or even anticommunity, like conventional suburbs and homeowner associations.[84] Urban planner Edward Blakely and others perceive these developments "gated communities" as weakening the public realm.[85] But gated communities also can reflect a desire for a community that feels secure and that has some controls on interaction. The desire to "wall off" an urban space is as ancient as the city itself.

Upon examination, gated communities and homeowner associations—which may house as many as forty million Americans—are not as ethnically exclusive and forbidding as Blakely and other critics fear. Social scientist Andrew Kirby notes that the residents of these communities come from a broad range of economic levels and ethnicities, not only from wealth.

Rather than dismiss these growing social forms, a far more reasonable approach would be to focus on how people define what they want from a community. To dismiss particular geographies—gated communities, small towns, or inner-city districts—just because they are not all-inclusive by class or age. is misguided. Populations that differ culturally and by age possess different conceptions of what community means and, sometimes, where best to find it.[86]

This approach makes particular sense in an America with longer life spans, ever greater diversity, and more kinds of residential choice. The traditional urbanist notion of one central community square around which a community revolves is clearly archaic. Community links will continue to morph, as population growth and technology expand people's options.

RECAPTURING ARCHITECTURE FOR COMMUNITY

The New Localism, in its many forms, will require a reevaluation of architecture. At the height of 20th-century industrialism, particularly after the Second World War, many buildings were constructed without regard to human needs. Even Minoru Yamasaki, who designed the World Trade Center, acknowledged that at least one of his largest projects, the massive Pruitt-Igoe residential development in St. Louis, was a failure in large part because he had "designed a housing project, not a community." Composed of thirteen eleven-story slabs, Pruitt-Igoe won awards from architects but had to be razed in 1972, seventeen years after its completion, because it had deteriorated into a crime-infested social disaster.

Ironically, the project was conceived as an example of progressive thinking and sought to model itself on similar projects in New York City. It was, as urban historian Alexander von Hoffman notes, part of an attempt to recast industrial St. Louis into a modern "Manhattan on the Mississippi." It was not intended to house solely African-Americans, but it ended up that way as much of the city's white population fled to the surrounding suburbs.[87]

At the heart of the Pruitt-Igoe's failure lay an enormous miscalculation. Its developers believed that poor people, many of them originally from the countryside, could adapt to life in constrained spaces, with little open area. This kind of large-scale housing project—an attempted architectural solution to a deep-seated social problem—has failed virtually all over the world. Such large projects have turned out to be disastrous not only in the United States but in the United Kingdom, France, and Brazil.[88]

More such housing projects are unlikely to be commissioned in the United States during the next few decades, but the tendency to decouple a specific location from its heritage and the everyday lives of its people has become ever more powerful. Some architects, such as Rem Koolhaas, see the emergence of a "generic city" indifferent to the issue of habitability and the specifics of place. It is based on the notion that all urban places are the same and can be designed without a strong connection to their surrounding historic or geographic context. This can be seen in the "iconic" architecture favored by some "starchitects" and critics who view buildings more for their arresting features—much like sculptures—than as habitats for people and business. At worst, as former Boston University president John Silber notes, these megastructures "trample over the lives of hundreds of thousands" in order to impose a stark, even absurd, urban landscape.

Urban neighborhoods, as Jane Jacobs noted, need landmarks or "eye-catchers"—even something as basic an old water tower—that are associated with their organic development. In contrast, the imposition of a grandiose, abstract vision contradicts the desire for a unique identifier, which can be an old theater, a simple statue, or a plaza. In contrast, the Forest City Company's proposals for massive high-rises in downtown Brooklyn in the early 2000s elicited strong opposition by those who loved the area's varied, organically developed, mid- and low-slung historic character. If architecture in the crowded mid-21st century is going to attract large numbers of permanent residents and families, particularly in dense urban areas, it will have to become more responsive to human needs and scale.[89]

Suburbia will face many of the same challenges, now that numerous communities have been made to look remarkably uniform. Some developers have shown little interest even in sidewalks, much less bike paths, attractive parks, or backyards. Families and individuals need to convince developers that they prioritize a coherent community life by demanding that they want, along with a security system, access to thriving community associations, or a neighborhood-oriented online social network.

Developers and city planners are unlikely to provide these features reliably by themselves. The successful community of the future will rely more on grassroots expressions of the New Localism. Residents' demands have already driven the proliferation of swap meets, farmers' markets, and festivals that define specific communities, even as they move away from more traditional retail settings.[90]

THE AMERICAN VALUE SYSTEM

The New Localism is part of the evolving set of values that will shape American society in the coming decades. From the earliest civilizations, successful communities—be they in classical times, Renaissance Italy, or Enlightenment Holland—have had a unifying belief system that has been a critical element of community, as well as a bulwark to families.

Over time a thriving civilization has to be built around something beyond the narrow interests of the individual. In America this belief system has revolved largely around religion.[91] Estimates of regular religious attendance vary widely, but Americans are clearly more likely to attend church than their counterparts in Europe. Roughly 60 percent of Americans, according to a Pew Global Attitudes survey, believe religion is "very important," twice the rate of Canadians, Britons, Koreans, or Italians, and six times the rate of French or Japanese.

This greater religiosity has become one of the most controversial aspects of American community. In the 1960s and 1970s social thinker Peter Berger predicted the nation would follow the European lead toward "secularization," defined as a society "removed from the domination of religious institutions and symbols," where individuals "look upon their world and their own lives without the benefit of religious interpretation."[92]

To be sure, since the 1960s the ranks of openly and even actively engaged secularists has grown. But religious communities, particularly evangelical elements, have undergone a considerable revival, and the search for spiritual experience has broadened.

This growth initially occasioned a civic divide, in which conservative evangelicals became shock troops for the Republican Party and its right wing, while secularists, if not as well organized, have flocked to the liberal wing of the Democratic Party.[93] Some have characterized the conflict as a "culture war" between believers and nonbelievers, a notably divisive view in a society that is becoming ever more complex and diverse. Focus on the Family sees salvation for a nation "on the verge of self-destruction" only in "family values," by which it essentially means a return to norms of the 1950s.[94]

At the same time many secular Americans, particularly in the urban centers and within academia, dismiss the validity of religious groups, preferring to emulate the secularism of Europe. Sociologist Phil Zuckerman equates the European rejection of religion with the continent's high level of social development, low crime rate, and welfare-state protections, which have undermined the traditional need for religious institutions. Many nonbelievers view religion as the enemy of science, rationalism, and tolerance. These views are as strongly felt in urban centers as they are disputed in more rural areas.[95]

But at the start of the 21st century the culture war is "waning," as one researcher observes.[96] Neither religion nor secularism has been defeated; rather, we are entering an era where these issues are dealt with in a less confrontational manner on both sides.

Over time religious influence is unlikely to decline much, since people who go to church are more likely to have offspring than those who don't.[97] This may explain, in part, the 60 percent rise in schools with a strong traditionalist Christian bent since the late 1980s, even as Catholic schools have been in decline.[98]

But the growth in the ranks of the religious does not suggest the ascendency of evangelical conservatism. Nontraditional faiths too have grown, as have smaller, less conventional institutions, while many join organized religious institutions after they have had children.[99] These diverse approaches to faith have gained adherents among the once secular. Likely due to the popularity of New Age mysticism, Eastern religious traditions, and hybrid spiritual approaches, relatively few Americans identify as atheists.

Ultimately, these shifts will reinforce the better understanding of Americans, not as religious zealots, but as spiritual searchers. A quarter of people in their twenties and thirties, notes sociologist Robert Wurthnow, have no interest in religion or spirituality, while an equal proportion consider themselves "very spiritual" even if they rarely attend church. Roughly three out of four college students, according to a 2003 UCLA study, consider their spiritual or religious views important, but most see their professors as largely indifferent to such concerns.

Longer life spans, later marriages, and postponing having children until their thirties or forties may keep young people away from churches longer; they may become members over their extra decades. Many view religion from an instructional, even therapeutic point of view: in 1965 half of Americans thought the primary purpose of a church was to teach people to live a better life; by 2005 almost three in four felt this way.[100]

The rise of interethnic, interracial, and homosexual marriages will serve to redefine spiritual life and make it more protean and adaptable. Even evangelical and fundamentalist churches may change as they adjust to new social realities. Shifts in attitudes, in part due to upward mobility among their own members, have lessened the glaring gulf in beliefs on homosexuality, abortion, and pornography between rural and small-town Protestants and the rest of society.

Once-rigid and conservative churches will be affected by immigration. Hispanics and Asians have already become important constituencies for conservative Christian groups; in southern California they have paced a revival of the Mennonites, constituting the vast majority of church members. Just as they have affected mainstream churches, these newcomers will affect, over time, the language, rituals, and attitudes of even the most tradition-minded churches.[101]

HOW RELIGION WILL INTEGRATE THE NEW AMERICANS

American religious institutions have long proved remarkably adaptable to a society without an official religion and with an ever-shifting racial and ethnic composition. On the frontier, churches brought a moral order to a difficult, often hostile environment. In Utah the Mormon Church oversaw not only moral education but the creation of rail lines, economic cooperatives, and irrigation systems. Mormonism, as Brigham Young suggested, made little distinction between "spiritual things" and "temporal things."

In the cities, churches and synagogues provided a sanctuary from often-turbulent settings. Since at least the mid-19th century the Catholic and Lutheran churches have worked as agents of charity, education, and ultimately integration for immigrant communities, helping raise them to the middle class and above.[102]

The Catholic Church was particularly important in helping the destitute arrivals from Ireland, those who John Hughes, the first Catholic archbishop of New York, described as "the scattered debris of the Irish nation." Similarly, in New York and other cities, the Hebrew Immigrant Aid Society helped Jewish immigrants with everything from job placement to protection from swindlers, many from their own community.[103]

Today, particularly among the poor and the newly arrived, religious organizations play a role that is, if anything, more important. As schools have declined, religious institutions have often picked up the slack for vulnerable populations. Organizations offer soup kitchens or AIDS hospices or low-cost housing are often based in churches and other spiritual institutions. "I would argue," notes one liberal academic, Brooklyn College's Anthony M. Stevens-Arroyo, "that life in New York would [not] be livable without the efforts of the religiously committed."[104]

GRAZING TO HEAVEN: 21ST-CENTURY RELIGION

In the next decades religious institutions will provide critical services to a growing population that is diverse across the demographic spectrum. The increasing number of young families in America indicates that there will be a strong demand for religious education. At the same time many aging baby boomers, including those who moved away from the faith of their parents, may have a greater need for the community that religious institutions provide.

Ever since the low point of the 1970s, boomers' religious commitments have grown gradually. Wade Roof, author of *Spiritual Marketplace*, points out that today's Americans, starting with the boomers, are less rigid and more flexible in their religious views than were earlier generations. Even those who embrace a religion, for example, tend to be skeptical of anthropomorphic views of God or the devil.

Some will embrace evangelical churches, whose members constitute almost a quarter of Americans. But others will shop around for other beliefs. More than one-quarter of all adult Americans, noted one 2008 survey, left their childhood faith to join another one or none at all. Among mainstream religious institutions, commitment to, say, Presbyterianism or Lutheranism now often shifts from one congregation to another. Many others will be "grazers," meeting their spiritual needs in online Bible study, meditation, Buddhism, and other expressions of what one author calls "America's cafeteria of alternative religions."

Rather than cling to a single religious community from childhood onward, Americans prefer to "make" or simply choose one. In this sense the religious experience parallels the evolution of our increasingly flexible families. "The picture that emerges," notes Roof, "is one of structural changes, fluidity and boundary crossings."[105]

Even evangelicals and fundamentalists may prove less rigid than is often suspected. Less than half of all conservative Christians believe that their faith should be the law of the land, and only a minority hold strict fundamentalist views on abortion or the role of women. Similarly, only a minority feel that public schools should teach religious values.

During the next few decades people will continue to embrace religions and drop them, to sample faiths and switch to others. Religious affiliation will be more akin to what marketing expert Chris Anderson calls the "world of abundant choices": many will embrace religious notions borrowed from Native Americans, Buddhism, or Taoism. This process will accelerate the diversification of religion.[106]

THE NEW ECUMENICALISM

An estimated 35 or 40 percent of Americans claim to attend church weekly. This number is likely exaggerated, but this small cadre will continue to play an outsize role in community life.

The religiously observant, according to the Harvard social capital survey, are more likely to be involved in community affairs, give blood, trust other people, and socialize with friends; they tend to have a wider social net than the nonobservant.[107] They are a primary reason why Americans, according to one recent study, are far more likely to volunteer their time to help others than are peoples of any country on the European continent, and more than twice as likely as those in Great Britain.[108]

In a world less dominated by organized, conventional religions, this role will take on an ever more ecumenical and nonreligious tone. In the future American religious attitudes, like those on racial matters, will demonstrate a greater degree of toleration between faiths and within. It will provide the basis for what Gregg Easterbrook has dubbed "the new ecumenicalism," a critical component in a successful 21st-century society.[109]

In order to fulfill the needs of America's current population, as well as the coming one hundred million, religious groups will find it necessary to work with others, including secular groups. They are already doing so in the Woodlands, the remarkable large planned development outside Houston. When the community was still young, the development's founder, George Mitchell, looked to create a charitable community group. He approached the Reverend Don Gebert, a Lutheran minister from Philadelphia. Thirty years later Gebert recalls that Mitchell told him, "I know how to do the hardware, but I need you to show me how to do the software, the people stuff."[110]

When Gebert arrived in 1975, according to Mitchell's longtime right-hand man Roger Galatas, the Woodlands had "no social structure" in terms of churches, community centers, or seniors groups.[111] In the ensuing years Gebert became a key architect of the city's large-scale volunteer effort, known as the Interfaith Council. Gebert built Interfaith into a powerful service organization with membership from forty-four religious institutions, the largest of which has roughly six thousand members. The Woodlands provided the initial space for some of these churches, and in ensuing years the group expanded to include Mormons and Jews. Hindus, Muslims, and Buddhists have also joined, which has caused objections from more hardline Christians, some of whom left the consortium.

Despite these problems, Interfaith has thrived. It coordinates many tasks usually associated with governments or for-profit organizations: family counseling, child care, job training, and senior citizen services. It visits new residents and is still helping new churches to start up. Its annual budget, which was hardly a few thousand dollars when Gebert began, in 2005 stood at $16 million. Although some of the funding comes from government sources, much of the work continues to be performed by thousands of volunteers.[112]

In the coming decades, as patterns of religious affiliation continue to change, this sort of flexible and open community organization will become increasingly critical. America today has, for example, more Muslims than Episcopalians. Mormons, once considered a fringe sect, have become a respected, rapidly expanding spiritual community. Jews, Buddhists, Muslims, and Hindus are now significant, well-recognized players in the nation's spiritual life.

Amid this diversity Christianity is hardly dying out; it will remain by far America's dominant religion. By some estimates, America has added one hundred million Christians in the past half century, which is as many as were added in the nation's first two hundred years. The difference now is that Christians are far less likely to see theirs as the only true faith. In the future Christians will likely view their faith more and more as a matter of choice.

COMMUNITY FOR THE NEXT HUNDRED MILLION

The nurturing of families, neighborhoods, and communities, and the broad spiritual and civic ground on which they rest, will become increasingly important as the nation copes with an expanding population. With a dispersed, growing, and ever-more-diverse society, and with more children than other developed countries, America's challenges will be of a different nature than those of the aging and generally more homogeneous cultures of Europe and East Asia.

This is not to say that our civilization is better or worse; it is born from different precedents and shaped by different imperatives. The strong American marketplace culture will continue to create opportunities, but many problems will defy simple economic solutions. "Technocrats," as the far-sighted futurist Alvin Toffler noted, "suffer from econo-think," and assume that the solution to every problem is a material one.[113]

Narrowly focused viewpoints, however helpful in any one aspect, have the potential to distract from society's fundamental social concerns. A more meaningful approach might be to adopt the notion of "existence value," in environmental economist John Kutilla's phrase. In this view, the intrinsic meaning of culture, family, environment, community, and the like must be considered alongside material well-being as determinants of a successful civilization.[114]

Similarly, we may place too much emphasis on planners, architects, industrialists, and scientists; even environmentalists can distort our view of the greater good. Aesthetes rightly criticize the crassness of much of our built environment, but they express little concern for the needs of families or the aged. Similarly, some environmentalists, seeing themselves as "secular prophets," define their quest not as a way to improve people's lives but as a crusade for the benefit of the natural world. To see human beings as "a disease, a cancer on nature," or as "the AIDS of the earth," as one prominent environmentalist put it, diverts our focus from improving the lives of current, not to mention future, generations.[115]

Aesthetics and the maintenance of the planet are critical priorities, but building a sustainable future has profound economic and social dimensions. Integrating another hundred million Americans will require us to balance those concerns against the aspirations of this newly expanded society. We need to create communities that work for all of us living here now and, most of all, for all those who will come next. In this quest Americans will have to employ their customary adaptability and optimism, along with something akin to faith.

CHAPTER SEVEN: AMERICA IN 2050

I n 1830 the *Illinois Monthly* published a vision of a future industrial St. Louis beset by social unrest. The newspaper deemed the story so disturbing that it asked the author to change his forecast to a cheerier one—that of a society harmonized by "the general spread of gospel, and its principles, among men."[1] A more popular vision of the American future was found in Edward Bellamy's *Looking Backward* (1888), the most widely read novel of its time. Set in the year 2000, Bellamy's socialistic prophecy of a just, egalitarian, and prosperous society represented the highest aspirations of its era.[2]

America is a country founded on and sustained by optimism. Remarkably, Americans have almost always maintained confidence in a bright future even when the present dimmed. Charles and Mary Beard, writing at the onset of the Depression, believed Americans felt "no doubt about the nature of the future of America. The most common note of assurance was belief in unlimited progress."[3] That optimism prevailed through the Depression and the devastation of the Second World War. As John Gunther observed in 1946, "It is a lucky country more than any other with an almost obsessive belief in the happy ending."[4]

This optimism has been revived to some extent by the election of President Barack Obama, even as a devastating recession has encouraged pessimism about the country's long-term prospects. But even a popular and widely appealing president may not be capable of reversing the sense of ennui that has built up over decades.

Today a typical science fiction account of America's future might be the technological dystopia in Philip K. Dick's 1968 novel *Do Androids Dream of Electronic Sheep?*, which served as the basis for the influential 1982 film *Blade Runner.* Popular futuristic visions feature chronic economic decline, devastating global warming, unceasing pestilence, a takeover by machines, or internal political collapse. Utopian visions along the lines of Bellamy's *Looking Backward* are difficult to find.[5]

Mainstream academic and journalistic predictions generally have not been much rosier, either from within the country or without. They have consistently portrayed a hapless America as losing out to a bewildering array of competitors, from Soviet Russia in the 1950s and 1960s, to Japan and Western Europe in the 1970s and 1980s, and more recently to a resurgent India or China or even the European Union.

For several decades the prevailing intellectual narrative has suggested that it is simply "time to get ready" for America's demise before other rising powers. The only difference has been the shift in the identity of the triumphant rival. Remarkably, this worldview was echoed in the National Intelligence Council's "2020 Project," which laid out a grim vision of an America overshadowed by both its new and traditional rivals.[6] Even if there idea of what country poses the greatest threat to America, what the declinists share most of all is a sense inevitability about the country's descent.[7]

AMERICA 2050: A RADICAL DEPARTURE

Such pessimistic ideas can serve as useful antidotes to complacency, and they may identify the profound challenges we face in everything from the economy to health care, education, and the environment. And lofty notions of unipolar global hegemony (a product of the widely unex-pected collapse of the Soviet Union) could certainly not persist in a world where new powers are always rising to assume greater influence on the planet.

But the unremittingly bleak vision of America's long-term future underestimates the nation's *sokojikara*, the self-renewing power gen-erated by its unique combination of high fertility, great diversity, and enormous physical assets.

The most critical factor may be demographics. In contrast to almost all its advanced rivals, America's population of working-age and young people is expected to continue upward. This trend could become more pronounced around 2050,[8] by which time the United States is likely to have a population bigger than the European Union and four times larger than its one-time great-power rival, Russia. While its popula-tion expands, as early as 2035 China may begin to experience a pro-cess of *decline*, first in workforce and then in actual population, due to the one-child policy and a growing surplus of boys over girls. By 2050, 31 percent of China's population will be older than sixty, compared to barely one-quarter in the United States. Even more remarkably, over 41 percent of Japanese will be that old.[9]

This demographic reality creates a set of issues for 21st-century America vastly different from those of its rivals. Their key challenges will be to cope with an aging population, fill labor shortages, and invest in growing economies. Like them, America will have to meet pension-ers' payments, although the problem here will be less severe than in other aging countries.

The United States' greatest priority will be to create entrepreneurial and workforce opportunities for its ever-expanding population. Sim-ply to keep pace with population growth in 2010, the New America Foundation estimates, the country needs to add more than 125,000 jobs a month. What the United States does with its "demographic dividend"—that is, its relatively young working-age population—will depend largely on whether the private sector can generate the incomes among the young to meet the needs of a larger aging population.[10]

THE FAMILY FACTOR

The most notable and important characteristic distinguishing Americans from most developed countries is the dynamics of its family formation. Between 1980 and 2000 the fertility rate of Americans of European ancestry—overwhelmingly native born—rose while immigrants also boosted the level of childbearing.[11] But it's about more than mere numbers. As the author Michael Chabon recently wrote, "In having children, in engendering them, in loving them, in teaching them to love and care about the world," parents are "betting" that life can be better for them and their progeny.[12]

This is not the first time a society has reaffirmed the importance of children and kinship after a period during which they were devalued. In the latter days of the Roman Empire, both pagans and Christians tended to be childless; pagans wanted to preserve the integrity of their estates from fratricidal divisions, while Christians celebrated the virtues of celibacy and continence. Medieval society, as historian Steven Ozment has observed, held "home and family" as "objects of widespread ridicule."

But early capitalist societies such as Holland and England, and ultimately the United States, dramatically reversed this trend. A renewed focus on family formation helped drive capitalist expansion and underpinned a growing faith in a future improved by human efforts.

Of course, pronatalist views are hardly universal in contemporary America.[13] Millions of Americans find the high financial costs of raising children so severe that they decide not to do so. This trend may grow as long as the economy remains stagnant. Even with a recovery, paying for education can place both children and their parents in such debt that they have little opportunity to support another generation. These pressures are particularly marked in urban areas, where raising children can mean paying for private day care and education all the way through high school.[14]

Many environmentally minded people in advanced countries see children as unwitting threats to the planet. Since the 1970s a growing chorus of environmentalists have regarded humans themselves as the fundamental problem and have sought to reduce their "carbon footprint" as much as possible. Some have a macabre fascination with the prospect of a postindustrial future with far fewer people—Gaia theorist James Lovelock predicts a massive die-off with only a few people left to live in the still-habitable arctic. Some foresee even no human presence at all, as in Alan Weisman's celebrated best seller, *The World Without Us*.[15]

This apocalyptic tendency grew in the 1970s as environmentalists reacted to the then rapidly worsening environment with growing pessimism; and that pessimism helped foster the notion of humans as "a rampant cancer" best isolated and limited. Although many of the widely accepted worst-case scenarios of the 1970s—including mass starvation and rapid depletion of the world's resources—have proven highly exaggerated, the tendency toward end-of-the-world scenarios has if anything grown more unrestrained.[16]

In 2008 the United States experienced the highest birthrate in forty-five years, which created consternation among some greens. One environmentalist and feminist asserted that these new parents were not taking responsibility for "their detrimental contribution" to both population growth and "resource shortages."[17] Similarly, Peter Kareiva, the chief scientist at the Nature Conservancy, compared reductions in carbon emissions from all possible sources—such as using fuel-efficient lightbulbs and cars—and concluded that not having children is the most effective way of reducing "carbon scenarios" and becoming an "eco hero."[18]

This deeply secular, "scientific" view may seem a far cry from the deep, otherworldly focus of the dark ages, but both reflect a deeply pessimistic assessment of humanity's role and future on earth. In contrast, the degree to which people are willing to have children, in the societies of the Reformation or today, reflects a more optimistic attitude toward the future.[19]

Where the antinatalist logic leads is not hard to discern. In Great Britain, where the population is growing more slowly than in the United States, Jonathon Porritt, the head of the government's Sustainable Development Commission, has openly called people who have more than two children "irresponsible" and has advocated that the country reduce its population to less than half its current total.[20]

Such antinatalist choices reflect a lack of understanding that depopulation and aging may be an even greater threat to the advanced countries. A too rapidly declining population could create a society excessively heavily weighted toward the elderly. Such a society might well be less concerned with the long-term future, since its predominant population would have shorter horizons and, in many cases, no progeny to worry about it. Although America too will age in the coming decades, it will do so far more slowly and will reinvent itself in ways not readily available to more geriatric states.

WHY AMERICA CANNOT EASILY ADOPT ANTIGROWTH ATTITUDES

Concern over resource depletion, or the impact of human development on global climate, are of course warranted and should inform future policies at the global, national, and local levels. But attempts to quickly reduce the carbon footprint or to "de-develop" the country could have major implications for economic growth.[21]

Preserving the quality of the environment should be a primary national concern, but strong economic growth remains a necessity for a nation that will be adding one hundred million people over the next decades. At the same time America's population growth necessitates a more aggressive pursuit of basic infrastructure and a focus on creating higher-wage employment.[22] A nation that must accommodate one hundred million more residents cannot do so with a slow-growth strategy. Rather, innovative technologies, and new ways of organizing work, may provide the key to achieving both economic growth and environmental sustainability.[23]

Without robust economic growth but with an expanding population, a country will have to accept a massive decline in living standards.[24] The kind of slow growth that has evolved in Europe may succeed for a continent whose population will decline, but its utility for one that still is growing is doubtful.[25]

To be sure, Americans should consider and, to some extent, emulate some elements of European social policy, like elements of the health care system and fuel economy standards. Civilizations can always learn from one another, and they have done so since ancient times. But overall profound differences in demographics and cultural traditions suggest that America cannot easily follow European or East Asian models of social organization and planning.

Reduced work hours and less economic growth could work, at least in the short run, in a rapidly aging society. And they certainly would be one way to cut back on consumption. But Americans—particularly those under fifty—seem unlikely to accept ever-diminishing prospects for themselves and their families. They may embrace means of growth that are less environmentally damaging, such as working close to or at home or conserving energy through technological innovation; but major cutbacks in economic output would not be *socially* sustainable over the longer term.[26]

This growing divergence in the best policies to be adopted among countries should not be viewed as a matter of right or wrong, better or worse. Rather it signifies how societies of different heritages, faced with different prospects, cope with their evolving futures. In Europe and much of East Asia, slow or negative population growth will almost inevitably reduce countries' ability to expand their economy. By 2050 Europe's economic growth rate is expected to fall 40 percent, due directly to the shrinking of its labor force.[27]

In contrast, there is no way the United States could rely on slow growth—by overregulating, taxing entrepreneurs, or rigidly limiting suburban development—without rapidly diminishing the quality of life.[28] Similarly, America's response to environmental challenges diverges from those in Europe as well as Japan, Korea, and other advanced Asian nations. Declining demographics may help these countries solve their numerous environmental problems, particularly those linked to energy use and land management. But a growing United States will have to seek out innovative environmental solutions in social organization and in technology, to maintain rising output at less detrimental ecological cost.

THE FUTURE THAT DIDN'T HAPPEN

At least since the 1950s social scientists, encouraged by the success of an increasingly centralized economic and political reality in Europe and America, have widely embraced the notion that the future will see the rise of universal standards and ever-greater concentrations of power. The late historian of the Progressive Era, Robert Wiebe, described "the great blend" that "so intermixed business and government that a practical, precise separation of the two is no longer possible." President Dwight D. Eisenhower also recognized this confluence, coining the phrase "military-industrial complex," although he wisely viewed it as ominous.

Wiebe noted that the success of this collaboration was marked by the existence of "so few signs of domestic upheaval at the beginning of the 1960s."[29] He said so just before the great convulsions of the end of that decade. But even after the 1960s upheavals Daniel Bell, in his pathbreaking *The Coming of Post-Industrial Society*, published in 1973, forecast the emergence of a carefully balanced economy administered by science-oriented corporations and government.[30]

The futurist Herman Kahn, writing in 1967, foresaw a vastly more concentrated society; control would be centralized in three megaregions—Boston-Washington, San Diego–San Francisco, and Chicago-Pittsburgh—that would include "roughly half of the total United States population." The story of America in 2000 would essentially be a "study" of these megaregions, which would reign from a commanding height in the new national hierarchy.[31]

This near-universal belief in geographic concentration and homogenization turned out to be far off the mark. Although the three megaregions are large and indeed influential, much of the growth in the country over the past several decades has been in the Southeast, the desert Southwest, the mountain states, and the Pacific Northwest.

Instead of the two or three dominant regions, Phoenix, Dallas, Houston, Miami, Seattle, and Atlanta arose from relative obscurity to emerge as major powers in the last part of the 20th century. The 21st century is likely to see more emerging powerhouse regions, including perhaps Charlotte, Austin, Tucson, and San Antonio. These metropolitan areas are unlikely to accept the predominance of the more established and well-entrenched centers. An ever-expanding field of competition and divergence is more likely to evolve among regions in everything from economic development to culture to approaches to the environment.[32]

Perhaps more important, even within regions there has been a growing shift toward local concerns, down to the neighborhood and even block level. This trend is reflected in the rise of Web-based community sites as well as the vitality of locally based new religious, community, and charitable organizations.[33]

The trend toward all things local is part of a distinct American tradition that sees the smaller units of society as absolutely vital. Most academic planners, policy gurus, and national media have a tendency to favor larger government units as the best way to regulate and plan for the future. They consistently seek to reduce the influence exercised by the plethora of villages, towns, and cities in the United States: well over 65,000 general-purpose governments. With so many "small towns," the average local jurisdiction population in the United States is 6,200, small enough that nonprofessional politicians can have a serious impact on local issues.[34]

In the 21st-century world many countries will tend toward a hierarchical system in which national (or global) elites simply dictate results. Here the American desire for local control could well seem an outlier and will be challenged by many in the policy community within the country, couched largely in environmental rationales. This style of top-down control is already well established in China, Russia, and many developing countries. A more benign trend toward continental centralization can be seen in Europe (although many Europeans are likely to strongly resist it), where the model calls for more power to be concentrated in Brussels.

The federal government has played an important role in developing the American landscape through public works, the interstate highways, and the defense and space programs. But, for the most part, Americans generally tend to believe that local communities, neighborhoods, and parents should possess the power to craft appropriate solutions to local problems. Democracy in America has been largely self-created and dispersed; in many countries in Europe, and more recently in parts of Asia, it was implemented by the state. As a result, in the United States the individual, the community, and even the political locality have been stronger and more fundamental.[35]

THE DECLUSTERED WORKFORCE

Over the past few decades this preference for decentralization has increasingly been reflected within the economy. U.S. employment has been shifting not to megacorporations but to smaller units and to individuals; between 1980 and 2000 the number of self-employed individuals expanded tenfold to include 16 percent of the workforce. The smallest businesses, the so-called microenterprises, have enjoyed the fastest rate of growth, far more than any other business category. By 2006 there were some twenty million such businesses, one for every six private sector workers.

The entrepreneurial urge, thought to be diminishing in the mid-20th century, has actually strengthened. In 2008, 28 percent of Americans said they had considered starting a business, more than twice the rate for French or Germans. Self-employment, particularly among younger workers, has been growing at twice the rate of the mid-1990s.

This trend has been exacerbated by the remarkable volatility within even the largest companies. Firms enter and leave the Fortune 500 with increasing speed. More and more workers will live in an economic environment like that of Hollywood or Silicon Valley, with constant job shifts, changes in alliances between companies, and the growth of job-hopping "gypsies." This trend will likely continue into the mid-21st century.[36]

Hard economic times could slow this trend, but historically recessions have served as incubators of innovation and entrepreneurship. At the same time the shift to localism could lead consumers to embrace new firms as well as existing regional ones in everything from banking to restaurants.[37]

Many of the individuals starting new firms will be those who have recently left or been laid off by bigger companies, particularly during a severe economic downturn. Whether they form a new bank, energy company, or design firm, they will do it more efficiently—with less overhead, more efficient use of the Internet, and less emphasis on pretentious office settings. In addition, they will do it primarily in places, from suburbs to hardscrabble old cities, that can scale themselves to a back-to-basics economy. "People are watching their companies go under. Therefore you get three vice presidents who get laid off but know their business," observes Texas entrepreneur Charlie Wilson. "They start a new company somewhere cheap that is more efficient and streamlined. These are the new companies that will survive and grow the next economy."[38]

Decentralization works well in the United States because of the country's ever-greater diversity in locally preferred lifestyles, environments, ethnic populations, and politics. South Dakotans may want to deal with local problems through grassroots community neighborhood action. San Franciscans may follow the path of government mandates and wealth redistribution, supported by nonprofits and ideologically oriented activist groups.[39]

Unless these uniquely American characteristics are unleashed, accommodating the needs of an unprecedentedly diverse and complex nation of four hundred million may prove impossible.[40] The economic crisis of 2008 has led to a rapid rise of federal power, but over time centralized authority will seem remote and ever more oppressive. This has occurred after each period of massive government intervention, most notably after the New Deal and the Great Society. Although a strong central response to an immediate crisis is often necessary, in the America of 2050 the personal and local will prove the most effective way to address the discrete problems of a diverse and complex society.

KEY TO THE FUTURE: CLASS, NOT RACE

For much of American history, race has been the greatest barrier to a common vision of community, and during the civil rights era it legitimized the centralization of power. Race still remains all too synonymous with poverty: higher poverty rates for blacks and Hispanics than for whites and Asians persist. But the future will likely see a dimming of economic distinctions based on ethnic origins.

Since the late 1960s the proportion of African-American households living in poverty has dropped from 70 percent to 46 percent, while the black middle class has grown from 27 percent to 37 percent. Perhaps more remarkable, the percentage who are considered prosperous—households making over $107,000 a year in 2007 dollars—has expanded from a mere 3 percent to 17 percent. Roughly 50 percent more African-Americans live in suburbs now than in 1980; most of these households are solidly middle class, and some are affluent.[41]

Instead of race, the most pressing social problem facing mid-21st-century America will be class, much as it was in the economically stressed 1890s and 1930s. Class lines will be different—and more subtle—than in the gilded age or even the 1920s. For one thing, the once-obvious visual barriers have largely dissolved. As Irving Kristol once noted, "Who doesn't wear blue jeans these days?" Today you can walk into a film studio, software firm, or high-end manufacturing firm and have trouble identifying those in upper tiers.

But diminished incomes affect all minorities, all ethnic groups, and even young, educated workers. The growth of low-wage professions particularly affects ethnic groups. At the same time the majority of house cleaners, as well as workers in other low-wage professions, are white, and they suffer much of the same economic deprivation that their nonwhite counterparts do.[42]

During the 20th century the middle class was ascendant, and many of the worst privations had been greatly reduced. Most families still spend a far smaller percentage of their income on food than they did in 1960, and the number of people earning more than $100,000 a year has risen by over 13 percent since 1979. By the century's end the poverty rate among the three hundred million Americans was slightly lower than in it was in 1967, when there were two hundred million.[43]

But trends over the past few decades suggest that the future trajectory may not be so positive.[44] Returns to capital and certain elite occupation incomes grew rapidly, while wages for lower-income and middle-class workers stagnated. Even after the 2008 downturn, largely engineered by Wall Street, it was primarily middle-class homeowners and jobholders who bore the brunt, often losing their residences. In contrast, considerable bonuses continued to be paid out to financial firms and, within a year, appeared to be back to historically high levels.[45]

These divergent results have created a sense of unease throughout the society. Even much of the upper middle class finds it difficult to maintain a "middle-class lifestyle" and keep pace with the rising costs of housing, education, and health insurance. In urban areas residents face high costs across the board, notably in real estate; in response to poor public schools, many parents pay for private education as well.[46]

Although they may dress casually and even shop at Costco, those at the top will remain radically different from the rest of society. Almost all the gains in wealth since 2000 have been achieved by the relatively small number of Americans with incomes seven times or more above the poverty level, while many middle-tier educated and skilled workers have lost ground.[47] Most disturbingly, the rate of upward mobility has stagnated overall, which means it is no easier for the poor and working class of any race to move up than it was in the 1970s.[48]

These trends threaten most of all the generations who will be entering the workforce over the next few decades. They will be most seriously affected by rising unemployment and underemployment, which may persist in a less-than-robust recovery. Although those without college educations or specialized training—particularly men—are most threatened, the returns even for college-educated younger people have also been in decline since 2000, even during relative boom periods.[49]

THE PRIMARY CHALLENGE: MAINTAIN UPWARD MOBILITY

The American middle class still subscribes to an individualist view of upward mobility, but if future generations and the millions of new workers face stagnant wage growth, it may not survive.[50] Traditionally Americans have addressed this problem by expanding opportunity. Americans tend to believe their efforts can lead to a better life, by margins of roughly two to one over residents of Germany, Italy, or France. Even in the midst of the great recession, over 70 percent told pollsters they had not lost faith in the basic belief that one can get ahead through hard work.[51]

The founders of the republic understood the critical importance of maintaining these aspirations, and European observers were struck by the remarkable social mobility in America's cities. In the 19th century American factory workers and their offspring had far better chances of entering the middle or upper classes than their European counterparts.[52] Expansion of opportunity was seen as essential to the American experiment. Writing in 1837, one Whig lawyer in Pittsburgh suggested, "If you deny the poor man the means to better his condition . . . you have destroyed republican principles in their very germ."[53]

The 19th-century agricultural and industrial expansion, both in the eastern cities and in the West, gave these principles added substance. Manufacturing value rose by nearly 10 percent during every decade from the 1840s to the 1880s, with the exception of the Civil War decade. But as the nation's economy grew, its wealth became increasingly concentrated, provoking a powerful reaction in the working and middle classes.[54]

From the Progressive Era onward, reformers looked to use government to achieve the goal of expanding opportunity for the working classes and between regions. The New Deal, the most important of the reform efforts, was fundamentally not an exercise in economic planning, but, as Richard Hofstadter observed, "a chaos of experimentation."[55]

The experimentation ultimately worked to expand the realm of wealth creation. Electrification programs such as the Tennessee Valley Authority spurred the modernization of vast areas of the country, including rural communities bypassed by earlier periods of economic expansion.

Critically, the New Deal programs did not try to reconcentrate people in cities (as was being done in Stalin's Russia and is now favored by many of today's "progressives") but rather sought to make more of the countryside productive and capable of supporting prosperous citizens. Roosevelt, himself a product of upper Hudson Valley gentry, held as his objective "the great fundamental of making country in every way as desirable as city life, an objective which will from the economic side make possible the earning of an adequate compensation."[56]

The New Deal, notes author and social critic Michael Lind, was designed to appeal to primarily rural, small-town-dwelling southern and western constituents. The promotion of conservation, he adds, was motivated not primarily by a romantic love of nature but to create a better environment for "the well-being of people."[57]

This focus on public investment—including greater access to education—reduced the concentration of wealth and ensured that more of the nation's income and productivity gains benefited the working and middle classes. Wealth concentration in the top 10 percent of all households fell from the mid-1930s through the immediate postwar years, and it remained at historically low levels until the mid-1970s. The Eisenhower administration continued broad public spending on defense-related projects, scientific research, and technology development. Most particularly, Eisenhower in 1956 initiated the interstate highway system, which by reducing transportation costs opened up much of the country to commerce and new settlement, particularly on the suburban fringe.[58]

In recent decades public investment in basic infrastructure construction and maintenance has declined, even in the face of considerable population growth.[59] "One looks back at that map 'Landscape by Moses,'" writes the noted sociologist Nathan Glazer, about the legacy of New York City's "master builder" Robert Moses, ". . . and if one asks what has been added in the fifty years since Moses lost power, one has to say astonishingly: almost nothing."[60]

Indeed, despite the staggering private wealth generated by the stock market and real estate in New York, the city's public infrastructure has been neglected—and could worsen during a prolonged economic slump. The city controller's office has estimated that infrastructure spending levels in the late 1990s and early 2000s were barely half of what was required to maintain the city's streets, main roads, and railways in "a systematic state of good repair." Subways and rail lines in America's richest city are frequently shut down after heavy rains due to floods caused by poor drainage.[61]

Similarly, California's once-envied water-delivery systems, roadways, airports, and education facilities are in serious disrepair, and the state, once known for its high degree of creditworthiness, is now virtually bankrupt. In the 1960s infrastructure spending accounted for 20 percent of all state outlays. But as the technocratic perspective—the belief that knowledge and technology businesses alone could fuel the economy—took hold in Sacramento, public infrastructure investment fell to just 3 percent of all expenditures, despite the rapid growth of the state's population.[62]

REVIVING THE REAL ECONOMY

To succeed in the mid-21st century, Americans will need to attend to the country's basic investments and industries. Some assume that the American future can be built around a handful of high-end "creative" jobs [63] and that it will not require reviving the "old industrial economy" or the basic infrastructure for the successful dispersion of the economy.[64] In the America envisioned by the advocates of the "creative economy," our productive facilities would serve mainly as tourist attractions, much as we now visit restored pioneer villages.[65]

In reality a more prosperous future is possible, but only if the country focuses *both* on developing the intellectual prowess of its citizenry *and* on maintaining the physical infrastructure necessary for basic production and transportation. A single-minded emphasis on nontangible industries is a dangerous delusion, particularly for a country that must accommodate one hundred million more people over the next few decades.

One dangerous sign of misguided priorities is the increasing dominance of finance over all other activities. By the mid-2000s finance accounted for some 41 percent of all American profits, three times the percentage in the 1970s. Financial activities' share of total income grew by a similar amount.[66]

But the massive collapse of the financial sector—and the ensuing gargantuan government effort to prop it up—reveals the limitations of this approach. An overemphasis on finance tends to create a misallocation of resources, and massive credit bubbles intensify a growing dependence on foreign countries for both manufactured goods and commodities. In 1970 the United States enjoyed a modest $3.4 billion manufacturing trade surplus. Just fourteen years later, it had amassed a then-unthinkably large $80 billion industrial deficit. That deficit now stands at more than $800 billion.[67]

This approach is unsustainable: an economy based on financial services cannot provide the necessary wealth for a growing population, or pay for the education of the young or the retirement of its elderly. After the great bubble crash that began in 2007, even some top corporate executives admitted that the finance-centered approach was severely limited. "I believe a popular, 30 year notion that the US can evolve from a technology and manufacturing leader into a service leader is just wrong," admitted Jeffrey Immelt, the CEO of General Electric, a company that had investments in both in early 2009.[68]

In addition, to expect that production-oriented economies will allow the United States and other western countries to dominate finance or any other high-end activity (from high-tech to fashion and culture) is very dangerous and plainly wrong,. In the 1980s Japanese firms that were widely written off as "copycats" became primary innovators, particularly in automobiles, semiconductors, and computer games.

In the coming decades Chinese and Indian companies, in everything from pharmaceuticals to fashion and finance, will seek to move from low-wage work to more specialized, and increasingly innovative, kinds of products. The enormous profits to be made from the less "sexy" activities will provide the funds to invest in both the hard infrastructure and the necessary training to move decisively into ever higher-end activities.

BACK TO BASICS: REHABILITATING "CINDERELLA"

The manufacture of hard goods, which requires a sophisticated infrastructure and is generally energy-intensive, could turn out to be relatively easy to salvage for American workers.[69] In the first decade of the 21st century many old-line "codger" companies—those making steel, farm equipment, and other basic industrial products—were doing far better before the economic crash than the much-ballyhooed high-tech and service industries. In the case of steel, the United States was becoming a low-cost producer in comparison not only with Europe but, to some extent, with China. As energy costs rise—and demand for lean inventories grows—this trend could well continue if American firms can make use of emerging competitive advantages.[70]

As Americans search for a future economic strategy, the example of Great Britain—home of the Industrial Revolution—should be considered a cautionary tale. In the 19th century and much of the 20th, even though the country depended on manufactured goods for its livelihood, British elite schools, financial institutions, and media all worked against "the needs of industry" to create what historian Martin Weiner has called "two unequal capitalist elites," the more powerful of which had little interest in and even disdain for industrial activities. The "best" talent, and the most social prestige, favored the financial sector over the industrial. Production was particularly looked down upon: it was "the Cinderella of British industry."[71]

This contempt for production underpinned the decline of Britain as a great power, and it could prove disastrous in mid-21st-century America as well. In a country lacking a strong productive economic base, tens of millions of workers, many of them minorities, would find few opportunities for useful employment. In contrast, policies that supported both old-fashioned manufacturing and new green infrastructure would spur positive impacts on employment across a broad spectrum.

Although manufacturing employment overall has dropped, in the last two decades the percentage of higher-wage, skilled industrial jobs has climbed.[72] In 2005 the National Association of Manufacturers, the Manufacturing Institute, and Deloitte Consulting surveyed eight hundred U.S. manufacturing firms: more than 80 percent reported that they were "experiencing a shortage of qualified workers overall." Nine in ten firms stated that they faced a "moderate-to-severe shortfall" of qualified technicians.[73] By 2020 this shortage could grow to thirteen million workers.[74]

A resurgent manufacturing sector would boost the technological workforce; by 2007 it employed about a quarter of the nation's scientists and related technicians. In the next few decades industry is likely to continue its trajectory, needing more workers qualified for high-skilled, well-paying positions.[75] Fortunately, compared to Europe and East Asia, America, with its vibrant demography, should produce a pool of more workers willing and able to do specific, necessary tasks.[76]

This revived focus on production will help the Great Plains as well as the beleaguered Great Lakes, which has suffered the greatest recent decreases in hourly incomes. Given the proper support in terms of infrastructure and skills training, these areas could once again exploit the natural resources and logistical advantages that turned them into productive centers in the first place. Similarly, the great rivers of the Northwest, the Midwest, and the Northeast could again generate power and provide transport—if upgraded and modernized—restoring some of the competitive edge that drove their former ascendancy.[77]

Government at every level can and should play a critical role in this great project, financing physical infrastructure and providing critical skills training.[78] But given the financial realities, the country will also need to take advantage of private capital here and abroad. Investors can be lured into the U.S. market in large part because a growing nation offers better long-term profit potential than one that is shrinking. Building toll roads or superfast train lines between burgeoning Texan or Californian cities has better prospects than doing the same in Japan or Germany, where the population is gradually diminishing.[79]

THE ENERGY CONNECTION

Perhaps the most immediate threat to an expanding American economy is its dependence on foreign energy sources. And in recent decades the country has been woefully short of the infrastructure to take advantages of its fossil as well as its renewable resources.[80] Producers with surplus power, such as electricity plants in North Dakota, lack the transmission capacity to deliver it to states that need it. California, New York City, and Chicago are vulnerable to blackouts and brownouts due to insufficient energy infrastructure.[81]

The costs of the nation's failure to invest in energy infrastructure are apparent in the state of its power transmission grid. From 1975 to 1999 the United States spent, on average, a minuscule $83 million a year on power lines and facilities that deliver electricity from generation plants to end users. Since 1999 spending increases on transmission have covered only a third of new demand. As a result, many regions of the country experience shortages; when power cannot be delivered from surplus regions to high-consumption areas, major metropolitan systems are left vulnerable to catastrophic failures. In August 2003, for example, the power grid failed across a huge swath of the Northeast, largely due to overtaxed and outdated transmission lines. All told, fifty million people lost power for up to two days in the biggest blackout in North American history. The event contributed to at least eleven deaths and cost an estimated $6 billion.[82]

This widespread vulnerability has been attributed to the lack of a mandatory national investment policy, as well as to the failure of individual utilities to voluntarily maintain the country's electrical grid capacity. On the other side of the coin, places that have invested in energy resources have seen a strong economic payoff. The cities in the Northwest's Columbia River region, with massive, cheap, and clean sources of hydroelectric power, have become attractive locations for high-technology firms.[83]

Such chronic energy infrastructure problems stem from a failure to seriously consider all policy options. In addition, environmental and aesthetic objections or jurisdictional conflicts contribute to serious delays in building new, more efficient facilities. Moreover, energy facilities are often built in regions that already possess significant resources or in undesirable geographic locations: along the storm-prone Gulf Coast, for example. Hurricane Katrina made it evident that the national infrastructure is frighteningly fragile.[84]

Compounding these problems are the direct and indirect costs of a reliance on nonmarket-driven producers such as Russian-, Saudi-, and Iranian-government-controlled energy firms to meet basic needs. A decrease in dependence would slow the massive transfer of American dollars to sovereign wealth funds, whose priorities may not coincide with those of this country.[85]

The way out of this predicament is multifaceted. Significant investment in domestic alternatives could drastically reduce the oil-import premiums now paid to overseas cartels. Relatively low-carbon natural gas could play a key role, while investments in research generate even cleaner fuel options and foster job and technology development at home. This course would reduce the possibility of armed conflict abroad and evolve into a tremendous relative advantage for the United States over emerging, less naturally endowed competitors such as India and China.[86]

THE FUTURE ROLE OF TECHNOLOGY

Technology, argues former vice president Al Gore, has increased human power in ways that "vastly magnif[y] the impact each individual has on the natural world" and threaten to cause a "violent destruction collision between our civilization and the Earth."[87] But the quest to forge a more competitive and environmentally sustainable America also will have to rely very much on technology.

Fortunately, no nation has been more prodigious than the United States—the term *technology* was even invented in America in 1829—in its ability to apply new methods and techniques to solve its fundamental problems. Americans, such as those who rebuilt Chicago and San Francisco after huge fires, tend to see themselves as capable of overcoming obstacles, and of turning even the worst challenges into "the prerequisite for its more glorious rebirth."[88]

This resilient attitude has been the response not only to natural or man-made disasters but to all the depredations of the industrial age. During the Progressive Era and the New Deal, conservation efforts helped preserve the countryside and make it more productive as well. Improved methods of irrigation, the planting of trees to cut wind erosion, and other techniques played important roles in reconstituting the ecologically devastated Great Plains. Over the past century significant national landscape and heritage that was thought to be endangered with extinction, from redwood forests to the buffalo herds of the Great Plains, have been much preserved. This effort has constituted, historian David Nye suggests, "a second creation . . . a managed site that seeks to recoup the virtues of the first creation while making it accessible to tourists and profitable for private enterprise."[89]

Technology will play a similarly critical role in meeting future challenges. "Peak oil" and a profound energy shortage, first predicted in the mid-1940s and then again in the 1970s and the early 21st century, has repeatedly diminished due to new discoveries, improved drilling techniques, and conservation driven by the price system. In the coming decades new energy finds, including unconventional sources, and better technology are likely to ameliorate the long-prophesied energy catastrophe.[90]

Finally, technology has helped produce remarkable improvements in water and air quality without needlessly lowering America's standard of living. With a population of three hundred million, the United States has cleaner air and water now than when it stood at two hundred million, forty years ago.[91] This suggests that, with proper planning and priorities, improvements are possible for an America with four hundred million or more residents.

PROSPECTS FOR SUBURBIA: BRIGHTER THAN GENERALLY THOUGHT

As our population grows to four hundred million, some "smart growth" advocates and urbanists, such as Brookings Institution fellow Chris Leinberger, have made it an article of faith that Americans should be crammed into high-density communities. Nobel laureate Paul Krugman and Harvard economist Edward Glaeser even argue that more Americans should give up the prospect of owning their homes and look forward to a lifetime of renting.[92]

It is also widely assumed that housing markets, particularly the demand for single-family suburban residences, will decline markedly during the coming decades, because of the aging of the baby boomers. But as argued in chapter 3, we are likely to see a continued strong popular interest in suburban-type living, albeit in a somewhat modified, more ecologically and socially sustainable form.

The key factor here will be the rise of the new generation, the millennials, who, according to recent surveys by Frank Magid and Associates, place an even stronger emphasis on home ownership than did previous generations.[93] Their preferences will become more important in the next decade. As the country ages, the population will continue to add large numbers of people aged 30 to 45, the prime home-buying and child-raising cohort. Between 2010 and 2025 this group will grow 13 percent; by 2050 it will increase 33 percent. By that year, too, twenty-two million more potential home owners and family formers seem likely to provide a market for America's ever-changing archipelago of suburban communities.[94]

Finally, rising costs are likely to drive further dispersion. As the population grows, the price pressure on land and housing in major metropolitan areas can only increase. Environmental and antidevelopment pressures, particularly in the Northeast and on the Pacific coast, are likely to further restrict supply for low-density housing. As a result, people will likely migrate farther from the prime metropolitan cores and seek a better life in a diverse set of locations across the country.

A GREENER, MORE HOME-BASED SOCIETY

None of this suggests that America's future suburbs and exurbs will be just like those of the past.[95] As argued in chapter 6, traditional "bedroom" communities on the periphery will evolve toward more efficient, more decentralized, and less commuter-dependent greenurbias. Houses may be smaller—lot sizes are already shrinking as a result of land prices—but they will remain, for the most part, single-family dwellings.[96]

The new suburbia will be far more environmentally friendly. Higher energy prices, produced either by the market or through government policies, will propel shifts toward more efficient cars, which will make commuting far less environmentally damaging. Similarly emerging work patterns, the greater use of trees for cooling, more sustainable architecture, and less wasteful appliances will make the suburban home of the future far less of a danger to ecological health than in the past.[97]

Many of the necessary changes do not need to be imposed from the central authorities but can be forged at the local level. Residents of low- and mid-density towns close to metropolitan areas can promote "greening" by acquiring open space, using funding from both public and private sources. Ultimately the goal would be to nurture communities that are separated from their neighbors by belts of open recreational or agricultural land.[98]

Arguably the greatest spur to successful dispersion will come from technology, as James Martin first saw in his pioneering 1978 book, *The Wired Society*. A former software designer for IBM, Martin foresaw the emergence of mass telecommunications that would allow a massive reduction in commuting, greater deconcentration of workplaces, and a "localization of physical activities . . . centered in local communities."

These communities, he noted, would reduce their consumption of fossil fuels as prices rose. They would seek to grow more of their own food or purchase it from nearby farms . Increasingly, residents would work at home or in the vicinity. Technology would allow skilled people to congregate in communities of their choice or at home. Today not only knowledge workers but many who work in construction trades, agriculture, and other professions are home-based, conducting their operations out of trucks or vans.[99]

This shift toward decentralized living will require changes in Americans' public and private lives. To recruit the best workers, companies will offer telecommuting and technology options that free up workers' time. By 2000 some companies had already moved in this direction. At IBM as much as 40 percent of the workforce operates full time at home or remotely at clients' businesses. Siemens, Compaq, Cisco, Merrill Lynch, and American Express have all expanded their use of telecommuting, with noted increases in productivity.

The potential energy savings—particularly in vehicle miles traveled—could be enormous. Telecommuters drive less, naturally; on telecommuting days, average vehicle miles are between 53 percent and 77 percent lower. Overall a 10 percent increase in telecommuting over the next decade will reduce forty-five million tons of greenhouse gases, while also dramatically cutting office construction and energy use. Only a gigantic shift to mass transit would produce comparable savings.

Teleconferencing as well could save additional millions of tons of emissions if it reduced air travel by just 10 percent over the next ten years. Simply put, telecommunications technology could provide the means to generate greater economic growth with markedly less energy demand and carbon emission. Looking forward, these changes may play the biggest role in reshaping American communities into a more sustainable model both for the environment and for family life.[100]

THE ECONOMY OF GREENURBIA

Greenurbia, a way of life that transcends the urban and the exurban, is not intrinsically anti-urban; nor is it opposed to all forms of planning. It would simply open up new economic opportunities for people who choose to live in communities that "leapfrog" the metropolis.[101]

For those who choose to live in cities, the dispersed future also increases their potential range of activities. Neighborhoods with concentrations of skilled workers would thrive, since home-based or dispersed workers can serve clients anywhere in the world from their home offices. This might be particularly useful to those who live in cities where the cost of doing business discourages large-scale corporate investment. Over the last thirty-five years, for example, payroll employment in San Francisco has dropped by 50 percent, but self-employment has shot up 150 percent, including a large number working in software, consulting, video games, and other higher-wage professions.[102]

Similarly, in close-in suburbs or in multipolar cities, home-based workers, many of them self-employed, would thrive; in the communities of the San Fernando Valley, for example, they already constitute upward of 10 percent of the total workforce.[103] In New York's outer boroughs, media, graphic arts, and other specialized service professionals have also been among the few groups with middle and upper-middle incomes to see rapid growth.[104]

These new, village-oriented employment centers will constitute an increasingly important part of the American economy in the next few decades. Telecommunications can create opportunities for long-distressed communities—in the scenic Appalachian belt, or in attractive older neighborhoods in former industrial cities—to find new ways to create higher-wage jobs. Ultimately the greenurban economy does not suggest the superiority of one place or another. Rather, it addresses the desire for quality of place, and expands the range of choices people and communities can enjoy.[105]

PREEMINENCE, NOT HEGEMONY

Over time the essential DNA of the decentralized model of life and governance will assert itself. America is simply too diverse, too large, and too complex to be controlled effectively from its center, except during times of emergency. The dispersed United States will operate in an environment where much of the world is dominated by outright autocracies or administrative dictatorships.

America in the 21st century may become, as it was in its first century, a great exception: a beacon and model to some, an abomination to many others. It will be exceptional in everything from culture and science to agriculture and politics. And although some countries may draw inspiration from American models, most will continue to follow patterns dictated by their own historical experiences and by perceptions of their own natural interest.

The Islamic world, rather than emulating an America model, has tended to become less and less tolerant of religious minorities, reversing centuries-old traditions that allowed Jewish, Christian, Baha'i, and other communities to flourish alongside one another.[106] Russia seems more likely to embrace neo-Czarism, and China authoritarianism, than a decentralized, democratic model. This may not be the world Americans would like, but it is probably the one they will have to inhabit.

By 2050 breathless talk of an "end of history" and the "inevitable" democratization that accompanied the fall of the Soviet Union may be replaced by recognition of ever-greater divergence between cultures and peoples.[107] History not only never ended but seems likely to create new models, some more friendly to American norms, others far less so.

Indeed, many developing countries have replaced faith in American-style capitalism with the "Beijing Consensus," a term invented by Henry Kissinger associate Joshua Cooper Ramo. Using China as opposed to America as the role model, the consensus places economic development ahead of even modest democratization. This approach may well prove to be an appealing alternative to American hectoring and self-righteousness, particularly after the George W. Bush years. But the appeal of autocracy and top-down planning also jibes with indigenous traditions that do not mesh easily with American ideals of law, due process, and human rights.[108]

How to respond to these trends? In the next decades Americans may have fewer options to apply military or economic power. The latter is now well dispersed throughout the world and is likely to become more so. As for military power, it will remain a key concern—and fundamental asset of America as a great power—but it has its limits as asymmetrical warfare allows terrorists to threaten even the most advanced states.

America's unique strengths will not fade quickly, and it's difficult to see how an aging Europe, with its own ethnic problems, out-migration of skilled workers, weak military, and less robust technological base could challenge our preeminent position.[109] India and China are more likely competitors, but both suffer from a legacy of poverty and underdevelopment that will take generations to overcome. In India's case, per capita income in 2005 ranked just slightly above that of sub-Saharan Africa; it endures chronic ethnic and religious conflict, as well as an often-deadly struggle with Pakistan.[110]

As for China, it seems likely to retain the essentially inward-looking "Middle Kingdom" characteristic of a singular racial culture, and it faces its own demographic crisis. Japan, Vietnam, and other Asian countries are unlikely to submit to "a Greater Chinese co-prosperity sphere," given traditional rivalries between those cultures.[111]

The America of 2050 may not stride the world like a hegemonic giant, but it will evolve into the one truly transcendent superpower in terms of society, technology, and culture. Its greatest power will be its identification with notions of personal liberty, constitutional protections, and universalism. The 21st-century world is likely to see a series of contending tribalisms: Chinese, Russian, Indian, Islamic, and even European. Although they may all prove contentious rivals, none will possess the essential strengths and universal appeal of the American ethos, not only in its own Heartland but across the world.

COUNTRIES OF ASPIRATION

In the emerging world of the 21st century, who will be our closest natural allies? Clearly America's character and demographic makeup necessitate some rethinking. The United States is no longer an offshoot of Europe and will be even less of one in 2050. Our historic tie with Britain may remain, but Canada, Australia, and New Zealand are likely to be the country's most reliable partners.

Like the United States, these countries are "countries of aspiration." They are blessed with ample land and natural resources and remain, along with the United States, the preferred location for immigrants, particularly educated ones, and the places where they are most likely to succeed.[112]

Our ties with Canada, the largest bilateral trading relationship in the world, seem likely to become particularly strong due to proximity. Millions of Canadians have relations with Americans; Canada, the largest source of visitors to the United States, ranks among the largest senders of immigrants as well; roughly 800,000 Canadians now have established themselves south of the border.[113]

Although Canada and the other aspirants were born to British colonialism, notes historian David Cannadine, they have "increasingly come to resemble the United States" much more than the United Kingdom, which over time may shift to a more European orientation. Like America, they knit together diverse legacies, including those of indigenous people. Pockets of anti-Americanism will remain in certain circles, but over time the similarities between these countries are likely to become more striking.[114]

AMERICAN INFLUENCE IN 2050

Over the next few decades the deep disdain for America that characterized the Bush years will no doubt fade, but other countries will likely have fewer military or economic imperatives to realign their societies in an American direction. The only thing that will prove persuasive internationally will be the success of America as a society, a concept that has been embraced at least notionally by President Obama.

A burgeoning, vital American entrepreneurial economy, for example, would be the best argument to convince countries that now follow a state-directed model to change their ways. A chaotic, failed economy would have the opposite effect, leading more countries to reject the American "model" for something more akin to that of the European Union or even China.

Immigration is one area where America could extend its influence most effectively. If Europe and parts of East Asia do not wish to shrink as societies and suffer ever-more-onerous pension burdens, they may look to the immigration model forged in the United States, Canada, and Australia.

Germany, for example, where the number of births in 2006 plunged below the levels at the end of the Second World War, will have to accommodate millions of young immigrants in the coming decades in order to avoid a catastrophic reduction of population. The Netherlands, Spain, Italy, and most eastern European countries face a similar dilemma.[115]

But such a change in policy may prove difficult, given many European countries' long-standing preference for homogeneity. Muslims, a primary immigrant group in Europe and the United Kingdom, bring deep religious values to societies where devotion to God and traditional morality are becoming vestigial. As the popular European saying goes, "Alcoholics outnumber practicing Christians, and more Czechs believe in UFOs than believe in God."[116]

The American immigration model, for all its many flaws, may provide a strong alternative scenario. In the coming decades Arabs, British Pakistanis, Dutch Surinamese, Filipinos, and Indians in Tokyo, Shanghai, or Berlin could create something akin to the "multiculturalism of the streets" so clearly evident in Los Angeles, New York, Houston, and for that matter Toronto or Sydney.

America's successful evolution to a post-ethnic society will prove critical in U.S. relations with developing nations, our largest source of immigrants. Unlike Britain at the height of its empire, America remains fundamentally a meritocracy; its influence extends not primarily from an imperial core of elites but rather from traffic between the middle class and those who aspire to it.[117]

This can be seen in the fact that the United States has more than twice as many foreign students as any other country; Asia is the source for nearly two out three. Attracting and retaining a more skilled immigrant base should be relatively easy. No country has proven as "sticky" as the United States in retaining skilled foreign immigrants.[118]

The role of America's non-Western emigrants—Indian and Middle Eastern entrepreneurs, African intellectuals and scientists, Chinese technologists, Mexican skilled workers—cannot be easily overestimated. Even as they return home, they retain strong familial and business ties to the United States. They are evidence that America maintains a special ability to integrate all varieties of people into its society.[119]

"LOUSY WITH GREATNESS"

The path to constructing a successful America for the next hundred million lies in understanding what Robert Bellah has called America's "civil religion," its ability to forge a unique focus amid great diversity of people and place.[120] To make this future work will require energetic central and local governments, as well as community organizations, which can lay down the pathways of critical human and physical infrastructure. Washington must play a role in this process, but it cannot be the primary determinant of the final destination. In 2050 the country will be primarily driven not by the central state but by families, individuals, and communities. During the industrial age Ralph Waldo Emerson observed, "The age has an engine, but no engineer."[121] Much the same may be said in the coming decades.

Ultimately, the success of 21st-century America will rely on its ability to take advantage of the ethos that differentiates it from much of the rest of the world. In the process Americans may feel like outsiders in a world that often craves central direction and accepts the legitimacy of autocracy. But this singularity has defined America from the beginning. It is what propelled the earliest settlements on this continent, the movement west, the ascendancy of industry and science, and the defeat of both fascism and communism.

None of it will be easy, and certainly much can go wrong. Still, we have no reason to lose faith in the possibilities of the future. For all its problems, America remains, as the journalist John Gunther suggested over sixty years ago, "lousy with greatness."[122] The elements essential to forge a successful nation of four hundred million remain very much within our reach, there for the taking.

ACKNOWLEDGMENTS

This book, which so often took me out on a multitude of limbs, has needed many helping hands. Yet perhaps no one has been more important than Scott Moyers, who originally bought this book for Penguin Press and later became my agent. Scott's steadfast commitment—along with that of Penguin Press's publisher, Ann Godoff—has been critical to this project from beginning to end.

Once Scott had left Penguin, the book fell into the capable hands of first Vanessa Mobley and then Laura Stickney, who steered it into port. Laura's tough editing, although often a challenge to the writer, has been an essential part of turning a series of ideas into a coherent book.

Parts of this book was made possible by assignments from some of the nation's most distinguished publications. Most critical has been my "New Geographer" column in Forbes.com, the brainchild of editor Tunku Varadarajan and edited mostly by Hana Alberts and Raquel Laneri. Other editors of note include Howard Dickman at the *Wall Street Journal*, Nick Schultz at the *American*, David Mark of Politico .com, Dan McGinn at *Newsweek*, Connie Rosenbloom at the *New York Times*, Gary Spieker at the *Los Angeles Times*, Zofia Smardz at the *Washington Post*, and Phil Boas at the *Arizona Republic*.

The project also has been helped by many people and organizations that funded critical research critical to its progress. I am particularly proud that these included organization that spanned across both the ideological spectrum and the vast breadth of the American geography. Hopefully this reflects on my decidedly nonpartisan and fundamentally fabian approach to the material.

Overall, this project would not have taken off without the stalwart support of my colleagues at Chapman University in Orange, California. Chapman faculty, students, and administrators have all become valued supporters and sometime critics of my work. I am particularly indebted to the school president, James Doti; the chancellor, Daniele Struppa; and my campus "rabbi," vice chancellor for undergraduate education, Jeanne Gunner.

On urban issues, I am particularly grateful to the Center for an Urban Future in New York City, including its president, Jonathan Bowles, and chairman, Andy Breslau. I also have relied repeatedly on the advice of my friend and mentor Fred Siegel, professor of history at Cooper Union, also in New York. I also want to express my appreciation to my mother, Loretta Kotkin, and my brother Mark as well as his wife, Pamela Putnam, for providing me with "a home away from home" while on frequent sojourns to the greatest of American metropolitan regions.

Houston has inspired many of the ideas for this project. I owe a debt of gratitude to the Greater Houston Partnership and its president, Jeff Mosley, and Caroll Robinson of the Mickey Leland–Barbara Jordan School of Public Affairs at Texas Southern University. My knowledge of this great Texas city was greatly enhanced by my coauthor of the Opportunity Urbanism report, Tory Gattis, as well as Andrew Segal, Charlie Wilson, Tim Cisneros, Jan Leger, and two great American mayors, Bill White and Bob Lanier.

On the issue of dispersion, suburbs, and demographics I would like to express my gratitude to Bill Frey at the Brookings Institution in Washington; Sam Staley of the Reason Foundation; Steve Pontell of the La Jolla Institute in Ontario, California; and the staff at the Goldwater Institute in Phoenix. Particular note should be made of the many contributions from the indefatigable Wendell Cox of Demographia.com, based outside St. Louis, whose willingness to share data and discuss ideas has been essential to this project. Thomas Tseng of New American Dimensions of Los Angeles helped shape many ideas about the evolution of race and ethnicity in America.

The discussion of the Heartland could not have been made without the enormous contributions of my consulting partners at the Praxis Strategy Group in Grand Forks, North Dakota. In particular I would like to thank Praxis's president and CEO Delore Zimmerman, as well as Dave Roby, Douglas McDonald, Matthew Lephion, and, most particularly, our resident research maven, Mark Schill. Praxis has also been an essential partner in developing newgeography.com, whose many writers also have enriched this volume and deserve my profound thanks.

In terms of policy and the role of industry, I owe a particular debt to my colleagues at the New America Foundation in Washington, D.C., particularly Michael Lind, Phil Longman, Gregory Rodriguez, and Sherle Schwenniger. My longtime associate David Friedman, an attorney in Los Angeles and an expert on industrial development worldwide, has been a constant source of wise counsel. My global perspectives have also been enriched by association with the Danish Confederation of Industry and Benny Damsgaard and, more recently, with the London, UK-based Legatum Foundation, and senior fellow Ryan Streeter, which has been supporting ongoing work on the issue of upward mobility in cities across the world.

Closer to home in the San Fernando Valley section of Los Angeles is where I received the greatest encouragement and inspiration. I am particularly thankful for the work of Zina Klapper, a veteran editor who organized the files and the research, reviewed first drafts, and provided critical direction from early on in the process of putting the book together. Zina's contributed also her even temperament and a willingness to challenge my assumptions, almost always resulting in a better result.

Finally, there are those closest to me. A writer who works primarily at home depends most on those with whom he shares a household. In my case I have been blessed by my two wonderful daughters, Ariel and Hannah, who have inspired me, perhaps more than anything, to write this book. But nothing would be possible for me without the support, love, and sometimes critical attentions of my beloved wife, Mandy, who has bequeathed to me all the blessings of a great and enduring life partnership, the bedrock of my existence.

NOTES

CHAPTER ONE: FOUR HUNDRED MILLION AMERICANS

1. Sam Roberts, "In a Generation, Minorities May Be the U.S. Majority," *New York Times,* August 14, 2008.
2. Walt Whitman, *Leaves of Grass* (1855), preface.
3. Thomas Jefferson to Barre de Marbois, June 14, 1817, in Andrew A. Lipscomb and Albert E. Bergh, eds., *The Writings of Thomas Jefferson* (Washington, D.C.: Thomas Jefferson Association, 1903–04), pp. 15:130–31.
4. Arthur C. Nelson, *Toward a New Metropolis: The Opportunity to Rebuild America* (Washington, D.C.: Brookings Institution Press, 2004), p. 5.
5. "Five Hundred Million Americans," *Economist,* August 22, 2002; *World Population Prospects: The 2004 Revision,* Population Division, Department of Economic and Social Affairs, United Nations, February 24, 2005; Phil Longman, *The Empty Cradle* (New York: Basic Books, 2004), p. 60; Dmitry Zaks, "Russia-Population: Russia Says Population Drop Now Key Security Threat," Agence France-Presse, February 15, 2001.
6. David E. Bloom and David Canning, "Booms, Busts and Echoes: How the Biggest Demographic in History Is Affecting Global Development," *Finance and Development* 43, no. 3 (September 2006); *World Population Prospects: The 1998 Revision,* vol. 2, *Sex and Age,* Population Division, Department of Economic and Social Affairs, United Nations, 1999; CIA, *The World Factbook;* U.S. Bureau of the Census, *U.S. Census 2008;* Nicholas Eberstadt, "The Population Implosion," *Foreign Policy* 123 (March-April 2001); "UN Revises World Population Forecast for 2050 Down by 400 Million," Agence France-Presse, February 26, 2003; Eurostat, *World Population Prospects: The 2004 Revision,* United Nations, February 24, 2005; Longman, *Empty Cradle,* pp. 26–27, 53.
7. Katherine Sheram and Tatyana P. Soubbotina, *Beyond Economic Growth: Meeting the Challenges of Global Development* (World Bank, 2000).
8. Rome, for example, fell into a severe demographic and economic decline after the 3rd century. One primary cause of the decline lay with the reluctance of the middle and upper classes to marry and raise families. Neither the agricultural population, which produced the wealth, nor the army, which protected it, had the bodies to operate at the levels of previous centuries. As a result, the world's greatest empire was "unable to defend itself from within and without" and thus "staggered slowly on to its inevitable dissolution." The same observation can be made of other declining societies, such as Venice in the 17th century, Amsterdam in the 18th, and much of Europe since the 1970s. Depopulation, it turns out, can be as destabilizing over time as overpopulation. See Arthur E. R. Bock,

Manpower Shortage and the Fall of the Roman Empire in the West (Ann Arbor: University of Michigan Press, 1955), pp. 17–21, 129; John Bagnell et al., *Cambridge Economic History* (Cambridge, U.K.: Cambridge University Press, 2000), pp. 14:388–89; Peter Burke, *Venice and Amsterdam* (Cambridge, U.K.: Polity, 1994), p. 139; Frederic C. Lane, *Venice: A Maritime Republic* (Baltimore: Johns Hopkins University Press, 1973), p. 430; Theodor Mommsen, *The History of Rome* (New York: Meridian, 1958), p. 549.

9. Iain Macwhirther, "Of Course Scotland's Birth Rate Is Low—So Are Our Spirits," *Sunday Herald*, November 13, 2005; Susan H. Greenberg, "The Rise of the Only Child," *Newsweek*, April 23, 2001.

10. CIA, *The World Factbook* 2008.

11. Samuel Hays, *The Response to Industrialism, 1885–1914* (Chicago: University of Chicago Press, 1957), pp. 22–24, 71–72.

12. "2005 Nen Wa Nihon No Tagagore," *Shokun*, February 1987.

13. NBC News/*Wall Street Journal* poll, July 27, 2006; Adam Widman, "Poll Reveals Environmental Pessimism," *Stanford Daily*, April 6, 2006.

14. Deborah Zabarenko, "U.S. Population to Top Three Hundred Million This Month," Reuters, October 2, 2006; Paul Kennedy, *The Rise and Fall of the Great Powers* (New York: Random House, 1987).

15. Robert J. Lieber, "Falling Upwards: Declinism," *World Affairs*, Summer 2008; Morris Berman, *Dark Ages America: The Final Phase of Empire* (New York: Norton, 2006); Parag Khanna, "Who Shrank the Superpower?" *New York Times Magazine*, January 27, 2008; Fareed Zakaria, "How Long Will America Lead the World?" *Newsweek*, January 12, 2006: David Rieff, "Superpower Failure," *Los Angeles Times*, September 9, 2007.

16. Laura Secor, "That Sinking Feeling: The View That America Is on the Skids Is on the Rise. But Does the New Declinism Tell Us Anything About How We Live?" *Boston Globe*, July 14, 2003.

17. Andrew Hacker, *The End of the American Era* (New York: Atheneum, 1971), p. 6; Rieff, "Superpower Failure."

18. Khanna, "Who Shrank the Superpower?"

19. Berman, *Dark Ages*, p. 24.

20. Immanuel Wallerstein, "The Eagle Has Crash Landed," *Foreign Policy*, July–August 2002; Immanuel Wallerstein, *The Decline of American Power: The U.S. in a Chaotic World* (New York: New Press, 2003), p. 209.

21. Jeffrey Garten, *A Cold Peace: America, Japan, Germany and the Struggle for Supremacy* (New York: Twentieth Century Fund, 1992); Guy Dinmore, "Chinese See Nation Becoming as Influential as U.S.," *Financial Times*, October 12, 2006; Jacques Attali, *Millennium: Winners and Losers in the Coming World Order*, trans. Leila Conners and Nathan Gardels (New York: Times Books, 1991), p. 3; Gordon G. Chang, "China in Revolt," *Commentary*, December 2006; Andrew Osborn, "As If Things Weren't Bad Enough, Russian Professor Predicts End of U.S.," *Wall Street Journal*, December 29, 2008; Pete Peterson, "Riding for a Fall," *Foreign Affairs*, vol. 83, no. 5 (Sept.–Oct., 2004), pp. 111–25; Edward Luttwak, *The Endangered American Dream* (New York: Simon & Schuster, 1994).

22. Paul Craig Roberts, "America's Lost Hegemony," *Human Events*, August 24, 2005; Pat Buchanan, *The Death of the West: How Dying Populations and Immigrant Invasions Imperil Our Country and Civilization* (New York: Thomas Dunne Books, 2002), pp. 1–3; Samuel Huntington, *The Clash of Civilizations and the Remaking of the World Order* (New York: Simon & Schuster, 1996), p. 305.

23. Paul Ehrlich, "The Population Bomb," Ballantine Books (New York: 1968); Donella H. Meadows, Dennis L. Meadows, Jorgen Randers, William W. Behrens III (Universe Books: New York, 1972).

24. Brad Knickerbocker, "The Environmental Load of 300 Million: Too Heavy," *Christian Science Monitor*, September 26, 2006; Lester Brown, "U.S. Population: Is Bigger Always Better?" *Globalist*, October 17, 2007; Juliet Eilperin, "Immigration Issue Sparks Battle at Sierra Club," *Washington Post*, March 22, 2004.

25. Lester Thurow, *Head to Head: The Coming Economic Battle Among Japan, Europe and America* (New York: Morrow, 1992); Robert Reich and Ira Magaziner, *Minding America's Business* (New York: Harcourt Brace Jovanovich, 1982); George C. Lodge, *The American Disease* (New York: Knopf, 1984); Clive Cook, "John Kenneth Galbraith Revisited," *Atlantic Monthly*, May 15, 2006.

26. Lawrence Krause, testimony to Joint Economic Committee of the Congress, December 11, 1986.

27. Tobias Buck, "European Record on Innovation Fifty Years Behind U.S.," *Financial Times*, January 12, 2006; George Parker, "Brussels to Set Out Why EU Is Trailing U.S.," *Financial Times*, January 21, 2004.

28. Christopher Rhoads, "U.S., EU Productivity Gap Is Widening," *Wall Street Journal*, January 10, 2004; John Micklethwait and Adrian Wooldridge, *The Right Nation: Conservative Power in America* (New York: Penguin, 2004), p. 392; C. Thomas, "Europe Sees Limit on Growth," *Wall Street Journal*, July 22, 2004; Stephan Richter, "En Finir avec l'Europe," *Les Echos*, May 21, 2003 (reprinted in *Globalist*); Karl Zinsmeister, "Old and In the Way," *American Enterprise*, December 2002; Joseph Stiglitz, "Fear and Loathing in Davos," *Guardian*, February 6, 2009; Joeleen Perry and Marcus Walker, "Euro-Zone Economy Registers a Grim Performance," *Wall Street Journal*, February 14, 2009.

29. Martin Jacques, *When China Rules the World: The Rise of the Middle Kingdom and the End of the Western World* (London: Allen Lane, 2009).

30. Chris Oliver, "China's GDP to Overtake U.S. by Early 2020s, Says Analyst," *Marketwatch*, April 23, 2009; David Kampf, "Not So Fast: Rethinking America's Decline," *World Politics Review*, May 7, 2008; Jason Dean, "How Capitalist Transformation Exposes Holes in China's Government," *Wall Street Journal*, December 18, 2006; Andrew Batson and Shai Oster, "As China Booms, the Poorest Lose Ground," *Wall Street Journal*, November 22, 2006; Shai Oster and Jane Spencer, "A Poison Spreads Among China's Boom," *Wall Street Journal*, September 30, 2006; Andrew Browne, "China Girds for Future Shock: Beijing Tackles Rural-Urban Divide, a Feared Source of Social Unrest," *Wall Street Journal*, April 4, 2005; Pankaj Mishra, "The Myth of the New India," *New York Times*, July 6, 2006; Gordon G. Chang, "China in Revolt," *Commentary*, December 2006; Jay Matthews, "Notable and Quotable," *Wall Street Journal*, April 14, 2005.

31. "Five Hundred Million Americans," *Economist*, August 22, 2002; Frederick Kempe, "Demographic Time Bomb Ticks On," *Wall Street Journal*, June 6, 2006; Elizabeth Rosenthal, "European Union's Plunging Birthrates Spread Eastward," *New York Times*, September 4, 2006; Mark Landler, "Empty Maternity Wards Imperil a Dwindling Germany," *New York Times*, November 18, 2004.

32. "Five Hundred Million Americans," *Economist*, August 22, 2002; "Falling Birth Rates Revive EU Debate on Immigration," *Hindu*, May 32, 2001; "Why Population Aging Matters: A Global Perspective," National Institute on Aging, March 2007, p. 14; Brad Knickerbocker, "Is a Bigger Nation Richer?" *Christian Science Monitor*, September 26, 2006;

"Banking the 'Demographic Dividend': How Population Dynamics Can Affect Economic Growth," *Population Matters: Rand Policy Brief,* May 2005.

33. Stuart Anderson and Michaela Platzer, "American Made: The Impact of Immigrant Entrepreneurs and Professionals on U.S. Competitiveness," National Foundation for American Policy, 2006; Louise Story, "Seeking Leaders, U.S. Companies Think Globally," *New York Times,* December 12, 2007.

34. Robert W. Fairlie, "Kauffman Index of Entrepreneurial Activity National Report 1996–2005," Ewing Marion Kauffman Foundation, p. 6; Glenn Ruffenach, "Growing Numbers of Americans Push Back Retirement Dates," *Wall Street Journal,* October 20, 2004.

35. Ann Hynek, "Senior Citizens Look to Re-Enter the Workforce," *Foxbusiness,* March 30, 2009.

36. Chris Leinberger, "The Next Slum?" *Atlantic,* March 2008; Richard Florida, "How the Crash Will Reshape America," *Atlantic,* March 2009.

37. John R. Logan, "The Suburban Advantage," Lewis Mumford Center for Comparative Urban and Regional Research, Albany, N.Y., June 24, 2002; "Violent Crime Rates in US Central Cities, Suburbs, and Metropolitan Areas," Demographia.com, http://www.demographia.com/db-crimecitysub.pdf.

38. "Consumers Survey on Smart Choices for Home Buyers," National Association of Realtors and National Association of Home Builders, April 22, 2002; John Kasarda, "Comment on Elvin K. Wyley and Daniel J. Hammel's 'Islands of Decay in Seas of Renewal: Urban Policy and the Resurgence of Gentrification,'" *Housing Policy Debate* 10, no. 4 (1999); Belden Russonello & Stewart, "2004 American Community Survey: National Survey of Communities," October 2004, p. 3.

39. June Kronholz, "The Coming Crunch," *Wall Street Journal,* October 13, 2006.

40. Peg Tyre, "Seniors and the City: An Urban Retirement," *Newsweek,* October 11, 2006.

41. Haya El Nasser, "Pew: Almost Half of Americans Want to Live Somewhere Else," *USA Today,* January 29, 2009.

42. Sandra Rosenbloom, "The Mobility Needs of Older Americans: Implications for Transportation Reauthorization," Center on Urban and Metropolitan Policy, Brookings Institution, July 2003, pp. 1–11; "Fast Facts: Baby Boomers Statistics on Empty Nesting and Retiring," *Del Webb Backgrounder,* Del Webb Corporation, 2005; Tracy M. Gordon, "Planned Developments in California: Private Communities and Public Life," Public Policy Institute of California, 2004.

43. Evan Ramstad, "South Korean Home Prices Spiral Higher," *Wall Street Journal,* December 20, 2006.

44. Mark Shill at the Praxis Strategy Group. Shill analyzed populations of children 5 to 17 based on 2004–05 American Community Survey data in leading metropolitan areas. In virtually all cases, the percent of children in suburbs was higher—often much more so—than in corresponding center cities. This is available at http://www.newgeography.com/content/00218-cities-children-and-future.

45. This estimate is based on 15 to 20 percent urban preference extrapolated on the growth of one hundred million people from various surveys William Frey based on census data; Belden Russonello & Stewart, "2004 American Community Survey: National Survey of Communities," October 2004, p. 3; "Consumers Survey on Smart Choices for Home Buyers," National Association of Realtors and National Association of Home Builders, April 22, 2002; Dowell Myers and Elizabeth Gearin, "Current Preferences and Future Demand for Denser Residential Environments," *Housing Policy Debate* 12, no. 4 (2001), p. 636.

46. Joe Gyourko, Christopher Mayer, and Todd Sinai, "Superstar Cities," Wharton School and National Bureau of Economic Research, June 16, 2006.

47. Anne S. Lewis, "What Dominique de Menil Wrought," *Wall Street Journal*, June 9, 2007.

48. "Trends in U.S. Agriculture," USDA, National Agricultural Statistics Service, 2005.

49. Kronholz, "Coming Crunch."

50. Belden Russonello & Stewart, "2004 American Community Survey," p. 3; "Perceptions of Rural America," W.K. Kellogg Foundation, n.d., pp.1, 5.

51. John Cromartie, "Rural Population and Migration: Rural Population Change and Net Migration," USDA, Economic Research Service, 1994; Nancy McArdle, "Outward Bound: The Decentralization of Population and Employment," Joint Center for Housing Studies, Harvard University, July 1999, pp. 8–9.

52. Thomas A. Horan, *Digital Places: Building Our City of Bits* (Washington, D.C.: Urban Land Institute, 2000), p. 99.

53. Alfred E. Eckes, *The United States and the Global Struggle for Minerals* (Austin: University of Texas Press, 1979), p. 241.

54. John J. Fialka, "Wildcat Producer Sparks Oil Boom in Montana Plains," *Wall Street Journal*, April 5, 2006; Ben Casselman, "U.S. Gas Fields Go from Bust to Boom," *Wall Street Journal*, April 30, 2009.

55. Thomas L. Friedman, "My Favorite Green Lump," *New York Times*, January 10, 2007; Robert Bryce, "The Good News About Energy That You Don't Hear," *American*, July-August 2008; Alan Murray, "Ascent of Sovereign Wealth Funds Illustrates New World Order," *Wall Street Journal*, January 28, 2008; Steven Mufson, "Oil Price Rise Cause Global Shift in Health," *Washington Post*, November 10, 2007.

56. *Biomass as Feedstock for a Bioenergy and Bioproducts Industry: The Technical Feasibility of a Billion-Ton Annual Supply*, a Joint Study by the U.S. Department of Energy and the U.S. Department of Agriculture, 2005.

57. "Census Bureau Projects Tripling of Hispanic and Asian Populations in Fifty Years; Non-Hispanic Whites May Drop to Half of Total Population," U.S. Census Bureau, March 18, 2004; June Kronholz, "Immigration's Latest Debate: Is U.S. Big Enough?" *Wall Street Journal*, July 11, 2006; Sam Roberts, "Asian and Hispanic Minorities Growing, but More Slowly," *New York Times*, May 14, 2009.

58. "Immigrants Flock to the Suburbs," *Chicago Sun-Times*, August 30, 2006; Alan Wolfe, *One Nation, After All* (New York: Viking, 1998), pp.158–59.

59. Ben Feller, "U.S. Immigrants Lag Behind in School, but Gaps Are Bigger in Other Nations," *Associated Press*, May 15, 2005.

60. Richard Florida, "The Real Economic Threat," *New Jersey Star-Ledger*, April 24, 2005.

61. "UN Revises World Population Forecast for 2050 Down by 400 Million," Agence France-Press, February 26, 2003; David Wessel, "Immigration's Attraction Lies in its Boost to Economic Vitality," *Wall Street Journal*, February 27, 2003.

62. Karen Arenson, "A Decline in Foreign Students Is Reversed," *New York Times*, November 13, 2006; David Bartlett, "The Global War For Talent," Finance Director Europe, January 1, 2007, http://www.the-financedirector.com/features/feature879/.

63. William Frey, "'Rainbow Nation': Mixed Race Marriages Among States," *Milken Institute Review* (2003). In New Mexico and Oklahoma more than 15 percent of marriages are mixed race.

64. Morley Winograd and Michael D. Hais, *Millennial Makeover: MySpace, YouTube and the Future of American Politics* (New Brunswick, N.J.: Rutgers University Press, 2008).

65. Allan Carlson, "The Family Factors: Lessons from History About the Future of Marriage and Family in the Untied States," *Touchstone Magazine*, 2006.

66. Phil Longman, "The Return of Patriarchy," *Foreign Affairs*, March-April 2006.

67. George Weigel, "Is Europe Dying?" *AEI Online*, March 17, 2005; Julian Glover and Alexandra Topping, "Religion Does More Harm Than Good—Poll," *Guardian*, December 23, 2006; Noelle Knox, "Religion Takes a Back Seat in Western Europe," *USA Today*, August 11, 2005; Leigh E. Schmidt, "Spirituality in America," *Wilson Quarterly* (2005); Carlson, "Family Factors."

68. Phil Zuckerman, "Atheism: Contemporary Rates and Patterns," Claremont Graduate School, 2005.

69. Mark Steyn, "O Come All Ye Faithless," *Spectator* [U.K.], December 2005.

70. David Rosnick, "Are Shorter Work Hours Good for the Environment?: A Comparison of U.S. and European Energy Consumption," Center for Economic and Policy Research, December 2006; John W. Miller, "Pension Systems Strain Europe," *Wall Street Journal*, June 17, 2004; Jeremy Rifkin, *The European Dream: How Europe's Vision of The Future Is Quietly Eclipsing the American Dream* (New York: Penguin, 2004), p. 3.

71. Ginny Parker Woods, "In Aging Japan, Young Slackers Stir Up Concerns," *Wall Street Journal*, December 29, 2005.

72. Harris interactive survey, 2003, cited in "Endangered Europe," *American Enterprise*, October-November 2005; Arthur C. Brooks, "Happy for Work," *Wall Street Journal*, June 20, 2007.

73. Stanley Rothman and Amy E. Black, "Elites Revisited: American Social and Political Leadership in the 1990s," *International Journal of Public Opinion* 11, no. 2 (Summer), pp. 169–95. This paper points out the rise to prominence of many working-class people, particularly white males, over the past generation. See also Douglas J. Besharov, "The Rio Grande Rises," *New York Times*, October 1, 2007; Jonathan Kaufman, "Rethinking Racial Progress," *Wall Street Journal*, August 28, 2008; John Gunther, *Inside USA* (New York: New Press, 1997), p. 691.

74. David Wessel, "Fed Chief Warns of Widening Inequality," *Wall Street Journal*, February 7, 2007; David Cay Johnson, "Report Says the Rich Are Getting Richer Faster, Much Faster," *New York Times*, December 15, 2007; Daniel Gross, "Income Inequality, Writ Larger," *New York Times*, June 10, 2007; "The Missing Rungs in the Ladder," *Economist*, July 16, 2005; David Wessel, "College Grad Wages Are Sluggish, Too," *Wall Street Journal*, May 18, 2005; Sara Murray, "The Curse of the Class of 2009," *Wall Street Journal*, May 9–10, 2009; Bradley R. Schiller, "The Futility of Class Warfare," *Policy Review*, October-November 2008.

75. David Wessel, "As Rich-Poor Gap Widens in U.S., Class Mobility Stalls," *Wall Street Journal*, May 13, 2005; "Ever Higher Society, Ever Harder to Ascend," *Economist*, December 29, 2004; Ron Haskins, Julia B. Isaacs, and Isabel V. Sawhill, "Getting Ahead or Losing Ground: Economic Mobility in America," Center on Children and Families, Brookings Institution, February 2008; Steven Greenhouse, "Many Entry-Level Workers Feel Pinch of Rough Market," *New York Times*, September 4, 2006.

76. Naazeen Barma and Ely Ratner, "China's Illiberal Challenge," *Democracy*, Fall 2006.

77. Sidney E. Mead, "The Nation with the Soul of a Church," in Russell E. Richey and Donald G. Jones, eds., *American Civil Religion* (New York: Harper & Row, 1974), p. 45; Russell E. Richey and Donald G. Jones, "The Civil Religion Debate," ibid., p. 28.

78. George Dangerfield, *The Awakening of American Nationalism* (New York: Harper Torchbooks, 1965), p. 101.

CHAPTER TWO: THE CITIES OF ASPIRATION

1. Tim Cisneros, interview by author.
2. Jane Jacobs, *The Death and Life of Great American Cities* (New York: Vintage Books, 1961), pp. 46, 354–55.
3. Christopher G. Boone and Ali Modarres, *City and Environment* (Philadelphia: Temple University Press, 2006), p. 151; Pietro S. Nivola, *Laws of the Landscape: How Policies Shape Cities in Europe and America* (Washington, D.C.: Brookings Institution Press, 1999), pp. 5–7.
4. Alexis de Tocqueville, *Democracy in America*, trans. Henry Reeve (New York: Bantam Books, 2000), p. 1:337.
5. Herman Kahn and Anthony J. Wiener, *The Year 2000: A Framework of Speculation on the Next Thirty Years* (New York: Macmillan, 1967), p. 61; Zina Klapper, Deputy Editor, www.newgeography.com, added regional numbers from 2000 U.S. Census.
6. Paul Kaihla and Krysten Crawford, "The $25 Trillion Land Grab," *Business 2.0*, November 2005.
7. Wendell Cox, www.demographia.com, see United States Municipalities (cities); U.S Cities Population History from 1790; U.S. Cities Achieving 300,000 or More; U.S Cities Ranked: 1850.
8. John Gunther, *Inside USA* (New York: New Press, 1997), pp. 42–43; Steven Longstreet, *An All Star Cast: An Anecdotal History of Los Angeles* (New York: Thomas W. Crowell, 1997), p. xii.
9. Dana W. Bartlett, *The Better City: A Sociological Study of a Modern City* (Los Angeles: Neuner Company Press, 1907), pp. 37, 211.
10. Ibid., p. 191.
11. David Gebhard and Harriette von Bretton, *Los Angeles in the Thirties, 1931–1941* (Los Angeles: Peregrine Smith, 1975), p. 28; Witold Rybczynski, *City Life: Urban Expectations in the New World* (New York: Scribner, 1995), p. 143.
12. Robert Caro, *The Power Broker: Robert Moses and the Fall of New York* (New York: Vintage Books, 1975); Gebhard and von Bretton, *Los Angeles in Thirties*, p. 26; Richard Longstreth, *City Center to Regional Mall* (Cambridge, Mass.: MIT Press, 1997), p. 13; Robert M. Fogelson, *Downtown: Its Rise and Fall, 1880–1950* (New Haven, Conn.: Yale University Press, 2001), p. 394; John D. Weaver, *El Pueblo Grande* (Los Angeles: Ward Ritchie Press, 1973), pp. 38–39.
13. John R. Logan and Harvey Molotch, *Urban Fortunes: The Political Economy of Place* (Berkeley and Los Angeles: University of California Press, 1987), p. 55.
14. Leo Rosten, *Hollywood: The Movie Colony, the Movie Makers* (New York: Harcourt Brace, 1941), pp. 3–4, 375; Carey McWilliams, *Southern California: An Island on the Land* (Salt Lake City: Gibbs-Smith, 1973), p. 339.
15. Quoted in Carey McWilliams, *The Great Exception* (Santa Barbara, Calif.: Peregrine Press, 1979), pp. 267–68.
16. Gebhard and von Bretton, *Los Angeles in Thirties*, p. 30.
17. McWilliams, *Southern California*, p. 113.
18. Kirkpatrick Sale, *Power Shift* (New York: Random House, 1975), pp. 31–32.
19. Tex Thornton, interview by author, 1981.
20. Steven Flusty and Michael Dear, "Invitation to a Postmodern Urbanism," in Robert E. Beauregard and Sophie Body-Gendrot, eds., *The Urban Moment: Cosmopolitan Essays on the Late 20th Century City* (Thousand Oaks, Calif.: Sage, 1999), p. 33.
21. Eugen Weber, "The Last Days of Los Angeles: Apocalypse in the City of Fallen Angels," *Times Literary Supplement*, July 9, 1999, pp. 5–6.

22. Kevin Ryan Byrd, "The Changing Role of Downtowns: An Examination on the Condition of Cities and Methods to Reinvent the Urban Core," paper submitted to Virginia Polytechnic Institute and State University, April 20, 2004, p. 17.

23. "Phoenix in Focus: A Profile from the 2000 Census," Metropolitan Policy Program, Brookings Institution, November 2003, p. 39.

24. Deb Weidenhamer, interview with author.

25. Elliot D. Pollack, "How We Got Here—A Triumph of the Will," paper presented to the Arizona Historical Foundation, February 23, 2005.

26. Andres Duany, Elizabeth Plater-Zyberk, and Jeff Speck, *Suburban Nation: The Rise of Sprawl and the Decline of the American Dream* (New York: North Point Press, 2000), pp. 95,137.

27. Stephanie Ebbert, "Bay State Exodus 2nd Only to New York," *Boston Globe*, April 20, 2006.

28. Jon Talton, "Urban Austin Powers: How the Valley Economy Froze in the 1960s," *Arizona Republic*, February 12, 2001; Jon Talton, "What Drives ASU's Chief to Place So Many Bets," *Arizona Republic*, June 6, 2004; Richard de Uriarte, "Reinvestment, Partnership Remade Downtown Philadelphia into a Place to Be," *Arizona Republic*, June 20, 2004; Andrew Jacobs, "A City Revived, But with Buildings Falling Right and Left," *New York Times*, August 30, 2000.

29. John Norquist, *The Wealth of Cities* (New York: Da Capo Press, 1999), p. 181.

30. Penny Phaezler, "Suburbs Must Not Forget the Importance of the Central City," *Arizona Republic*, January 7, 2005; Penny Phaezler, "Phoenix Won't Be a Place of Renown Till It Has Big IT," *Arizona Republic*, March 11, 2005.

31. "Phoenix in Focus: A Profile from the 2000 Census," Center on Urban and Metropolitan Policy, Brookings Institution, November 2003, p. 39.

32. Sharon Simonson, "High Rise Plans Reshape Downtown San Jose," *Silicon Valley/San Jose Business Journal*, May 21, 2001; Sharon Simonson, "Exodus from Downtown Signals San Jose Is Still Struggling," March 3, 2005; Mark Lacter, "Soft Core," *Los Angeles Magazine*, January 2009.

33. Andrew Kirby, "Celebrity Cities and B-List Boroughs," *Cities* 21, no. 6 (2004), p. 470.

34. "Phoenix Land Use Indicators 1975–2000," The Urban Environment, U.S. Environmental Protection Agency, http://www.epa.gov/urban/phx/indicators.htm; Michele L. Wichert, "Who Pays for Growth?: An Analysis of Housing in the City of Phoenix," thesis (MEP), Arizona State University, 1996, pp. 60, 66; Robert Franciosi, "Which is the Real Downtown?" *Arizona Republic*, December 14, 2003; Elliot D. Pollack, "How We Got Here—a Triumph of the Will," Presentation to the Arizona Historical Foundation, February 23, 2005.

35. Robert M. Fogelson, *Downtown: Its Rise and Fall, 1880–1950* (New Haven, Conn.: Yale University Press, 2001), pp. 11–12, 112–66.

36. "New Census Data Provides a Reality Check," *Innovation Briefs* 13, no. 4 (July-August 2002); Edward L. Glaeser and Matthew E. Kahn, "Sprawl and Urban Growth," Harvard Institute of Economic Research, May 2003, p. 5; Elisa Barbour, "Time to Work: Commuting Times and Modes of Transportation of California Workers," *California Counts* 7, no. 3 (February 2006), p. 3; Christopher Ferrell and Elizabeth Deakin, "Changing California Lifestyles: Consequences for Mobility," University of California Transportation Center, May 2001, p. 13; *American Community Survey 2004*, U.S. Census Bureau.

37. "Phoenix Land Use Indicators 1975–2000," Urban Environment, U.S. Environmental Protection Agency, http://www.epa.gov/urban/phx/indicators.htm.; Joel Kotkin, "Phoenix Rising: A City of Aspiration," Goldwater Institute, April 27, 2005.

38. Analysis of residential permits by Tory Gattis, Houston Strategies, March 29, 2007 (private communication), Tory Gattis, Houston Strategies, June 14, 2005; interview with author.

39. http://www.demographia.com/db-metrocore2005.htm," Demographia.com.

40. Rebecca Sohmer and Robert Lang, "Downtown Rebound," Fannie Mae Foundation and Center on Urban and Metropolitan Policy, Brookings Institution, May 2001.

41. James Sterling Young, *The Washington Community* (New York: Harcourt Brace & World, 1966), pp. 17, 24–25, 44.

42. E. Digby Baltzell, *The Protestant Establishment: Aristocracy and Caste in America* (New York: Random House, 1964), p. ix.

43. Fernand Braudel, *The Perspective of the World: Civilization and Capitalism: 15th–18th Century*, trans. Sian Reynolds (New York: Harper & Row, 1979), p. 3:30.

44. Ellis Lawrence Raesly, *Portrait of New Netherland* (New York: Columbia University Press, 1945), pp. 7, 40; Henri van der Zee and Barbara van der Zee, *A Sweet and Alien Land: The Story of Dutch New York* (New York: Viking Press, 1978), pp. 2–3; "New Amsterdam, Frontier Trading Post," from Nicholas van Wassenaer, *Historisch Verhael*, in Kenneth T. Jackson and David S. Dunbar, eds., *Empire City: New York Through the Centuries* (New York: Columbia University Press, 2002), p. 26; Raesly, *New Netherland*, pp. 53–55.

45. Henry Howard Kessler and Eugene Rachlis, *Peter Stuyvesant and His New York* (New York: Random House, 1959), p. 273; Oliver A. Rink, *Holland on the Hudson: An Economic and Social History of Dutch New York* (Ithaca, N.Y.: Cornell University Press, 1986), p. 263; van der Zee and van der Zee, *Sweet and Alien Land*, p. 473; Bernard Bailyn, *Voyagers to the West: A Passage in the Peopling of America on the Eve of the Revolution* (New York: Vintage, 1986), pp. 235–36; Reuven Brenner, *Rivalry: In Business, Science, Among Nations* (Cambridge, U.K.: Cambridge University Press, 1987), p. 39; Bailyn, *Voyagers to the West*, p. 575.

46. Braudel, *Perspective of the World*, p. 3:406.

47. Andrew Lees, *Cities Perceived: Urban Society in European and American Thought, 1820–1940* (New York: Columbia University Press, 1985), p. 97; Janet Lippman Abu-Lughod, "Comparing Chicago, New York, Los Angeles: Testing Some World City Hypotheses," in Peter Knox and Peter J. Taylor, eds., *World Cities in a World-System* (Cambridge, U.K.: Cambridge University Press, 1995), p. 173.

48. Roger L. Ransom and Richard Sutch, "The Decline in Fertility and Life Cycle Transition in the Antebellum United States," paper presented at the All-UC Group in Economic History Conference, Laguna Beach, Calif., 1986, pp. 3–4.

49. Rita Kramer, "Cathedrals of Commerce," *City Journal*, Spring 1996.

50. Jonathan Hughes, *American Economic History* (New York: HarperCollins, 1990), p. 315.

51. Gunnar Myrdal, *An American Dilemma: The Negro Problem and Modern Democracy* (New York: Harper & Row, 1962), pp. 998–99.

52. Thomas Piktty and Emmanuel Saez, "The Evolution of Top Incomes: A Historical and International Perspective," NBER Working Paper no. 11955, issued in January 2006; NBER Program(s). At first this growth could be ascribed to the effects of the Depression, which evaporated much of the "paper" wealth of the population's top 10 percent. From the end of the Progressive Era the income share of this decline had risen until it reached over 40 percent in late 1920s. This proportion stabilized and then fell markedly with the enactment of the New Deal reforms in the late 1930s, dropping to about 30 percent.

53. Tony Hiss, *The Experience of Place* (New York: Vintage Books, 1990), pp. 103–20.

54. William Julius Wilson, *When Work Disappears: The World of the Urban Poor* (New York: Knopf, 1996), pp. 37–39.

55. Jason D. Antos, *Whitestone* (Charleston, S.C.: Arcadia, 2006), pp. 7–8; Robert Caro, *The Power Broker: Robert Moses and the Fall of New York* (New York: Vintage Books, 1975),

pp.143–44, 329; C. J. Hughes, "Whitestone, Queens: Returning a Queens Neighborhood to Its Old Self," *New York Times*, June 4, 2006.

56. Howard Roberts Lamar, *The Far Southwest: A Territorial History* (New York: Norton, 1970), pp. 17, 415.

57. Ibid., p. 474; Bradford Luckingham, *Phoenix: A History of a Southwest Metropolis* (Tucson: University of Arizona, 1989), pp. 13, 28–33, 37, 56–57.

58. David G. McComb, *Houston: A History* (Austin: University of Texas Press, 1981), pp. 5–12; Marguerite Johnston, *Houston: The Unknown City* (College Station: Texas A&M Press, 1991), pp. 1–11.

59. Gunther, *Inside USA*, p. 827.

60. E. Digby Baltzell, *Philadelphia Gentlemen: The Making of a National Upper Class* (New Brunswick, N.J.: Transaction, 1995), p. 8.

61. G. William Domhoff, *Who Rules America?* (Englewood Cliffs, N.J.: Prentice-Hall, 1967), p. 139.

62. Robert W. Gilmer, "The Urban Consolidation of American Oil: The Case of Houston," Federal Reserve Bank of Dallas, Houston branch, June 6, 1998; "Oil Related Employment Long-term Adjustment in Nine Cities," *Houston Business*, September 1998; Robert W. Gilmer and Iram Siddik, "1982–1990: When Times Were Bad in Houston," *Houston Business*, June 2003.

63. Thomas Klier and William Testa, "Location Trends of Large Company Headquarters During the 1990s," *Economic Perspectives*, Federal Reserve Bank of Chicago, 2002.

64. E. Michael Jones, *The Slaughter of Cities: Urban Renewal as Ethnic Cleansing* (South Bend, Ind.: St. Augustine's Press, 2004), pp. 518–19.

65. Mariana Mogilevich, "Big Bad Buildings: The Vanishing Legacy of Minoru Yamasaki," *Next American City*, no. 3 (October 2003).

66. Saskia Sassen, *Cities in the World Economy* (Thousand Oaks, Calif.: Pine Force Press, 2000), pp. 5, 21.

67. Susanne MacGregor and Arthur Lipow, "Bringing the People Back In: Economy and Society in New York and London," in Susanne MacGregor and Arthur Lipow, eds., *The Other City: People and Politics in New York and London* (Atlantic Highlands, N.J.: Humanities Press, 1995), p. 5; Peter Hall, "Urban Growth and Decline in Western Europe," in Mattei Dogan and John D. Kasarda, eds., *A World of Giant Cities: The Metropolis Era* (Thousand Oaks, Calif.: Sage, 1998), p. 113; Anna Segre, "Turin in the 1980s," in High Clout, ed., *Europe's Cities in the Late 20th Century* (Utrecht: Royal Dutch Geographical Society, 1996), pp. 99–107; John R. Logan, "Still a Global City: The Racial and Ethnic Segmentation of New York," in Peter Marcuse and Ronald van Kempen, eds., *Globalizing Cities: A New Spatial Order?* (London: Blackwell, 2000), pp. 158–61; Saskia Sassen, "How Population Lies," *Newsweek International*, July 3, 2006; and Sewell Chan, "New York Tops 8 Big Cities in Taxes, Study Shows," *New York Times*, February 21, 2007.

68. Saskia Sassen, interview by author.

69. Joe Gyourko, Christopher Mayer, and Todd Sinai, "Superstar Cities," Wharton School and National Bureau of Economic Research, June 16, 2006, pp. 1–2, 31; Troy McMullen, "Nobody's Home: A Growing Number of Manhattan's Choice Apartments Are Being Bought by People Who Rarely Use Them," *Wall Street Journal*, February 9, 2007.

70. Terry Nichols Clark et al., "Amenities Drive Urban Growth," in Terry Nichols Clark, ed., *The City as Entertainment Machine* (Amsterdam, Netherlands: Elsevier, 2004), p. 201.

71. Mark Sappenfield, "In San Francisco, Pet Owners Recast as 'Guardians,'" *Christian Science Monitor*, December 20, 2001; "U.S. Cities Have Fewer Kids, More Singles," *USA Today*, June 13, 2001 ; Ilene Lelchuk, "Lots of Toddlers, Fewer School Age Kids in SF," *San*

Francisco Chronicle, May 30, 2006; John Ritter, "Some Cities Looking More Adult," *USA Today*, June 13, 2001; John Pomfret, "Where Did All the Children Go?" *Washington Post*, March 19, 2006.

72. Antonio Olivio, "Chicago Population Dips by 18,000," *Chicago Tribune*, June 21, 2006; Christopher Hawthorne, "Home Is Where the Height Is: Skyscrapers, No Longer Seen Just as Office Towers, Are Being Reshaped for Residences," *Los Angeles Times*, August 2, 2005.

73. Jonathan Bowles, Joel Kotkin, and David Giles, *Reviving the City of Aspiration: A Study of the Challenges Facing New York City's Middle Class*, Center for an Urban Future, February 2009. Based on ACCRA cost of living estimates, 2008.

74. William H. Frey, "Brain Gains, Brain Drains," *American Demographics*, June 2004; Greg Lacour, "'The Young and Restless' Flocking to Queen City," *Charlotte Observer*, December 7, 2006.

75. John Harris, interview by author.

76. Quoted in Howard Husock, "Jane Jacobs: New York's Indispensable Urban Iconoclast," *City Journal*, April 27, 2006.

77. David Wessel, "Fed Chief Warns of Widening Inequality," *Wall Street Journal*, February 2, 2007; George Galster, Jackie Cutsinger, and Jason C. Booza, "Where Did They Go?: The Decline of Middle-Income Neighborhoods in Metropolitan America," Metropolitan Policy Program, Brookings Institution, June 2006; Deborah Reed, "Poverty in California: Moving Beyond the Federal Measure," *California Counts* 7, no. 4 (May 2006), p. 8.

78. Bowles, Kotkin, and Giles, *Reviving the City of Aspiration*.

79. Patrick McGeehan, "Report Shows Quick Growth in New York Since 9/11," Citigroup Equity Research, *Revisiting Plutonomy* (March 2006); "Reviving the City of Aspiration: A Study of the Challenges Facing New York's Middle Class," Center for an Urban Future, New York, February 2009; Patrick McGeehan, "Top Executives Return Offices to Manhattan," *New York Times* July 3, 2006.

80. William Frey, conversation with author; Bowles, Kotkin, and Giles, *Reviving the City of Aspiration*.

81. David Dyssegaard Kallick, "Little in the Middle," *New York Times*, September 4, 2005; Sam Roberts, "Study Shows a Dwindling Middle Class," *New York Times*, June 22, 2006 : Fred Siegel, "Hell of a Town", *Commentary*, May 2009.

82. Bowles, Kotkin, and Giles, *Reviving the City of Aspiration*.

83. Interview with author.

84. Sam Roberts, "In Manhattan, Poor Make 2 Cents for Each Dollar to Rich," *New York Times Magazine*, September 4, 2005.

85. Galster, Cutsinger, and Booza, "Where Did They Go?"; Reed, "Poverty in California," p. 8.

86. Elizabeth Rhodes and Justin Mayo, "Only Nine Areas in King County Left for Middle-Income Buyers," *Seattle Times*, July 16, 2006; "U.S. Suburban Poverty Tops City Poverty for 1st Time," Associated Press, December 7, 2006.

87. Kate Swan, "Where Are You on the Talent Map," *Fast Company*, January 2001; Haya El Nasser, "Mid-sized Cities Get Hip to Attract Young Professionals," *USA Today*, October 10, 2003.

88. Jon C. Teaford, *Cities of the Heartland: The Rise and Fall of the Industrial Midwest* (Bloomington: Indiana University Press, 1994), pp. 216–18.

89. Dennis Powell, "Suburbs Thriving, Cities Stagnating in Keystone State," Newgeography .com, July 15, 2008.

90. Gordon T. Anderson, "The Milwaukee Effect," *CNN Money*, August 6, 2004; Eugenie L. Birch, "Who Lives Downtown," Metropolitan Policy Program, Brookings Institution,

November 2005; Sam Staley, "Ground Zero in Urban Decline," *Reason*, November 2001; Bishop Douglas Miles and Reverend Marshall Prince, "Carry the Flight to City's Blight," *Baltimore Sun*, July 11, 2005; Heywood Sanders, "Space Available: The Realities of Convention Centers as Economic Development Strategy," Metropolitan Policy Program, Brookings Institution, January 2005; Michael Norman, "Cleveland Rocks After Museum Brings It Fame," *Los Angeles Times*, March 15, 1999; Christopher Conkey, "Snapshot of America: Whose Richest, Poorest, Where Single Men Area," *Wall Street Journal*, August 30, 2006; Rich Exner, "Cleveland Population Lowest Since 1900," *Cleveland Plain Dealer*, June 30, 2005; Tod Blumer, "Why Ohioans Are Voting with their Feet," Pajamasmedia .com, May 1, 2009; Ed Morrison, "Cleveland: How the Comeback Collapsed," Newgeography.com, February 2, 2009; Sam Dillon, "Large Urban Suburban Gap Seen in Graduation Rates," *New York Times*, April 22, 2009.

91. Pam Radtke Russell, "The Bigger, Easier: The Migration of Oil and Gas Companies to Houston Picked Up Steam After Hurricane Katrina," *New Orleans Times-Picayune*, August 5, 2007.

92. www.epodunk.com New Orleans Income, based on 2000 U.S. Census.

93. Nicole Gelinas, "Katrina's Real Lesson: Blame Inadequate Infrastructure, Not Poverty, for the Storm's Devastation," *City Journal*, August 28, 2006.

94. Sonya Heisser, interview by author.

95. Richard C, Hula, "Privatizing Regeneration," in Dennis Judd and Michael Parkinson, eds., *Leadership and Urban Regeneration: Cities in Europe and North America* (Thousand Oaks, Calif.: Sage, 1990), p. 203; Gary Dorsey, "Can a Troubled City Remake Its Image Through Marketing?" *Baltimore Sun*, January 12, 2003.

96. William Frey, interview by author.

97. Bowles, Kotkin, and Giles, *Reviving the City of Aspiration*; Richard Florida, "How the Crash Will Reshape America," *Atlantic*, January 2009.

98. "Homeownership and Living," Zogby International, September 2005.

99. Ian Frazier, "Someplace in Queens," in Kenneth Jackson and David Dunbar, eds., *Empire City: New York Through the Ages* (New York: Columbia University Press, 2002), p. 920.

100. Beth DeBetham, interview by author.

101. Lewis Mumford, *The Urban Prospect* (New York: Harcourt Brace, 1956), p. 18.

102. Braudel, *Perspective of the World*, p. 3:629.

103. Edwin G. Burrows and Mike Wallace, *Gotham: A History of New York to 1898* (Oxford, U.K.: Oxford University Press, 1999), pp. 660–62, 744–46.

104. Dan Fost, "Where Neo-Nomads Ideas Percolate: New Bedouins Transform a Laptop, Cell Phone and Coffeehouses into Their Office," *San Francisco Chronicle*, March 11, 2007; Ilana DeBare, "Small Businesses Helped SF During Dot-com Bust: Layoffs Less Likely when Employer Knows Workers," *San Francisco Chronicle*, August 9, 2006; interview with Leslie Parks, consultant, City of San Francisco.

105. Dan Blake, CSU Northridge, interview with author.

106. Praxis Strategy Group analysis based on census date, 2008.

107. Alistair MacDonald, Aaron Lucchetti, and Edward Taylor, "Long City-Centric, Financial Exchanges Are Going Global: Mergers Are in the Air as Goal Is to Offer One-Stop Shops to Sophisticated Investors; Appeal to 'Black Box' Traders," *Wall Street Journal*, May 27, 2006; "Goodbye to All That: Will Technology and Competition Kill Traditional Financial Exchanges?" *Economist*, January 30, 1999.

108. Judy Markowitz, interview by author.

109. Thomas Horan, *Digital Places: Building Our City of Bits* (Washington, D.C.: Urban Land Institute, 2000), p. 11.

CHAPTER THREE: **THE ARCHIPELAGO OF VILLAGES**

1. Malcolm Gladwell, "The Terrazzo Jungle," *New Yorker*, March 15, 2004.
2. Patrick Wirtz, "Valencia, California: From New Town to Regional Center," School of Policy, Planning and Development, University of Southern California, June 1999, pp. 15–18.
3. Ibid., pp. 2–3, 34; Steve Zimmer, interview by author and Colin Drukker.
4. Wirtz, "Valencia," p. 124.
5. C.B. Richard Ellis, Valencia Gateway Industrial Market Overview, May 31, 2006; Claritas http://www.claritas.com/Default.jsp, 2003 Estimates, August 2003. Provided by Newhall Land.
6. Interview with Newhall Land and Farming.
7. Julie Weith, interview by author.
8. "The Cultura in the United States (USA): Domesticated Land in 2000 and 1950," Demographia.com; Samuel R. Staley, "Sustainable Development in American Planning: A Critical Appraisal," *Town Planning Review* 77, no. 1 (2005).
9. Daniel Akst, "He Built It and They Came," *Wall Street Journal*, August 19, 2004.
10. Robert Cervero, "Planned Communities, Self-containment and Commuting: A Cross National Perspective," *Urban Studies* 32, no. 7 (1995), 1135–61.
11. Ibid.; Bill Geist, *From Way Off the Road* (New York: Broadway Books, 2007), p. 191.
12. Steven Hayward, "Legends of the Sprawl," *Policy Review*, September-October 1998; Thomas Frank, *The Conquest of Cool: Business Culture, Counterculture and the Rise of Hip Consumerism* (Chicago: University of Chicago Press, 1997), p. 13; Paul Knox, "Vulgaria: The Re-enchantment of Suburbia," *Opolis* 1, no. 2 (2005).
13. Michael Southworth and Eran Ben Joseph, "Reconsidering the Cul-de-Sac," *Access*, Spring 2004, p. 31.
14. Christopher P. Leinberger, "Sprawl Is the Root Cause of the Financial Crisis," *Eco-Compass Blog*, September 22, 2008; Florida, "How the Crash Will Reshape"; David Villano, "The Slumming of Suburbia," Miller-McCune, February 20, 2009.
15. Piers Scholfield, "The Most Dangerous Gang in America," BBC News, April 5, 2008; Dan Mitchell, "Suburbia's March to Oblivion," *New York Times*, February 23, 2008; Lara Farmar, "Is America's Suburban Dream Collapsing into a Nightmare?" CNN.com, June 21, 2008; Christopher B. Leinberger, "The Next Slum?" *Atlantic*, May 1, 2008.
16. Brad Knickerbocker, "The Environmental Load of 300 Million: How Heavy?" *Christian Science Monitor*, September 26, 2006; Peter S. Goodman, "Life on the Fringes of U.S. Suburbia Becomes Untenable with Rising Gas Prices," *International Herald Tribune*, June 24, 2008.
17. Daniel Pimlott, "As Cities Revive America's Poor Are Forced to the Periphery," *Financial Times*, April 4, 2008.
18. John Rebchook, "Downtown Real Estate Engine Sputtering," *Rocky Mountain News*, February 21, 2009; Azam Ahmed and Darnell Little, "Foreclosures Spur Neighborhood Ghost Towns," *Chicago Tribune*, February 22, 2009; Robert Seina, "SF Construction Slows to a Crawl," *San Francisco Chronicle*, March 9, 2009; Joan Gralla, "New York City Fears Return to the 1970s," *Reuters*, January 27, 2009; Abby Goodnough, "Hard Times for New England's 3-Deckers," *New York Times*, June 20, 2009; "Will Condo Market Be Slower to Recover than the Market for Single Family Homes?" Themariogrecogroup.com, June 18, 2009.
19. John R. Logan, "The Suburban Advantage," Lewis Mumford Center for Urban and Regional Research, Albany, N.Y., June 24, 2002.
20. David Dyssegaard, "Little in the Middle," *New York Times*, September 4, 2005; Sam Roberts, "Study Shows a Dwindling Middle Class," *New York Times*, June 22, 2006.

21. "'Job Sprawl' Undermines Long-term Regional, National Prosperity," Metropolitan Policy Program, Brookings Institution, April 6, 2009.

22. William Frey, interview by author; Belden Russonello & Stewart, "2004 American Community Survey: National Survey of Communities," October 2004, p. 3; Richard Morin and Paul Taylor, "Suburbs Not Most Popular, but Suburbanites Most Content," Pew Research Center, February 26, 2009.

23. "Urban Sprawl: Aren't City Centres Great," *Economist*, August 14, 1999; "Back to the City—Baby Boomers Are Leaving the Suburbs," *AARP Magazine*, July 22, 2004; Robert E. Lang, James W. Hughes, and Karen A. Danielson, "Targeting the Suburban Urbanites: Marketing Central-City Housing," *Housing Policy Debate* 8, no. 2 (1997); John Kasarda, "Comment on Elvin K. Wyley and Daniel J. Hammel's 'Islands of Decay in Seas of Renewal: Housing Policy and the Resurgence of Gentrification,'" *Housing Policy Debate* 10, no. 4 (1999); *National Housing Study*, Fannie Mae Foundation, 1997; Kirkpatrick Sale, *Human Scale* (New York: Coward, McCann & Geoghegan, 1980), pp. 204–06; Belden Russonello & Stewart, "2004 American Community Survey," p. 3; Jeffrey K. Hadden and Josef J. Barton, "Thoughts on the History of Anti-Urban Ideology," in Irving Lewis Allen, ed., *New Towns and the Suburban Dream* (Port Washington, N.Y.: University Publications, 1977); Dowell Myers and Elizabeth Gearin, "Current Preferences for Denser Residential Environments," *Housing Policy Debate* 12, no. 4 (2001), p. 642; Alan B. Kirschenbaum. "A Flight from Suburbia," in Paul Meadows and Ephraim H. Mizruchi, eds., *Urbanism, Urbanization and Change: Comparative Perspectives* (Reading, Mass.: Addison Wesley, 1969), pp. 113–17.

24. Scott Donaldson, *The Suburban Myth* (New York: Columbia University Press, 1969), p. 3.

25. E. Digby Baltzell, *Philadelphia Gentlemen* (New Brunswick, N.J.: Transaction Press, 1950), pp. 196–209; John Modell, "An Ecology of Family Decisions: Suburbanization, Schooling and Fertility in Philadelphia, 1880–1920," *Journal of Urban History* 6, no. 4 (August 1980), pp. 397–417; Robert Bruegmann, *Sprawl: A Compact History* (Chicago: University of Chicago, 2006), pp. 26–29; Leo Marx, *The Machine in the Garden: Technology and the Pastoral Ideal of America* (Oxford, U.K.: Oxford University Press, 1994), p. 5; Jon Teaford, *Creating Suburbia* (New York: Routledge, 2007), p. 3; Ann Durkin Keating, *Building Chicago: Suburban Developers and the Creation of a Divided Metropolis* (Columbus: Ohio State University Press, 1988), pp. 16, 28.

26. Kenneth T. Jackson, *Crabgrass Frontier: The Suburbanization of the United States* (New York: Oxford University Press, 1987), p.176; Donaldson, *Suburban Myth*, pp. 3–4; Fred Siegel, *The Future Once Happened Here: New York, D.C., L.A., and the Fate of America's Big Cities* (New York: Free Press; 1997), p. x.

27. Adam Rome, *The Bulldozer in the Countryside: American Sprawl and the Rise of American Environmentalism* (Cambridge, U.K.: Cambridge University Press, 2001), p. 257; Alexander von Hoffman and John Felkner, "The Historical Origins and Causes of Urban Decentralization in the United States," Joint Center for Housing Studies, Harvard University, January 2002, p. 17; Dolores Hayden, *Building Suburbia: Green Fields and Urban Growth, 1820–2000* (New York: Vintage, 2004), p. 34.

28. M. P. Baumgartner, *The Moral Order of a Suburb* (New York: Oxford University Press, 1988), p. 94.

29. Nicole Stelle Garnett, "Suburbs as Exit, Suburbs as Entrance," *Michigan Law Review* 106 (November 2007).

30. Edward L. Glaeser and Janet E. Kohlhase, "Cities, Regions and the Decline of Transportation Costs," Harvard Institute of Economic Research, July 2003, p. 23.

31. Demographia.com; statistics courtesy of William Frey; Nancy McArdle, "Outward Bound: The Decentralization of Population and Employment," Joint Center for Housing Studies, Harvard University, July 1999, p. 14; "Outlying Counties Grew Faster than Central Counties Between 2000 and 2007," U.S. Census Bureau, June 17, 2009; www.demographia.com/db_msacore.pdf.

32. Jonathan D. Miller and Myron Orfield, "Suburbs in Flux," *Urban Land*, March 1998.

33. Marx, *Machine in the Garden*, p. 5.

34. Joel Garreau, *Edge City: Life on the New Frontier* (New York: Doubleday, 1991), pp. 206–07.

35. "Consumers Survey on Smart Choices for Home Buyers," National Association of Realtors and National Association of Home Builders, April 22, 2002; Myers and Gearin, "Current Preferences for Denser Residential Environments," p. 636.

36. *Los Angeles Times* poll, October 19, 1999; *Kansas City Star* poll, November 19, 2005; Ken McCall, "Satisfaction: The City-Suburb Great Divide: Inside Dayton, Fewer Like It Compared with Those in the Suburbs," *Dayton Daily News*, February 12, 2006; Kelly Zito, "Study Reveals What Buyers Want," *San Francisco Chronicle*, November 7, 2004; Michele Derus, "Generation Has High X-pectations," *Contra Costa Times*, January 10, 2005.

37. Arthur C. Nelson, *Toward a New Metropolis: The Opportunity to Rebuild America* (Washington, D.C.: Brookings Institution Press, 2004); Patrick O'Gilfoil Healy, "Far Flung Houses for Very Young Buyers," *New York Times*, January 1, 2006.

38. Eric Heisler, "The New Suburbanism," *St. Louis Post-Dispatch*, January 12, 2004. Heisler writes that a four-story apartment development in Webster Groves, Missouri, may seem out of scale to local residents who wish to "protect" their suburban lifestyle.

39. Peter Dreier, John Mollenkpf, and Todd Swanstrom, *Place Matters: Metropolitics of the 21st Century* (Manhattan: University of Kansas Press, 2000), p. 60.

40. Mark Baldassare, "Citizen Preferences for Growth Controls: Trends in U.S. Suburban Support for a New Political Culture Movement," in Terry Nichols Clark and Vincent Hoffmann-Martinot, eds., *The New Political Culture: Urban Policy Challenges* (Boulder, Colo.: Westview Press, 1998), pp. 261–75; Terry Nichols Clark and Edward Goetz, "The Anti-Growth Machine," in Terry Nichols Clark, ed., *Urban Innovation: Creative Strategies for Turbulent Times* (Thousand Oaks, Calif.: Sage, 1994), p. 113; Teaford, *Creating Suburbia*, p. 94.

41. Fred Hirsch, *Social Limits to Growth* (Cambridge, Mass.: Harvard University Press, 1999), pp. 1,4, 33–34; Berny Morson, "Desire for More Space Fuels Sprawl, But Many Who Don't Like Being Close to Neighborhors Don't Want Uncontrolled Urban Spread Either," *Rocky Mountain News*, October 1, 2000; Jenifer Ragland, "Voters Stick to Middle Ground in Growth Debate," *Los Angeles Times*, November 7, 2002.

42. Hirsch, *Social Limits to Growth*, p. 39.

43. John D. Landis, Lan Deng, and Michael Reilly, "Growth Management Revisited," Institute of Urban and Regional Development, University of California, 2002, p. 9; C. J. Hughes, "Merging the Old with the New in a Washington Suburb," *New York Times*, January 28, 2007.

44. Alexander von Hoffman and John Felkner, "The Historical Origins and Causes of Urban Decentralization in the United States," Joint Center for Housing Studies, Harvard University, January 2002, p. 23.

45. William Peterson, "The Ideological Origins of Britain's New Towns," in Irving Lewis Allen, ed., *New Towns and the Suburban Dream*, (Port Washington, N.Y.: University Publications, 1977), pp. 62–65.

46. Ibid.; Carl E. Schorske, "The Idea of the City in European Thought," in Oscar Handlin and John Burchard, eds., *The Historian and the City* (Cambridge, Mass.: MIT Press, 1963), p. 108.

47. H. G. Wells, *Anticipations of the Reaction of Mechanical and Scientific Progress upon Human Life and Thought* (London: Chapman & Hall, 1902), pp. 33–62.

48. Robert Fishman, *Bourgeois Utopias: The Rise and Fall of Suburbia* (New York: Basic Books, 1987), pp. 127, 129–33.

49. Peterson, "Ideological Origins of New Towns"; Robert Fishman, "America's New City," *Wilson Quarterly* (Winter 1990), p. 38; Fishman, *Bourgeois Utopias*, pp. 188–89.

50. http://www.radburn.org/geninfo/history.html.

51. "Radburn: A Town for the Motor Age in Fair Lawn, N.J., U.S.A.," Radburn.org.

52. Scott Donaldson, "City and Country: Marriage Proposals," in Irving Lewis Allen, ed., *New Towns and the Suburban Dream* (Port Washington, N.Y.: University Publications, 1977), pp. 82–103.

53. Charles C. Bohl, "A Downtown for the 21st Century," in Alan Ward, ed., *Reston Town Center: A Downtown for the 21st Century* (Washington, D.C.: Academy Press, 2006), p. 34; Roger Biles, "New Towns for the Great Society: A Case Study in Politics and Planning," *Planning Perspectives* 13 (1998).

54. James Rouse, "Building a Sense of Place," in Donald C. Klein, ed., *Psychology of the Planned Community: The New Town Experience* (New York: Human Science Press, 1978), pp. 51–55.

55. http://www.columbia-md.com/columbiahistory.html; "James Wilson Rouse: Urban Visionary," *Blueprints Magazine*, National Building Museum, Spring 1998.

56. Roger Galatas with Jim Barlow, *The Woodlands: The Inside Story of Creating a Better Hometown* (Washington, D.C.: Urban Land Institute, 2004), pp. 1–14, 22.

57. Vicki Fullerton, interview by author and Colin Drukker.

58. Wally Siembab, "The Smart Sprawl Strategy," *Planetizen*, August 31, 2005.

59. Randal O'Toole, "Dense Thinkers," *Reason*, January 1999; Ann Carrns, "Architects Attack Development Style," *Wall Street Journal*, June 14, 1997; Staley, "Sustainable Development," p. 113.

60. Karrie Jacobs, "The Manchurian Main Street," *Metropolis*, June 2005.

61. Edward L. Glaeser, "Green Cities, Brown Suburbs," *City Journal*, February 20, 2009; Ariamalar Selvakumar and Michael Borst, "Land Use and Seasonal Effects on Urban Stormwater Runoff Microorganism Concentrations," *ASCE Publications*, 2004, http://www.pubs.asce.org/WWWdisplay.cgi?0410354#; Werner H. Terjung, "Urban Energy Balance Climatology: A Preliminary Investigation of the City-Man System in Downtown Los Angeles," *Geographical Review* 60, no. 1 (January 1970), pp. 31–53; Donald Morgan et al., "Microclimates Within an Urban Area," *Annals of the Association of American Geographers* 67, no. 1 (1977), pp. 55–65; Werner H. Terjung and Stella S.-F. Louie, "Solar Radiation and Urban Heat Islands," *Annals of the Association of American Geographers* 63, no. 2 (1973), pp. 181–207; Stanton E. Tuller, "Microclimatic Variations in a Downtown Urban Environment," *Geografiska Annaler, Series A, Physical Geography* 55, no. 3–4 (1973), pp. 123–35; Brian Stone and John M. Norman, "Land Use Planning and Surface Heat Island Formation: A Parcel-based Radiation Flux Approach," *Atmospheric Environment* 40 (2006), pp. 3561–73; Sharon L. Harlan et al., "Neighborhood Microclimates and Vulnerability to Heat Stress," *Social Science and Medicine* 63 (2006), pp. 2847–63; Wendell Cox, "Enough 'Cowboy' Greenhouse Gas Reduction Policies," Newgeography.com, March 20, 2009.

62. For a recent study of energy consumption and greenhouse gas emissions in Sydney, Australia, which compares high- and low-density areas, see Paul Myors, Rachel O'Leary, and

Rob Helstroom, "Multi Unit Residential Buildings Energy and Peak Demand Study," Energy Australia, 2005; David M. Chapman, "It's HOT in the City!" *GeoDate* 18, no. 2 (May 2005); Heat Island Group, "Energy Use," http://eetd.lbl.gov/HeatIsland/Energy Use/; Witold Rybczynski, "The Last Landscape."

63. William D. Solecki et al., "Mitigation of the Heat Island Effect in Urban New Jersey." *Environmental Hazards* 6 (2005), pp. 39–49.

64. Edward L. Glaeser and Matthew E. Kahn, "Sprawl and Urban Growth," Harvard Institute of Economic Research, May 2003, p. 6.

65. Jim Carlton, "Many Voters Agree to Raise Money for Green Space," *Wall Street Journal*, November 7, 2003.

66. Christopher G. Boone and Ali Modarres, *City and Environment* (Philadelphia: Temple University Press, 2006), p. 172; Glaeser and Kahn, "Sprawl and Urban Growth," p. 36.

67. Randall G. Arendt, *Conservation Design for Subdivisions: A Practical Guide to Creating Open Space Networks* (Washington, D.C.: Island Press, 1996), pp. 10, 13, 28, 47, 124.

68. Galatas and Barlow, *Woodlands*, pp. 30–42; Phaedra Friend, "The Woodlands Is on the Rise," *Texas Magazine*, April 2005; Vicki Fullerton, interview by author and Colin Drukker.

69. Jeff Speck, "Sprawl and the Future of the Old Neighborhood," *Asheville Citizen-Times*, September 3, 2000.

70. Becky Nicolaides, "How Hell Moved from the City to the Suburbs," in Kevin M. Kruse and Thomas J. Sugrue, eds., *The New Suburban History* (Chicago: University of Chicago Press, 2006), p. 91.

71. Jan K. Brueckner and Ann Largey, "Social Interaction and Urban Sprawl," Department of Economics, University of California Irvine, October 2006 abstract; Wendell Cox, "City Violent Crime Rate 3.3 Times Suburbs in U.S.," *Urban Policy*, July 4, 2007.

72. Hayward, "Legends of the Sprawl"; Edward J. Blakely and Mary Gail Snyder, *Fortress America: Gated Communities in the United States* (Washington, D.C.: Brookings Institution Press, 1997), p. 132; Daryl Kennedy, "Suburbia Lost," *Los Angeles Times*, October 24, 1999.

73. Ken McCall, "Satisfaction: The City-Suburb Great Divide: Inside Dayton, Fewer Like It Compared with Those in the Suburbs," *Dayton Daily News*, February 12, 2006.

74. Real estate reporter Nancy Sarnoff of Houston Chronicle, interview by author; Demographia.com, "Portland: Urban Growth Boundary Keeps Out Growth 98 Percent of Domestic Movers Settle Outside Urban Growth Boundary," 2005; Dylan Rivera, "Office Presence Grows in Suburbs," *Portland Oregonian*, January 26, 2006. Wendell Cox, "Death of Suburbia: Part Nauseum," www.Newgeography.com, July 6, 2009.

75. Lewis Mumford quoted in Kevin M. Kruse and Thomas J. Sugrue, "The New Suburban History," in Kruse and Sugrue, eds., *The New Suburban History* (Chicago: University of Chicago Press, 2006), p. 3.

76. Jackson, *Crabgrass Frontier*, p. 42; William H. Whyte, "The Anti-City," in C. E. Elias, James Gillies, and Svend Riemer, eds., *Metropolis: Values in Conflict* (Belmont, Calif.: Wadsworth, 1965), pp. 69; John C. Clark et al., *Three Generations in Twentieth Century America: Family, Community, and Nation* (Homewood, Ill.: Dorsey Press, 1977), p. 469; Greg Hise, *Magnetic Los Angeles* (Baltimore: Johns Hopkins University Press, 1997), p. 7; Hayden, *Building Suburbia*, pp. 68–69.

77. Al Ehrbar, "The Housing Boom: Another 20 Years of Growth," Stern Stewart & Co., 2003, executive summary; George J. Borjas, "Homeownership in the Immigrant Population," Research Institute for Housing America, March 2002.

78. Christine Cipriani, "Homeownership and Association Living: HOA Members and Homeowners Nationwide," Zogby International, September 2005; William H. Frey, "Married with Children," *American Demographics*, March 2003.

79. Audrey Singer et al., "The World in a Zip Code: Greater Washington, D.C., as a New Region of Immigration," Center on Urban and Metropolitan Policy, Brookings Institution, April 2001; "Into the Suburbs," *Economist*, March 11, 2004; Nicole Stelle Garnett, "Suburbs as Exit, Suburbs as Entrance," *Michigan Law Review* 106 (November 2007).

80. Truman Hartshorn and Keith R. Ihlanfeldt, "Growth and Change in Metropolitan Atlanta," in David L. Sjoquist, ed., *The Atlanta Paradox* (New York: Russell Sage Foundation, 2000), p. 26; Mary Lou Pickel and Megan Clarke, "Gwinett Moving to Majority Minority," *Atlanta Journal Constitution*, August 9, 2007; Robin Fields and Erin Texeira, "White Flight Is Giving Way to Civic Diversity," *Los Angeles Times*, May 20, 2001; Alan Wolfe, *One Nation, After All* (New York: Viking, 1998), p. 165; William Frey, "Melting Pot Suburbs: A Census 2000 Study of Suburban Diversity," Center on Urban and Metropolitan Policy, Brookings Institution, June 2001.

81. Todd Swanstrom et al., "Pulling Apart: Economic Segregation Among Suburbs and Central Cities in Major Metropolitan Areas, 1980–2000," in Alan Berube, Bruce Katz, and Robert Lang, eds., *Redefining Urban and Suburban America: Evidence from Census 2000* (Washington, D.C.: Brookings Institution Press, 2006); Becky Gaylord, "For Carless in City, Jobs Are Far Away," *Cleveland Plain Dealer*, July 10, 2005; Robert Puentes and David Warren, "One Fifth of America: A Comprehensive Guide to America's First Suburbs," Metropolitan Policy Program, Brookings Institution, February 2006; "U.S. Suburban Poverty Tops City Poverty for 1st Time," Associated Press, December 7, 2006.

82. Frey, "Melting Pot Suburbs"; Anne-Marie O'Connor, "Learning to Look Past Race," *Los Angeles Times*, August 25, 1999.

83. Heath Foster, "The 2000 Census: Looking for Kids? Baby Booms in the Cities and Towns," *Seattle Post-Intelligencer*, July 21, 2001; Tara Malone, "Suburban Sprawl Continues Among Collar Counties," *Daily Herald*, March 22, 2007.

84. William Frey and Alan Berube, "City Families and Suburban Singles: The Emerging Household Story from Census 2000," Center on Urban and Metropolitan Policy, Brookings Institution, February 2002, pp. 9–10.

85. "Fast Facts: Baby Boomers Statistics on Empty Nesting and Retiring," *Del Webb Backgrounder*, Del Webb Corporation, 2005.

86. "Urban Sprawl: Aren't City Centres Great," *Economist*, August 14, 1999; "Back to the City—Baby Boomers Are Leaving the Suburbs," *AARP Magazine*, July 22, 2004.

87. Chris Farrell, "Choosing Where to Grow Old," *BusinessWeek*, July 3, 2008; William Frey, "Boomer Havens and Young Adult Magnets—Baby Boomers and Post-Baby Boomers Geographical Information," *American Demographics*, September 2001; Linda Baker, "Retirement Homes Go High-Rise and Urban," *New York Times*, April 1, 2007; "Empty Nesters Flock to Cities," CBS News, July 9, 2004; "NAHB Study Finds Boomers Aren't Downsizing by Much," Buildingonline.com, March 5, 2008; "Baby Boomer Survey Shows Big Appetite for Real Estate," National Association of Realtors, 2006; Al Heavans, "Active-Adult Boomers Still Favor Suburbs," *Realty Times*, October 14, 2004; Peg Tyre, "Seniors and the City: An Urban Retirement," MSNBC.com, April 7, 2007; Gary V. Engelhardt, "Housing Trends Among Baby Boomers," Research Institute for Housing, 2006; William R. Taylor, *In Pursuit of Gotham: Culture and Commerce in New York* (Oxford, U.K.: Oxford University Press, 1992), p. xvii; "Second and Urban Homes Not a Big Lure for Baby Boomers," *National Building News Online*, December 11, 2006; Gail Marks Jarvis, "Second Thoughts About Second Homes," *Chicago Tribune*. November 12, 2006; William H. Frey, "Boomers and Seniors in the Suburbs: Aging Patterns in Census 2000," Center on Urban and Metropolitan Policy, Brookings Institution, January 2003; Joel Hirschhorn, "Sprawl Politics Traps Americans in Blandburbs," *Newtopia Magazine*, January 1, 2006;

"Moving Rates Lowest in Fifty Plus, the Census Bureau Reports," *U.S. Census Bureau News*, March 23, 2004.

88. Jennifer Lisle, "Adult-Adult Builders Target Urban Locales," *Real Estate Journal*, January 29, 2005; Sandra Rosenbloom, interview by author; William H. Frey, "Mapping the Growth of Older America: Seniors and Boomers in the Early 21st Century," Metropolitan Policy Program, Brookings Institution, May 2007; Gary V. Engelhardt, "Housing Trends Among Baby Boomers," Research Institute for Housing, 2006.

89. Sandra Rosenbloom, interview by author.

90. Gerald A. Carlino, "From Centralization to Deconcentration: People and Jobs Spread Out," Federal Reserve Bank of Philadelphia, November-December 2000, p. 19; Margaret Pugh O'Mara, "Uncovering the City in the Suburb," in Kevin M. Kruse and Thomas J. Sugrue, eds., *The New Suburban History* (Chicago: University of Chicago Press, 2006), p. 77; Edward L. Glaeser and Jesse Shapiro, "Is There a New Urbanism? The Growth of U.S. Cities in the 1990s," Harvard Institute of Economic Research, June 2001, pp. 2–3.

91. "The State of the Nation's Housing," Joint Center for Housing Studies, Harvard University, 2001, p. 8; Bruce Katz and Alan Berube, "Cities Rebound—Somewhat," *American Enterprise*, June 2002; Edward Glaeser, Matthew Kahn, and Chenghuan Chu, "Job Sprawl: Employment Location in U.S. Metropolitan Areas," Center on Urban and Metropolitan Policy, Brookings Institution, May 2001.

92. Manuel Castells, *The Informational City* (London: Blackwell, 1989), pp. 153–66, 306.

93. O'Mara, "Uncovering City in Suburb," pp. 69–75; Teaford, *Creating Suburbia*, p. 101; U.S. Census Bureau, "Percent of People 25 and Over Who Have Completed a Bachelor's Degree and Over (County Level)," 2003; Dowell Myers and Elizabeth Gearin, "Current Preferences for Denser Residential Environments," *Housing Policy Debate* 12, no. 4 (2001), p. 642; Sam Dillon, "Large Urban Suburban Gap Seen in Graduation Rates," *New York Times*, April 22, 2009.

94. Peter Muller, "The Suburban Transformation of the Globalizing American City," *Annals of the American Academy of Political and Social Science* 551, no. 1 (May 1997), pp. 44–58; Jonathan Friedmann, *The Prospect of Cities* (Minneapolis: University of Minnesota Press, 2002), p. 41.

95. Robert Fishman, "America's New City," *Wilson Quarterly*, Winter 1990, p. 28.

96. Thomas Klier and William Testa, "Location Trends of Large Company Headquarters During the 1990s," *Economic Perspectives*, Federal Reserve Bank of Chicago, 2002; Ron Martin and Peter Sunley, "Deconstructing Clusters: Creative Concept or Policy Panacea?" *Journal of Economic Geography* 3 (2003), pp. 5–35.

97. Hongmian Gong and James O. Wheeler, "The Location and Suburbanization of Business and Professional Services in the Atlanta Metropolitan Area," *Growth and Change*, Summer 2002; Ianthe Jeanne Dugan and Robert Frank, "Big Hedge Funds Feel Right at Home in Greenwich, Connecticut," *Wall Street Journal*, August 3, 2004; "Downtowns Versus Edge Cities: Spatial Competition for Jobs in the 1990s," Torto Wheaton Research, March 13, 1997.

98. Robert E. Lang, "Edgeless Cities: Exploring the Elusive Metropolis," *Greater Philadelphia Regional Review*, Summer 2002.

99. Andres Duany, Elizabeth Plater-Zyberk, and Jeff Speck, *Suburban Nation: The Rise of Sprawl and the Decline of the American Dream* (New York: North Point Press, 2000), p. 5; William H. Lucy and David Phillips, "Suburban Decline: The Next Urban Crisis," *Issues in Science and Technology* (Fall 2000).

100. Robert Zur Schmeide, interview by author.

101. Christine Jeffries, interview by author.

102. James Howard Kunstler, "Remarks in Providence," October 19, 2001; James Howard Kunstler, *Home from Nowhere* (New York: Simon & Schuster, 1996), coda; James Howard Kunstler, "Atlanta: Does Edge City Have a Future?" http://www.kunstler.com/excerpt_atlanta.htm.

103. Kris Hudson and Vanessa O'Connell, "Recession Turns Malls into Ghost Towns," *Wall Street Journal*, May 22, 2009.

104. Matt Valley, "The Remalling of America," *National Real Estate Investor*, May 1, 2002; Haya El Nasser, "New Growth Sprouts on USA's Brownfields," *USA Today*, October 6, 2005.

105. Sam Truitt, "Lifestyle Focus: Every Force Evolves a Center," Reis.com, August 11, 2004; Jamie Reno, "Scenes from a Mall: Urban Shopping in Suburbia: Shoppers Can Now Find Downtown in Suburbia," *Newsweek*, December 4, 2006; Thaddeus Herrick, "Fake Towns Rise, Offering Urban Life Without the Grit," *Wall Street Journal*, May 31, 2006; Andrew P. Cohen and Marty Borko, "The Community Mall," *Urban Land*, November–December 2002.

106. Lisa Mascaro, "Revival in the Valley," *Daily News*, May 28, 2005; David Flick, "Burbs, Cities May Be Able to Learn from Each Other," *Dallas Morning News*, February 26, 2005; Joey Bunch and Chuck Plunkett, "Desperate for Downtowns: All Along the Front Range, Communities Are Drafting Plans for a Sense of Identity," *Denver Post*, February 6, 2005.

107. O'Mara, "Uncovering City in Suburb," p. 77.

108. David Fanagel, interview by author.

109. Patricia Leigh Brown, "Megachurches as Minitowns," *New York Times*, May 9, 2002; David Hamer, *New Towns in the New World* (New York: Columbia University Press, 1990), p. 211.

110. J. L. Koch, R. Miller, K. Walesh, and E. Brown, "Historic Survey Measures Social Connections and Civic Involvement in Silicon Valley," Business Wire, March 1, 2001; Jonathan Mahlet, "The Soul of the New Exurb," *New York Times*, March 27, 2005; Jacqueline Trussell, "The Changing Face of Religion: The Suburbanization of the Black Church," BlackandChristian.com, September 8, 2006; Nikita Stewart, "Muslims Find Room to Grow in D.C.'s Outer Suburbs," *Washington Post*, August 1, 2005; "Social Capital Benchmark Survey," National Survey Data, 2000, http://www.cfsv.org/communitysurvey/docs/marginals.pdf; Elizabeth Schwinn, "A Snapshot of Civic Ties," *Chronicle of Philanthropy*, March 8, 2001.

111. Duany, Player-Zybeck, and Speck, *Suburban Nation*, pp. xii, 59.

112. Jane Jacobs, *The Economy of Cities* (New York; Random House, 1969), pp. 163–64; David Hamer, *New Towns in the New World* (New York: Columbia University Press, 1990), p. 211.

113. Robert J. Hughes, "Give Me Discards from Broadway," *Wall Street Journal*, June 17, 2005; Barbara Jepson, "Will a Suburban Outpost Save the Symphony?" *Wall Street Journal*, March 9, 2005; Douglas Tallman, "Montgomery's New Aria," *Gazette*, February 4, 2005.

114. "Geographic and Political Distribution of Arts-Related Jobs in Illinois," Illinois Arts Foundation, March 2003.

115. "A New Angle: Arts Development in the Suburbs," McKnight Foundation, Minneapolis, 2002.

116. Neal Cuthbert, interview by author.

117. Patricia Jones, interview by author.

118. Quoted in Blakely and Snyder, *Fortress America*, p. 12.

119. Ann Forsyth, "Grading the Irvine Ranch," *Planning*, May 2005.

120. Eric Pryne, "Despite Planners' Best Efforts, Many People Choose the Commute," *Seattle Times*, September 10, 2006; Robert Cervero, "Planned Communities, Self Contain-

ment and Commuting: A Cross National Perspective," *Urban Studies* 32, no. 7 (1995), 1135–61.

121. David Bombach, interview by author.

122. "Telework: Part of the Work-Life Balance Equation," *Balancing Act*, Employment Policy Foundation, March 11, 2004; Christopher Rhoads and Sara Silver, "Advances in Technology Make Telecommuting More Feasible," *Wall Street Journal*, December 29, 2005; "Home-based Telework by U.S. Employees Grows by Nearly 40 Percent Since 2001," International Telework Association and Council, September 3, 2004; Rachael King, "Working for Home: It's in the Details," *Business Week*, February 12, 2007.

123. Robert Cervero, "Coping with Complexity in America's Urban Transportation Sector," paper for the second international conference on the Future of Urban Transport, Göteborg, Sweden, September 22–24, 2003.

124. Peter Stearns, *The Industrial Revolution in World History* (Boulder, Colo.: Westview Press, 1998), p. 61.

125. Philippe Ariès, *Centuries of Childhood* (New York: Vintage Books, 1962), p. 351.

CHAPTER FOUR: **THE RESURGENT HEARTLAND**

1. Bill Richards, "Many Rural Regions Growing Again A Reason: Technology," *Wall Street Journal*, November 21, 1994.

2. "When Staying Put Trumps Off Shoring," CNET, December 7, 2004; Mike McPhate, "Indian Call Center Workers Suffer Abuse," *San Francisco Chronicle*, November 17, 2005; Adam Geller, "Offshore to a Small Town," Associated Press, June 21, 2005; Ryan Chittum, "Call Centers Phone Home," *Wall Street Journal*, June 9, 2004; interview with author.

3. Richard Rubin, "Not Far from Forsaken," *New York Times*, April 9, 2006.

4. Andrew Haeg, "Farm Towns Look for Ways to Survive," Minnesota Public Radio, July 10, 2001.

5. Florence Williams, "Frank and Deborah Popper's 'Buffalo Commons' Is Creeping Towards Reality," *High Country News*, January 15, 2001.

6. Deborah Epstein Popper and Frank J. Popper, "The Great Plains: From Dust to Dust," *Planning Magazine*, December 1987.

7. Census data compiled by Praxis Strategy Group. based on Census and Demographia 2000–2008 Metropolitan Area Population & Migration, www.demographia.com.

8. Quoted in Henry Nash Smith, *Virgin Land: The American West as Symbol and Myth* (Cambridge, Mass.: Harvard University Press, 1950), p. 40.

9. *CIA Factbook: 2002*; Samuel R. Staley, "The 'Vanishing Farmland' Myth and the Smart Growth Agenda," Reason Public Policy Institute, January 2000, p. 4. According to "Stop Sprawl: Sierra Club Sprawl Report" (1999): "Sprawl is carving up our farm land, too. Developments are replacing farmers' fields, disrupting small-town agriculture and a way of life. An astounding 70 percent of prime or unique farm land is now in the path of rapid development, according to the American Farmland Trust. While it may sound like parks and open space in America are going, going, gone." The Smart Growth Gateway reads: "Remember back when your town was surrounded by forests, fields, and farms? Ever wonder how that all got turned into parking lots, malls, and office parks?" http://www.smartgrowthgateway.org/local.shtml#openspace.

10. Leslie Whitener, "Policy Options for a Changing Rural America," *Amber Waves* (Economic Research Service, USDA, April 2005).

11. James McDonald, Robert Hoppe, and David Banker, "Growing Farm Size and the Distribution of Commodity Program Payments," *Amber Waves* (Economic Research Service, USDA, February 2005).

12. "Trend Broken or at Least Leveled; the Number of U.S. Farms Increases," *Purdue University News*, February 5, 2009; Andrew Martin, "Farm Life Subsidized by a Job Elsewhere," *New York Times*, February 8, 2009.

13. Carolyn Dimitri and Catherine Greene, "Recent Growth Patterns in the U.S. Organic Foods Market," *Agriculture Information Bulletin*, no. 777 (September 2002).

14. "Organic Production," Economic Research Service, USDA, http://www.ers.usda.gov/Data/Organic/.

15. Nigel Hunt and Brad Dorfman, "How Green Is My Wallet?" Reuters, January 28, 2009.

16. Frederick Merk, *History of the Westward Movement* (New York: Knopf, 1978), p. 565.

17. Steve Mufson, "Oil Price Rise Causes Global Shift in Wealth," *Washington Post*, November 10, 2007; Steven Raabe, "Georgia Gives OK to Wood Alcohol," *Denver Post*, July 3, 2007.

18. Robert D. Perlack et al., "Biomass as Feedstock for a Bioenergy and Bioproducts Industry: The Technical Feasibility of a Billion-ton Annual Supply," Joint Study by the U.S. Department of Energy and the U.S. Department of Agriculture, April 2005.

19. John J. Fialka, "Wildcat Producer Sparks Oil Boom in Montana Plains," *Wall Street Journal*, April 5, 2006; Stephen Power and Ben Casselman, "Quest for Oil: Where to Look Is the Question," *Wall Street Journal*, June 16, 2008.

20. "States Show Sharp Contrasts in Income, Economic Fortunes," *USA Today*, May 4, 2006.

21. April Reese, "The U.S. Is the Saudi Arabia of Wind Power," Beyondfossilfuel.com, July 16, 2008; "Some Tribes Try Their Hands at renewable Energy, but Traditional Energy Sources Hold More Allure Than Ever," *High County News*, April 4, 2003; Leslie Brooks Suzakamo, "Huge Wind-Energy Transmission Line Proposal Gets Mixed Reaction Around the State," Twincities.com, March 8, 2009; Matthew Leiphon, "The Transmission Infrastructure Dilemma," Newgeography.com, November 21, 2008; Kate Galbraith, "Texas Approves a $4.93 Billion Wind Power Project," *New York Times*, July 19, 2008.

22. For an excellent account of this process, see Jared Diamond's description of changes in his native Montana in Diamond, *Collapse: How Societies Choose to Succeed or Fail* (New York: Viking Press, 2005), pp. 56–70.

23. Karl Marx, *The Communist Manifesto*, http://www.marxists.org/archive/marx/works/1848/communist-manifesto/ch01.htm, p. 2.

24. Leo Marx, *The Machine in the Garden: Technology and the Pastoral Ideal of America* (Oxford, U.K.: Oxford University Press, 1964), pp. 124–25; Daniel M. Friedenberg, *Life, Liberty, and the Pursuit of Land* (Buffalo, N.Y.: Prometheus Books, 1992), pp. 177, 199–202.

25. Henry Nash Smith, *Virgin Land: The American West as Symbol and Myth* (Cambridge, Mass.: Harvard University Press, 1950), p. 125; Marx, *Machine in the Garden*, p. 147.

26. Alexis de Tocqueville, *Democracy in America*, trans. Henry Reeve, 2 vols. (New York: Bantam Classic, 2002), vol. 1, p. 213.

27. Jonathan Hughes, *American Economic History* (New York: HarperCollins, 1990), pp. 19, 97, 89; Charles Beard and Mary Beard, *The Rise of American Civilization* (New York: Macmillan, 1930), p. 391.

28. Hughes, *American Economic History*, pp. 161–68, 184.

29. Jon C. Teaford, *Cities of the Heartland: The Rise and Fall of the Industrial Midwest* (Bloomington: Indiana State University Press, 1994), pp. 1–4; Lawrence R. Larsen, "Chicago's Midwest Rivals: Cincinnati, St. Louis and Milwaukee," *Chicago History* 5, no. 3 (Fall 1976), p. 144.

30. Hughes, *American Economic History*, pp. 182–94.
31. Ibid., pp. 194–98.
32. De Tocqueville, *Democracy in America*, vol. 2, p. 684.
33. Beard and Beard, *Rise of American*, p. 2:257.
34. Elwyn B. Robinson, *History of North Dakota* (Lincoln: University of Nebraska Press, 1966), pp. xv, 146.
35. Beard and Beard, *Rise of American*, pp. 2:269, 257.
36. William Appleman Williams, *The Roots of the Modern American Empire: A Study of the Growth and Shaping of Social Consciousness in a Marketplace Society* (New York: Random House, 1969), pp. 204–05; Richard Hofstadter, op. cit., pp. 48–50.
37. Robert E. Pierre, "Homesteading Reborn for a New Generation," *Washington Post*, April 5, 2004.
38. Hughes, *American Economic History*, pp. 285–96.
39. Robinson, *North Dakota*, p. 12.
40. Donald Worster, *Dust Bowl: The Southern Plains in the 1930s* (New York: Oxford University Press, 1979), pp. 35, 185.
41. Hughes, *American Economic History*, pp. 287, 380; Patrick Barta, "Australia Wheat Trade Squeezed by Iraq Scandal," *Wall Street Journal*, March 27, 2006.
42. Elizabeth Becker, "Land Rich in Subsidies, but Poor in Much Else," *New York Times*, January 22, 2002; Dick Lugar, "The Farm Bill Charade," *New York Times*, January 21, 2002; "Farm State Pig Out," *Wall Street Journal*, May 2, 2002.
43. Local businessmen, did not want to use name; interview by author.
44. John Cromartie, "Changing Nonmetro Definitions Affect Population Counts," *Amber Waves* (Economic Research Service, USDA), February 2006; Haya El Nasser and Paul Overberg, "Metro Area 'Fringes' Are Booming," *USA Today*, March 17, 2006.
45. John Herbers, *The New Heartland: America's Flight Beyond the Suburbs and How It's Changing Our Future* (New York: Times Books, 1978), pp. 5–7.
46. Wendell Cox, "United States Metropolitan Area Internal (Domestic) Migration Report: 2000–05," Demographia.com.
47. Candy Evans, "Are Farms the Suburban Future?" Newgeography.com, March 23, 2009; Greg Ramsey, "Community Supported Agriculture and the Return of the Small Farm," Villagehabitat.com, May 19, 2008.
48. Robert Lang, "Open Spaces, Bounded Places: Does the American West's Arid Landscape Yield Dense Metropolitan Growth?" *Housing Policy Debate* 13, no. 4 (2002), p. 759.
49. John Markoff, "Hiding in Plain Sight, Google Seeks More Power," *New York Times*, June 14, 2006; Dave Kolpack, "An Outpost on the Plains," Associated Press, April 2, 2007; "Servers as High as an Elephant's Eye," *Business Week*, June 12, 2006; Jay Kirschenbaum, "A Silicon Valley Is Growing on the Silicon Prairie," *Sioux Falls Argus-Leader*, February 23, 2003; Jim Carlton, "One Tiny Town Becomes an Internet Age Power Point," *Wall Street Journal*, March 7, 2007.
50. Haya Al Nasser, "Life on the Great Plains is Anything but Plain, Simple," *USA Today*, August 13, 2007.
51. Quoted in Matthew Grimm, "The Cloning of Austin, TX," *American Demographics*, July 1, 2004.
52. "Wenatchee's Technology Future Lies in Local Resources," press release, Washington Technology Center, May 25, 2005.
53. Praxis Strategy Group analysis of census trends and BLS job trends; Richard Rathge et al., "Demographic Chartbook: Profiling Change in the Great Plains," prepared for the Great Plains Population symposium, Bismarck, N.D., October 15–17, 2001; Sean Moore,

"Regional Asset Indicators: Tapping the Skills Surplus in Rural America," *The Main Street Economist*, February 2005.

54. Interview with author.

55. William Yardley, "Slump Dashes Oregon Dreams of Californians," *New York Times*, June 18, 2008.

56. Michael Taus, interview by author; "Bend, Oregon, Tech Scene Blowing Up," G5 Search Marketing, http://www.g5searchmarketing.com/blog/?p=122.

57. "Major Market Housing Affordability: United States: 1995–2005," table, Demographia International Housing Affordability Survey, Demographia.com.

58. "Rural America at a Glance, 2005," *Economic Information Bulletin* (USDA), no. 4 (September 2005).

59. "Size Doesn't Matter," *American Demographics*, May 1, 2001.

60. William Frey, conversation with author; Belden Russonello & Stewart, "2004 American Community Survey: National Survey of Communities," October 2004, p. 3; Michael Morin and Paul Taylor, "Suburbs Not Most Popular, but Suburbanites Most Content," *Pew Research Center*, February 26, 2008.

61. Belden Russonello & Stewart, "2004 American Community Survey," p. 3; "Perceptions of Rural America," W. K. Kellogg Foundation, n.d., pp. 1, 5.

62. Jim Sylvester, "The Migration Behavior of Great Plains Residents," Bureau of Business and Economic Research, University of Montana-Missoula, April 12, 2002.

63. Interview with author.

64. William Frey, "America's Emerging Demography: Immigration, Migration and the Aging of the Population," Presentation to *America's Americans: The Populations of The United States of America*, a two-day conference organized by the Institute for the Study of the Americas and the British, Library Eccles Centre, 8–9 May 2006, British Library Conference Centre.

65. Mark Houser, "Hispanic Heartland," Pittsburgh Tribune Review, November 20, 2005; Leif Jensen, "New Immigrant Settlements in Rural America: Problems, Prospects and Policies," *Carsey Institute Reports on Rural America* 1, no. 3 (2006).

66. "When State's Educated Young Adults Move Out, Immigrants Move In," Associated Press, March 22, 2004; "Rural America at a Glance, 2005," *Economic Information Bulletin* (USDA), no. 4 (September 2005).

67. Nancy McArdle, "Outward Bound: The Decentralization of Population and Employment," Joint Center for Housing Studies, Harvard University, July 1999, p. 20.

68. Gerald A. Carlino, "From Centralization to Deconcentration: People and Jobs Spread Out," Federal Reserve Bank of Philadelphia, November-December 2000, p. 19.

69. Analysis of BLS numbers by Mark Schill, Praxis Strategy Group, 2008.

70. Michael Shires, "The New Boomtowns," *Inc.*, May 2006.

71. Ibid. Such micropolitan areas are experiencing some of the country's fastest job growth. *Inc.* magazine's analysis of the 393 fastest-growing regions in the country found that 15 of the top 20 were micropolitan, while only one—sprawling Las Vegas—ranked among the country's largest metros.

72. Donghwan An, Peter Gordon, and Harry W. Richardson, "The Continued Decentralization of People and Jobs in the United States," paper presented at the 41st annual meeting of the Western Regional Science Association, Monterey, Calif., February 17–20, 2002, pp. 50–57; McArdle, "Outward Bound," pp. 12–13; Annette Steinacker, "Economic Restructuring of Cities, Suburbs and Non-metropolitan Areas, 1977–1992," *Urban Affairs Review*, November 1998.

73. Herbers, *New Heartland*, pp. 151–52; McArdle, "Outward Bound," p. 12.

74. Richard Deitz and James Orr, "A Leaner, More Skilled U.S. Manufacturing Workforce," *Current Issues in Economics and Finance*, February-March 2006; Mark Trumbull, "America's Midsized, 'Inner Sunbelt' Cities Growth," *Christian Science Monitor*, July 11, 2007.

75. Donnelle Eller, "More Jobs Lift Outlook for Three Cities," *Des Moines Register*, January 7, 2007.

76. Interview with author.

77. Sam McMahon, interview by author.

78. Amy Zuckerman, "Hidden Tech: Move Over, Silicon Valley. Wenatchee, Washington Is About to Steal Your Thunder," *Red Herring*, February 5, 2004.

79. Quoted in Amy Zuckerman, "Hidden Tech: On the Trail of the Pioneer Valley's Low-Profile High Technology Community," *Boston Globe Magazine*, February 10, 2002.

80. Sean Moore, "Regional Asset Indicators: Tapping the Skills Surplus in Rural America," *Main Street Economist*, February 2005.

81. Donnelle Eller, "High Tech Workers Abound in Iowa. Why Aren't Workers Filling Them?" *Des Moines Register*, February 12, 2007; "National Center for Higher Education Management Systems Information Center for Higher Education Policymaking and Analysis," http://www.higheredinfo.org/; "Mortenson Seminar on Public Policy Analysis of Opportunity for Postsecondary Education," http://www.postsecondary.org.

82. Moore, "Regional Asset Indicators."

83. Mark Swanson, interview by author; Doug McDonald; "Paper to Paperless: Realigning the Stars," Newgeography.com, September 9, 2008.

84. Scott Thurm, "Toll of Tech Bust Has Been Severe, Survey Shows," *Wall Street Journal*, October 8, 2004; Sherri Cruz, "Twin Cities Lose Cost Edge as Location for Tech Firms," *Minneapolis Star Tribune*, January 19, 2002.

85. Mark Weinraub, "U.S. Rural Economy Holds Fast in Recession," Reuters, March 17, 2009.

86. Ellen McCarthy, "Mining Coal County for Tech Workers," *Washington Post*, January 2, 2006; Scott Thurm, "Toll of Tech Bust in California Has Been Severe, Survey Shows," *Wall Street Journal*, October 8, 2004.

87. M. Leanne Lachman, "The New Exports: Office Jobs," Paul Milstein Center for Real Estate at Columbia Business School and Urban Land Institute, 2008.

88. Erin White, "A Cheaper Alternative to Outsourcing," *Wall Street Journal*, April 10, 2006; "Kempthone Celebrates the Opening of Dell Computer's Tech Support Center," press release, Dell Computer Corporation, February 21, 2002.

89. "Outsourcing to Arkansas," CNET News, November 11, 2004.

90. John Larkin, "India's Talent Pool Drying Up," *Wall Street Journal*, January 4, 2006.

91. Jason Crawforth, interview by author.

92. Mark Singer, "True North," *New Yorker*, February 26, 2002.

93. Carole Burgum, interview by author.

94. Elizabeth Stevenson, *The Park Maker: A Life of Frederick Law Olmsted* (New York: Macmillan, 1977), p. 298.

95. Brad Carlson, "Boise's Urban Renewal Agency Develops Series of Buildings on Front Street," *Idaho Business Review*, August 23, 2004.

96. Patricia Leigh Brown, "If This Is the Swap Meet, Then It Must Be Monday," *New York Times*, April 28, 2002; Patrick O'Driscoll, "Sioux Falls Powers South Dakota's Growth," *USA Today*, March 12, 2001.

97. "America the Creative," *Economist*, December 19, 2006.

98. Frederick Jackson Turner, *The Significance of the Frontier in American History* (New York: Frederick Ungar, 1963), p. 57.

CHAPTER FIVE: POST-ETHNIC AMERICA

1. Interview with author.
2. David A. Hollinger, *Post-ethnic America: Beyond Multiculturalism* (New York: Basic Books, 2000), p. 3.
3. Jeremy Rifkin, *The European Dream: How Europe's Vision of the Future Is Quietly Eclipsing the American Dream* (New York: Penguin, 2004), pp. 256–57.
4. Nina Bernstein, "Record Immigration Is Changing the Face of New York Neighborhoods," *New York Times*, January 24, 2005.
5. Ibid.; Gregory Korte, "Can Immigrants Save a City?" *Cincinnati Enquirer*, April 13, 2006.
6. Marjorie Valbrun, "New Blood: A Wave of Refugees Lubricates the Economy of Rusty Utica, New York," *Wall Street Journal*, March 8, 1999; Chinki Sinha, "Bosnians Find a Place to Worship," *Utica Observer-Dispatch*, December 20, 2007; Paul Zielbauer, "Looking to Prosper as a Melting Pot; Utica Long in Decline, Welcomes an Influx of Refugees," *New York Times*, May 7, 1999.
7. Ron Takaki, *A Different Mirror: A History of Multicultural America* (Boston: Little, Brown, 1993), p. 418; Thomas Sowell, *Preferential Policies: An International Perspective* (New York: William Morrow, 1990), p. 141; Steven Lee Myers, "In Anti-Immigrant Mood, Russia Heeds Gadfly's Call," *New York Times*, October 22, 2006.
8. Flemming Rose, "Europe's Politics of Victomology," *Real Clear Politics*, May 27, 2006; Peter Marcuse and Ronald van Kempen, "Conclusion: A Changed Spatial Order," in Marcuse and van Kempen, eds., *Globalizing Cities: A New Spatial Order?* (London: Blackwell, 2000), p. 261.
9. Stefan Theil, "Idle by Law," *Newsweek*, Atlantic Edition, August 13, 2001; Christopher Caldwell, "A Swedish Dilemma" *Weekly Standard*, February 8, 2005; Christopher Caldwell, "Islam on the Outskirts of the Welfare State," February 5, 2006; Ben Feller, "U.S. Immigrants Lag in School, but Gaps Are Bigger in Other Nations," Associated Press, May 15, 2006.
10. Haeyoun Park, "Recession's Toll on Hispanic Immigrants," *New York Times*, March 22, 2009; Steven A. Camarota, "Unemployment for Immigrants and the U.S. Born: Picture Bleak for Less Educated Black and Hispanic Americans," Center for Immigration Studies, February 2009.
11. Farrukh Dhondy, "An Islamic Fifth Column," *Wall Street Journal*, December 26, 2001.
12. Grace Sung, "Ageing Europe Forced to Open Door to Immigrants," *Straits Times*, March 3, 2004; Rüdiger Falksohn et al., "What's Wrong with Europe," *Der Spiegel*, November 7, 2005; "The Enemy Within," *Economist*, July 16, 2005.
13. Xavier de Souza Briggs, "'Some of My Best Friends Are . . .': Interracial Friendships, Class, and Segregation in America," *City & Community* 6 , no. 4 (2007), p. 274.
14. Reed Ueda, "The Permanently Unfinished Country," Worldandi.com, October 1992.
15. "Signs of Increased Social Tension," *Economist Intelligence Unit*, March 7, 2007.
16. Irshad Manji, "Muslim Melting Pot," *Wall Street Journal*, June 4, 2007; Neil MacFarquhar, "Pakistanis Find U.S. an Easier Fit Than Britain," *New York Times*, August 21, 2006; Haya El Nasser, "American Muslims Reject Extremes," *USA Today*, May 23, 2007; Marie Valla, "France Seeks Path to Workplace Diversity," *Wall Street Journal*, January 3, 2007.
17. "New Citizenships," Nationmaster.com, February 27, 2006; "Citizenship Applications Soar Since 9-11," *Los Angeles Daily News*, July 17, 2002.
18. Frédéric Docquier and Abdeslam Marfouk, "Measuring the International Mobility of Skilled Workers 1990–2000," World Bank, n.d.

19. Department of City Planning, New York; Julia Chaplin, "The New Eurofestation," *New York Times*, December 8, 2002.

20. Jeff Chu, "How to Plug Europe's Brain Drain," *Time Europe*, January 19, 2004; William Broad, "U.S. Is Losing Its Dominance in the Sciences," *New York Times*, May 3, 2004; Mark Landler, "Germany Agonizes Over Brain Drain," *New York Times*, February 6, 2007.

21. U.S. Census 2005; for example, an editor at a New York Polish newspaper estimated the illegal Polish population at one-fifth the total for the entire metropolitan area, or roughly 250,000.

22. Julia Chaplin, "The New Eurofestation," *New York Times*, December 8, 2002.

23. Nick Fraser, "The New Americans," BBC News, April 2, 2004; Sam Roberts, "In a Generation, Minorities May Be the U.S. Majority," *New York Times*, August 14, 2008.

24. "Into the Suburbs," *Economist*, March 11, 2004.

25. Anne-Marie O'Connor, "Learning to Look Past Race," *Los Angeles Times*, January 25, 1999; D'Vera Cohn and Tara Bahrampour, "Of U.S. Children Under 5, Nearly Half Are Minorities," *Washington Post*, May 10, 2006; Roberts, "In a Generation."

26. Ruben G. Rubaut, "Origins and Destinies: Immigration to the United States Since World War II," *Sociological Forum* 9, no. 4 (December 1994).

27. Leslie Casimir, "In America, Nigerians' Education Pursuit Is Above Rest," *Houston Chronicle*, May 20, 2008.

28. Eli Lehrer, "We Want to Depend on Ourselves," *American Enterprise*, November–December 1998; Genero C. Armas, "Cultural Divide Seen in Black Groups," Associated Press, May 9, 2003.

29. Interview and conversations over years with author.

30. John F. Burns, "Top Anglican Seeks a Role for Islamic Law in Britain," *New York Times*, February 8, 2008.

31. Irshad Manji, "Muslim Melting Pot," *Wall Street Journal*, June 4, 2007.

32. Cary Wintz, "Blacks in Houston Today," online, April 9, 2006, Houstonhistory.com.

33. Quoted in Edward Hegstrom, "In Houston, Money Spoke Louder Than Parks," *Houston Chronicle*, October 26, 2005.

34. Patricia Everidge Hill, *Dallas: The Making of a Modern City* (Austin: University of Texas Press, 1996), pp. x–13, 170; Carolyn Brown and David A. Padgett, "What's Your Favorite U.S. City?" *Black Enterprise*, July 2004.

35. Janny Scott, "Census Finds Immigrants Lower City's Income Data," *New York Times*, August 6, 2002; Steven A. Camorata, "Immigration From Mexico," Center for Immigration Studies, July 2001; "Wage Gaps Between Racial and Ethnic Groups Are Not Diminishing," research brief, Public Policy Institute of California, May 2003; George J. Borjas, "For a Few Dollars Less," April 18, 2006; John R. Logan, "Regional Divisions Dampen 90s Prosperity," Lewis Mumford Center for Comparative Urban and Regional Research, Albany, N.Y., June 5, 2002.

36. Peter D. Salins, *Assimilation American Style* (New York: Basic Books, 1997), p. 193; Ron Takaki, *A Different Mirror: A History of Multicultural America* (Boston: Little, Brown, 1993), p. 415; John R. Logan, "New York: Racial and Ethnic Segregation," in Peter Marcuse and Ronald van Kempen, eds., *Globalizing Cities: A New Spatial Order* (London: Blackwell, 2000), pp. 159–63; Bridget Johnson, "Loaded Rhetoric Harms Immigrant Movement," *USA Today*, May 3, 2006.

37. Joe Matthews, "Immigrant Education Gap Could Be Closing," *Los Angeles Times*, December 5, 2002; George J. Borjas, "Homeownership in the Immigrant Population," Mortgage Bankers Association, March 2002; Douglas Besharov, "The Rio Grande Rises," *New York Times*, October 1, 2007.

38. "A World of Opportunity," Center for an Urban Future, February 2007, p. 4.

39. Gary Shteyngart, "The New Two Way Street," in Tamar Jacoby, ed., *Reinventing the Melting Pot: The New Immigrants and What It Means to Be American* (New York: Basic Books, 2003), pp. 258–59.

40. Peter D. Salins, *Assimilation American Style* (New York: Basic Books, 1997), pp. 19, 24–25.

41. Hughes, *American Economic History*, pp. 103–5; Tamar Jacoby, "What It Means to Be American in the 21st Century," in Jacoby, ed., *Reinventing the Melting Pot*, p. 273; William V. Shannon, *The American Irish* (New York: Macmillan, 1966), p. 37.

42. Sven Beckert, *The Monied Metropolis: New York City and the Consolidation of the American Bourgeoisie, 1850–1896* (Cambridge, U.K.: Cambridge University Press, 2001), p. 65.

43. Hughes, *American Economic History*, pp. 312–16; J. W. Gregory, *Human Migration and the Future: A Study of the Causes, Effects and Control of Emigration* (Philadelphia: J. B. Lippincott, 1928), pp. 27–28; Caroline Golab, *Immigrant Destinations* (Philadelphia: Temple University Press, 1977), p. 11.

44. H. Brett Melendy, *The Oriental Americans* (New York: Hippocrene Books, 1972), pp. 120–22; Thomas J. Archdeacon, *Becoming American: An Ethnic History* (New York: Collier Macmillan, 1983), p. 162.

45. Richard Hofstadter, *Social Darwinism in American Thought* (Boston: Beacon Press, 1992), pp. 177–89.

46. Quoted in Maurice C. Davie, *World Immigration, with Special Reference to the United States* (New York: Macmillan, 1936), p. 237.

47. Irving Howe, *World of Our Fathers* (New York: Harcourt Brace Jovanovich, 1976), pp. 406–7; Randolph Quirk, *The English Language and Images of Matter* (London: Oxford University Press, 1972), pp. 32–33; Henry James, *The American Scene* (Bloomington: Indiana University Press, 1969), p. 132.

48. Daniel Hata and Nadine Hata, "Indispensable Scapegoats: Asians and Pacific Islanders in Pre-1945 Los Angeles," in Martin Schiesl and Mark M. Dodge, eds., *City of Promise: Race and Historical Change in Los Angeles* (Claremont, Calif.: Regina Books, 2006), pp. 41–44.

49. Melendy, *Oriental Americans*, p. 121.

50. M. B. Starr, *The Coming Struggle, or What People on the Pacific Coast Think of the Coolie Invasion* (San Francisco: Bacon & Co., 1873), p. 20.

51. Gloria Miranda, "Mexican Immigrant Families: Cultural Conflict, Sociological Survival and the Formation of Community in Los Angeles 1900–1954," in City of Promise: Race and Historical Change in Los Angeles, Martin Schiesl and Mark M. Dodge, eds., (Claremont, Calif.: Regina Books, 2006), pp. 12–21.

52. Philippe Legrain, *Immigrants: Your Country Needs Them* (Princeton, N.J.: Princeton University Press, 2006), p. 55.

53. "Public's View of Immigration," Center for Immigration Studies," November 2006; "Poll: Immigration a Growing Public Concern," Associated Press, April 9, 2006.

54. Victor Davis Hanson, "Do We Want Mexifornia?" *City Journal*, Spring 2002.

55. Pat Buchanan, *The Death of the West: How Dying Populations and Immigrant Invasions Imperil Our Country and Civilization* (New York: Thomas Dunne Books, 2002), pp. 3, 12.

56. Samuel P. Huntington, *The Clash of Civilizations: Remaking of World Order* (New York: Simon & Schuster, 1996), pp. 204–6. Toward the end of his career the late historian Arthur Schlesinger expressed fears that immigrants would stoke "a cult of ethnicity" that would threaten continued "national integration." A similar danger was identified by former Colorado governor Richard Lamm, who in the early 1980s denounced immigration both on environmental grounds and as a threat to "American culture."

57. Morley Winograd and Michael D. Hais, *Millennial Makeover: MySpace, YouTube and the Future of American Politics* (New Brunswick, N.J.: Rutgers University Press, 2008), p. 95; Julia Preston, "Poll Surveys Ethnic Views Among Chief Minorities," *New York Times*, December 13, 2007.

58. Gregory Rodriguez, "Mexican Americans Are Building No Walls," *Los Angeles Times*, February 29, 2004; Eduardo Porter, "Army's Hispanic-Recruitment Ads Cater to Mom," *Wall Street Journal*, May 24, 2002.

59. Quoted in Rowland Tappan Berthoff, *British Immigrants in Industrial America, 1790–1950* (New York: Russell & Russell, 1953), pp. 123, 137–40.

60. Lisa A. Keister, "Upward Wealth Mobility: Exploring the Roman Catholic Advantage," *Social Force* 85, no. 3 (March 2007); "U.S. Census Shows Euro-Americans Losing Their Identity," *Canadian Press*, June 7, 2002.

61. "U.S. Census Shows Euro-Americans."

62. Robert C. Christopher, *Crashing the Gates: The De-Wasping of America and the Rise of the New Power Elite in Politics, Business, Education, Entertainment and the Media* (New York: Simon & Schuster, 1989), pp. 51–53.

63. Michael Barone, *The New Americans: How the Melting Pot Can Work Again* (Washington, D.C.: Regnery, 2001), pp. 132, 148.

64. Roger Daniels, *Asian America: Chinese and Japanese in the United States Since 1850* (Seattle: University of Washington Press, 1988), p. 77.

65. Thomas Muller, *Immigrants and the American City* (New York: Twentieth Century Fund, 1993), pp. 86–87.

66. Howe, *World of Our Fathers*, pp. 59, 139, 165.

67. "Asian-Owned Biz Booming in U.S.," Rediff.com, May 17, 2006.

68. Stuart Anderson and Michaela Platzer, "American Made: The Impact of Immigrant Entrepreneurs on U.S. Competitiveness," National Foundation for American Policy, 2007.

69. Ariana Eunjung Cha and Ken McLaughlin, "Diversity Hits Home," *San Jose Mercury*, May 13, 1999.

70. "Silicon Valley Mentorship Program Aims to Build Future High-tech Leaders," *Asia Week*, November 23, 2008.

71. John Tu, interview by author.

72. Marguerite Johnston, *Houston: The Unknown City* (College Station: Texas A&M Press, 1991), p. 37; David G. McComb, *Houston: A History* (Austin: University of Texas Press, 1981), pp. 171–72; Arnoldo de Leon, *Ethnicity in the Sunbelt: Mexican Americans in Houston* (College Station: Texas A&M Press, 2001), pp. 250–51.

73. "Mexicos Cultural Landscapes: A Conversation with Carlos Monsivais," *Journal of American History* 86 (September 1999), p. 620; Jonathan Kandell, "Mexico's Megalopolis," in Gilbert M. Joseph and Mark D. Szuchman, eds., *I Saw a City Invincible: Urban Portraits of Latin America* (Wilmington, Del.: SR Books, 1997), p. 183.

74. Robert W. Fairlie and Bruce D. Meyer, "Ethnic and Racial Self-Employment: Differences and Possible Explanations," *Journal of Human Resources* (September 1996); Jonathan Bowles with Tara Colton, "A World of Opportunity," Center for an Urban Future, February 2007.

75. "Immigrants Fueling Job Growth in U.S. Inner Cities," Initiative for a Competitive Inner City, November 15, 2005; Edward Iwata, "Study Shows Immigrants' Real 'Engine' for Growth: Highly Skilled Immigrants Create 'Enclave' Economies," *USA Today*, Feb 7, 2006.

76. Joel Millman and Will Pinkston, "Mexicans Transform a Town in Georgia," *Wall Street Journal*, August 30, 2001.

77. Daniels, *Asian America*, p. 321.

78. Javier Reyes, interview by author.
79. Jeffrey M. Humphreys, "The Multicultural Economy 2003," Selig Center for Economic Growth, Terry College of Business, University of Georgia, 2003.
80. "Serving Diverse Taste Buds," *Houston Chronicle*, December 31, 2006.
81. Teresa Bouza and Gabriel Sama, "America Adds Salsa to Its Burgers and Fries," *Wall Street Journal*, January 2, 2003.
82. David Schwartz, "Bok Choy: Southland Farmers Cash in on Asian Staple," *Los Angeles Daily News*, September 14, 2004; Candice Choi, "Customers Opting for Ethnic Markets' Tailored Offerings," *Daily News*, August 17, 2004; Debbie Howell, "Vertical Food Formats Begin to Reveal Viability," *DSN Retailing Today*, March 24, 2003; Julie Jargon, "General Mills Tries to Persuade Americans to Cook Chinese," *Wall Street Journal*, May 29, 2007.
83. José Cárdenas, interview by author.
84. Jesus Cárdenas, interview by author.
85. Jargon, "General Mills Tries to Persuade Americans."
86. Andrew Cherng, interview by author; Jerry Hirsch, "Chinese Fast-Food Chain Panda Express Thrives on Orange Chicken," *Los Angeles Times*, August 13, 2008.
87. Sarah Filius, "What's Black and White and Ready to Get Fancy," *Los Angeles Business Journal*, August 13, 2007.
88. Eric Schmitt. "Whites in Minority in Largest Cities, the Census Shows," *New York Times*, April 1, 2001.
89. Daniels, *Asian America*, p. 173; "Racial Changes in the Nation's Large Cities," Brookings Institution, April 2001.
90. Gloria Miranda, "Mexican Immigrant Families: Cultural Conflict, Sociological Survival and the Formation of Community in Los Angeles, 1900–1954," in Martin Schiesl and Mark M. Dodge, eds., *City of Promise: Race and Historical Change in Los Angeles* (Claremont, Calif.: Regina Books, 2006), pp. 33–34.
91. Sam Roberts, "In Shift, 40% of Immigrants Move Directly to Suburbs," *New York Times*, October 17, 2007; Beth Barrett, "Immigrant Population Balloons in the Valley," *Daily News*, August 28, 2008.
92. William H. Frey, "Melting Pot Moves to the Suburbs," *Newsday*, August 4, 1999; E. Michael Jones, *The Slaughter of Cities: Urban Renewal as Ethnic Cleansing* (South Bend, Ind.: St. Augustine's Press, 2003), pp. 424–528; Suzanne Wasserman, "Déjà Vu: Replanning in the Lower East Side in the 1930s," in Janet Abu-Lughod et al., ed., *From Urban Village to East Village: The Battle for New York's Lower East Side* (London: Blackwell, 1994), p. 102; Albert Saiz, "Immigration and Real Estate Markets," *Wharton Real Estate Review*, Fall 2006, p. 67.
93. "Into the Suburbs," *Economist*, March 11, 2004; Antonio Olivio and Oscar Avila, "Latinos Choosing Suburbs Over City," *Chicago Tribune*, November 1, 2005; Diane Wedner, "Back to the 'Burbs," *Los Angeles Times*, January 29, 2006; Audrey Singer et al., "The World in a Zip Code: Greater Washington, D.C. as a New Region of Immigration," Center on Urban and Metropolitan Policy, Brookings Institution, April 2001; William H. Frey, "Melting Pot Suburbs: A Census 2000 Study of Suburban Diversity," Center on Urban and Metropolitan Policy, Brookings Institution, June 2001; Mike Swift, "Other Tongues Overtaking English as Language Spoken in Majority of Santa Clara Homes," *San Jose Mercury News*, March 2, 2007; Beth Barrett, "Immigrant Population Balloons in California's San Fernando Valley," *Los Angeles Daily News*, August 28, 2002.
94. Juliet Eilperin, "Immigration Issue Sparks Battle at Sierra Club," *Washington Post*, March 22, 2004.

95. Tamar Jacoby, "Assimilation: A Progress Report," p. xxvii; Audrey Singer, "The Rise of New Immigrant Gateways," Brookings Institution, February 2004; Mary Lou Pickel and Megan Clarke, *Atlanta Journal-Constitution*, August 9, 2007; Haya El Nasser, "Asian Immigrants Changing the Makeup of the South," *USA Today*, May 19, 1998; Jonathan Kaufman, "America's Heartland Turns to Hot Location for the Melting Pot," *Wall Street Journal*, October 15, 1995.

96. "Into the Suburbs," *Economist*, March 11, 2004; Nicole Stelle Garnett, "Suburbs as Exit, Suburbs as Entrance," *Michigan Law* Review 106 (November 2007), p. 17.

97. Garnett, "Suburbs as Exit," p. 12.

98. Ayse Pamuk, "Immigrant Clusters and Homeownership in Global Metropolises: Suburbanization Trends in San Francisco, Los Angeles and New York," Institute of Urban and Regional Development, University of California at Berkeley, 2004.

99. Robin Fields and Erin Texeira, "White Flight Is Giving Way to Civic Diversity," *Los Angeles Times*, May 20, 2001; Jon Teaford, *The American Suburb: The Basics* (New York: Routledge, 2008), p. 83; Allie Shah, "In Blaine, a Global Village," *Minneapolis Star-Tribune*, June 18, 2007.

100. Frey, "Melting Pot Suburbs."

101. Lori Rodriguez, "Language Barriers," *Houston Chronicle*, September 18, 2006; K. Anthony Appiah, "The Multiculturalist Misunderstanding," *New York Review of Books*, October 9, 1997; Tyler Cowen and Daniel M. Rothschild, "Latinos Really Do Succeed at Moving Up, Blending In," *Houston Chronicle*, July 6, 2006; Leon Lazaroff, "English Enters into Media for Latinos," *Chicago Tribune*, August 5, 2005; Shirin Hakimzadeh and D'Vera Cohen, "English Usage Among Hispanics in the United States," Pew Hispanic Center, 2007; Julia Preston, "Latino Immigrants Children Found Grasping English," *New York Times*, November 30, 2007.

102. "Once More, with Feeling: Latino Voters Watch English-Language TV," Pineda Consilating, June 16, 2006.

103. Quoted in Gregory Rodriguez, "The Overwhelming Allure of English," *New York Times*, April 7, 2002.

104. Phillip Longman, address to the Long Now Foundation, San Francisco, August 13, 2004; Sam Roberts, "What's in a Name? For Hispanics, a Generational Shift," *New York Times*, May 29, 2009.

105. Rodriguez, "Overwhelming Allure of English"; Haya El Nasser, "U.S.-born Hispanics Propel Growth," *USA Today*, May 10, 2006.

106. Brent Staples, "Why Race Isn't as 'Black' and 'White' as We Think," *New York Times*, October 31, 2005; Emma Daly, "DNA Tells Students Who They Aren't," *New York Times*, April 13, 2005; Jennifer Lee and Frank D. Bean, "America's Changing Color Lines: Immigration, Race/Ethnicity, and Multiracial Identification," *Annual Review of Sociology* 30 (August 2004), pp. 221–42; Mireya Navarro, "Who Are We? New Dialogue on Mixed Race," *New York Times*, March 31, 2008; Hope Yen, "Multiracial People Become Fastest Growing U.S. Group," Associated Press, May 28, 2009.

107. Hollinger, *Post-ethnic America*, p. 233; Arthur Schlesinger, *The Disuniting of America: Reflections on a Multicultural Society* (New York: Norton, 1992), p. 133; Legrain, *Immigrants: Your Country Needs Them*, p. 243; Ben Stocking, "Hope for Greater Unity Increases: Mixed-race Births Could Make Old Divisions Obsolete," *San Jose Mercury News*, May 13, 1999.

108. Thomas Tseng, interview by author; Mike Swift, "Other Tongues Overtaking English as Language Spoken in Majority of Santa Clara Homes," *San Jose Mercury*, March 4, 2007.

109. Jonathan Birtchell, "Hip Operator of Cultured Taste," *Financial Times*, August 1, 2007.

110. Greg Ip, "Blacks Trail in Growth of Income," *Wall Street Journal*, November 12, 2007.

111. Ellis Close, *The Rage of a Privileged Class: Why Do Prosperous Blacks Still Have the Blues?* (New York: HarperCollins, 1993), p. 163.

112. Quoted in Howe, *World of Our Fathers*, p. 407.

113. Roman Ghishman, *Iran,* Penguin (New York: 1954) pp. 208–9.

114. Edward Gibbon, *The Decline and Fall of the Roman Empire,* Modern Library, (New York: 1931) vol. 1, p. 33; G. W. Bowerstock, "The Dissolution of the Roman Empire," in Norman Yoffee and George L. Cowgill, eds., *The Collapse of Ancient States and Civilizations* (Tucson: University of Arizona Press, 1988), p. 169; Michael Grant, *Ancient Mediterranean* (New York: Scribner's, 1959), pp. 297–99; Richard P. Saller, "Roman Class Structures and Relations," in Michael Grant and Rachel Kitzinger, eds., *Civilization of the Ancient Mediterranean: Greece and Rome* (New York: Charles Scribner's Sons, 1988), p. 569; Muller, *Immigrants and the American City,* p. 218.

115. Gunnar Myrdal, *An American Dilemma: The Negro Problem and Modern Democracy* (New York: Harper & Row, 1962), pp. 3–5.

116. Shannon, *American Irish,* pp. 179–80.

117. Louise Story, "Seeking Leaders, U.S. Companies Think Globally," *New York Times,* December 12, 2007.

118. John F. Kennedy, *Immigrants* (New York: Harper & Row, 1964), p. 3; from preface of Walt Whitman, "Leaves of Grass," 1855.

CHAPTER SIX: THE 21ST-CENTURY COMMUNITY

1. Ellen Moncure, e-mail to author, June 15, 2008.

2. Gabrielle Birknew, "Renovations Follow Families to Victorian Flatbush," *New York Sun,* September 21, 2006.

3. "Defining America: Why the U.S. Is Unique," *USA Today,* July 4, 2004.

4. "The Internet's Growing Role in Life's Major Moments," Pew Internet and American Life Project, April 19, 2006; Mary Macdden and Susannah Fox, "Riding the Waves of Web 2.0," Pew Internet Project, October 5, 2006; Keith Hampton and Barry Wellman, "Neighboring in Netville: How the Internet Supports Community and Social Capital in a Wired Suburb," *City and Community* 2, no. 4 (December 2003), p. 284.

5. Michael Winerip, "Helping Families Right Where They Live," *New York Times,* July 27, 2008, Newark Family Success Centers, Newarkfamilysuccess.org, March 28, 2009.

6. Alan and Michelle Shaw, "Social Empowerment through Community Networks," in Donald A. Schon, Bish Sanyal, and William Mitchell, eds., *High Technology and Low Income Communities* (Cambridge, Mass.: MIT Press, 1999), pp. 328–33.

7. Hampton and Wellman, "Neighboring in Netville," pp. 286, 301.

8. Phillip Longman, address to the Long Now Foundation, San Francisco, August 13, 2004; "Half a Billion Americans," *Economist,* December 22, 2002.

9. Allison Stein Wellner, "The Mobility Myth," *Reason,* April 2006.

10. Robert Putnam, *Bowling Alone: The Collapse and Revival of American Community* (New York: Simon & Schuster, 2000), p. 200; "The Glue of Society," *Economist,* July 16, 2005, pp. 25–27.

11. "Moving Rates Lowest in 50+ Years," U.S. Census Bureau, March 23, 2004; Sam Roberts, "Data Show Steady Drop in Americans on Move," *New York Times,* December 21, 2008; "Corporate Relocation Survey 2009," http://www.atlasworldgroup.com/survey.

12. Wendell Cox, "Special Report: Domestic Migration Bubble and Widening Dispersion: New Metropolitan Area Estimates," Newgeography.com, March 25, 2009; Susan Chan-

dler, "Economy Influences the Decision to Have Babies," *Chicago Tribune*, December 23, 2008.

13. Stephanie Coontz, *The Way We Never Were: American Families and the Nostalgia Trap* (New York: Basic Books, 1992), pp. xiv, 15; Stephanie Coontz, "The American Family and the Nostalgia Trap," *Phi Beta Kappan*, March 2005; "More Americans Staying Put," U.S. Census Bureau, March 23, 2004; D'Vera Cohn and Rich Morin, "Who Moves? Who Stays Put? Where's Home?" Pew Research Center, December 17, 2008; Sharon Jayson, "When It Comes to Family, There's No Place Like Your Hometown," *USA Today*, December 18, 2008.

14. Gail Rosenblum, "For Single Women, Right Now Trumps Mr. Right," *Minneapolis Star-Tribune*, February 4, 2007; Sam Roberts, "To Be Married Means to Be Outnumbered," *New York Times*, October 15, 2006.

15. Laura Vanderham, "Do Smart Girls Finish Last in Love?" *USA Today*, October 18, 2006.

16. Mary Engel, "Moms Over 40 a Risky Trend," *Los Angeles Times*, December 3, 2007; Darragh Worland, "Egg Freezing May Offer Fertility Freedom," Fox.com, April 9, 2005; Salynn Boyles, "After 44, Fertility Successes Are Few," Fox.com, August 26, 2005; "More IVF Keeps the Birth Rate Up," *New Scientist*, April 7, 2007; Sharon Jackson, "Society Switches Focus Away from Children," *USA Today*, July 12, 2006.

17. William Frey, "Married with Children," *American Demographics*, March 1, 2003.

18. Eugene Kennedy and Sara Charles, M.D., *Authority: The Most Misunderstood Idea in America* (New York: Free Press, 1997), p. 53; Phillip Longman, "The Return of Patriarchy," *Foreign Policy*, March-April 2006.

19. Coontz, *The Way We Never Were*, p. xiv.

20. Jane Jacobs, *Dark Age Ahead* (New York: Random House, 2004), pp. 28–29.

21. Francis Fukuyama. *The End of History and the Last Man* (New York: Free Press, 1992), p. 324; Caroline Bledsoe, Susana Lerner, and Jane I. Guyer, eds., *Fertility and the Male Life-Cycle in the Era of Fertility Decline* (New York: Oxford University Press, 2000); Wellner, "Mobility Myth."

22. William J. Bennett, "Quantifying America's Decline," *Wall Street Journal*, March 15, 1993.

23. "Child Well-Being in Rich Countries: A Summary Table," UNICEF Innocenti Research Center, 2007; Janet C. Gornick, Alexandra Heron, and Ross Eisenbrey, "The Work-Family Balance: An Analysis of European, Japanese and U.S. Work-Time Policies," Economic Policy Institute, May 24, 2007.

24. Sheila Dewan, "Cities Compete in Hipness Battle to Attract Young," *New York Times*, November 25, 2006; Laura Vanderkam, "Cities Covet Young Urban Single Professionals," *USA Today*, December 16, 2003.

25. Peter Calthorpe, *The Next American Metropolis: Ecology, Community and the American Dream* (Princeton, N.J.: Princeton Architectural Press, 1995), pp. 15–18.

26. Tim O'Brien, "Empty Nesters Return to the Busy City Life," *Albany TimesUnion*, December 13, 2004; Peg Tyre, "Seniors and the City: An Urban Retirement," *Newsweek*, October 11, 2006; Michael Corkery, "King of the Suburban McMansions Follows Boomers Back to the City," *Wall Street Journal*, December 15, 2006.

27. Kennedy and Charles, *Authority*, p. 55; Sharon Jackson, "Society Switches Focus Away From Children," *USA Today*, July 12, 2006.

28. Terry Nichols Clark and Ronald Inglehart, "The New Political Culture," in Terry Nichols Clark and Vincent Hoffman-Martinet, eds., *The New Political Culture* (Boulder, Colo.: Westview Press, 1998), pp. 58–59.

29. Deborah Zabarenko, "U.S. Population to Top 300 Million This Month," Reuters, October 2, 2006; "More IVF Keeps the Birth Rate Up," *New Scientist*, April 7, 2007.

30. Phillip Longman, *The Empty Cradle: How Falling Birthrates Threaten World Prosperity* (New York: Basic Books, 2004), p. 83.

31. Frey, "Married with Children"; Sam Roberts, "25th Anniversary Mark Elusive for Many Couples," *New York Times*, September 20, 2007; Neil Swidey, "Full House: Three Is the New Two and in Some Towns—Especially Affluent Ones—Four or More Is the New Three," *Boston Globe*, May 28, 2006; Phillip Longman, "The Return of Patriarchy," *Foreign Policy*, March-April 2006; James P. Vere, "Having It All No Longer: Fertility, Labor Supply and the New Life Choices of Generation X," *Demography* 44, no. 4 (2007), pp. 821–28; "The Dadprenerial Urge," *New York Crain's Business*, November 3, 2007; Stephanie Armour, "Some Moms Quit as Offices Scrap Family-friendliness," *USA Today*, October 12, 2006; Sue Shellenberger, "More New Mothers Are Staying Home Even When It Causes Financial Pain," *Wall Street Journal*, November 30, 2006; Daniel McGinn, "Twenty Years Later," *Newsweek*, May 23, 2006; "Stay-at-home Moms, Staying Even More," *Associated Press*, August 11, 2008.

32. Morley Winograd and Michael Hais, *Millennial Makeover: My Space, YouTube and the Future of American Politics* (New Brunswick, N.J.: Rutgers University Press, 2008), pp. 81–83.

33. Jocelyn Noveck and Trevor Tompson, "Poll: Family Ties Key to Youth Happiness," Associated Press, August 20, 2007; Associated Press–MTV poll, April 16–23, 2007.

34. Steven Greenhouse, "Many Entry Level Workers Feel Pinch of Rough Market," *New York Times*. September 4, 2006; Bob Herbert, "Here Come the Millennials," *New York Times*, May 13, 2008.

35. Asa Briggs, *Victorian People* (Chicago: University of Chicago Press, 1955), p. 13.

36. Frederick Jackson Turner, *The Significance of the Frontier in American History* (New York: Frederick Ungar, 1973), pp. 44, 52; Charles Beard and Mary Beard, *The Rise of American Civilization* (New York: Macmillan, 1930), vol. 1, p. 757.

37. Roger L. Ransom and Richard Stauch, "The Decline of Fertility and the Life Cycle Transition in the Ante-Bellum United States," paper for the All-UC Group in Economic History conference, Laguna Beach, May, 1986; Irving Howe, *World of Our Fathers* (New York: Harcourt Brace Jovanovich, 1976), pp. 262–63.

38. Coontz, *The Way We Never Were*, pp. 12–15; William V. Shannon, *The American Irish* (New York: Macmillan, 1966), p. 37.

39. Beard and Beard, *Rise of American Civilization*, pp. 2:726–27; Alvin Toffler, *Power Shift: Knowledge, Wealth and Violence at the End of the 21st Century* (New York: Bantam Books, 1990), p. 208.

40. F. Scott Fitzgerald, "The Jazz Age" in John Tipple, ed., *Crisis of the American Dream: A History of American Thought, 1920–1940* (New York: Pegasus, 1968), pp. 268–369; Martine Segalen, "Kinship Ties in European Families," in David I. Kertzer and Marzio Bargbagli, eds., *The History of the European Family*, vol. 3, *Family Life in the Twentieth Century* (New Haven, Conn.: Yale University Press, 2003), pp. 350–51.

41. Lewis Mumford, *The City in History* (San Diego: Harcourt Brace, 1961), pp. 511–513; Nicole Stelle Garnett, "Suburbs as Exit, Suburbs as Entrance," *Michigan Law Review* 106 (November 2007).

42. Coontz, *The Way We Never Were*, pp. 96–97, 183–85.

43. Rachel L. Swarns, "Family Mainstay to Move In to White House," *New York Times*, January 10, 2009.

44. Ibid., pp. xiv, 15; Al and Tipper Gore, *Joined at the Heart* (New York: Henry Holt, 2002), p. 38; Coontz, "American Family and Nostalgia Trap"; Adam P. Romero et al., "Census Snapshot," Williams Institute, University of California at Los Angeles, December 2007.

45. Philip S. Gutis, "What Is a Family? Traditional Limits Are Being Redrawn," *New York Times*, August 31, 1989; "Parents Doing Better with Child Support Payments," *USA Today*, October 18, 2007; Tamar Lewin, "Families Help Care for Half of U.S. Preschoolers, Census Says," *New York Times*, February 29, 2008; "Anti-nuclear Reaction," *Economist*, December 31, 1999.

46. Laura M. Holson, "Text Generation Gap," *New York Times*, March 9, 2008; Amanda Lenhart, Mary Madden, and Lee Rainie, "Teens and the Internet," Pew Internet and American Life Project, July 11, 2006.

47. Alan Wolfe, *One Nation, After All: What Middle Class Americans Really Think About* (New York: Penguin, 1998), pp. 103–4, 132; Wellner, "Mobility Myth."

48. Barbara Beck, "Options: Payroll or Pasture," *Urban Age* 7 (Winter 2000); Robert Fairlie, Kauffman Index of Entrepreneurial Activity by Age, 1996–2005, Kauffmann Foundation, 2006, "Working After Retirement: The Gap Between Expectations and Reality," Pew Research Center, September 21, 2006; Stephen Ohlemacher, "Working Longer: Boomers Staying on," Associated Press, June 12, 2007; Angel Jennings, "Nest Eggs Emptying, Not the Nests," *New York Times*, July 14, 2007.

49. "The MetLife Survey of American Attitudes Towards Retirement," Zogby International, 2001; Avrun D. Lank and Karen Herzog, "Boomerang Kids: Grown Children Move Back with Parents to Save Money for a House," Jsonline.com, June 28, 2008; Naomi Schaefer Riley, "A New Generation of the Young and the Restless," *Wall Street Journal*, January 18, 2008.

50. Marc Freedman, *How Baby Boomers Will Revolutionize Retirement and Transform America* (New York: Public Affairs Press, 1999), pp. 13–16.

51. Lewis Mumford, *The Urban Prospect* (New York: Harcourt Brace, 1956), pp. 45–47; Emily Fredrix, "Last Hope in a Weak Economy? Mom and Dad," Associated Press, March 21, 2008; Coontz, "American Family and Nostalgia Trap"; "Why Population Aging Matters: A Global Perspective," National Institute on Aging, March 2007; Sandra Block, "Elder Care Shifting Away from Nursing Homes," *USA Today*, February 1, 2008; Sharon Graham Niederhaus and John L. Graham, *Together Again: A Creative Guide to Successful Multigenerational Living*, (Lanham, Md.: Evans, 2007), pp. xvii, 8–40, 94–95, 118, 196; Chip Jacobs, "Here to Stay," *Los Angeles Times*, July 1, 2007; Jane Gross, "Boomerang Parents," *New York Times*, November 18, 2008.

52. John Ritter, "Some Cities Are Looking More Adult," *USA Today*, June 13, 2001; Kay S. Hymowitz, "Marriage and Caste: America's Chief Source of Inequality," *City Journal*, Winter 2006; Blaine Harden, "Numbers Drop for the Married with Children," *Washington Post*, March 4, 2007; Kay S. Hymowitz, *Marriage and Caste in America* (Chicago: Ivan R. Dee, 2006), pp. 25, 50–71; William A. Galston, "Causes of Declining Well-Being Among U.S. Children," in David M. Estlund and Martha C. Nussbaum, eds., *Sex, Preference and Family* (New York: Oxford University Press, 1997), p. 300; Julie Bosman, "Obama Calls for More Responsibility from Black Fathers," *New York Times*, June 16, 2008.

53. James J. Heckman, "Catch 'Em Young," *Wall Street Journal*, January 10, 2005.

54. Julie Scelfio, "As More People Work at Home, Design Evolves," *New York Times*, January 3, 2008; Ralph Gardner, Jr., "Home Office Life and Its Discontents," *New York Times*, January 3, 2008; Joseph P. Fuhr and Stephen Pociask, "Broadband Service: Economic and Environmental Benefits," American Consumer Institute, October 31, 2007, p. 18;

Margaret Walls and Elena Safirova, "A Review of the Literature on Telecommuting and Its Implications for Vehicle Travel and Emissions," Resources for the Future, December 2004, p. 3; Ralph Gregory, "It's Not Your Father's Office Anymore," *Intelligent Office*, January 2004; Ryan Chittum, "Office Space as Cost Cutting Tool: Less Is Less," *Wall Street Journal*, July 27, 2005.

55. Alvin Toffler, *The Third Wave* (New York: William Morrow, 1980), p. 195.

56. Ibid., pp. 42–45, 353–54; Ivonne Audirac, "Information Technology and Urban Form: Challenges to Smart Growth," International Regional Science Review 28, no. 2 (April 2005), pp. 119–45; Alvin Toffler, *The Third Wave* (New York: William Morrow, 1980), p. 195.

57. "The Dadpreneurial Urge," *Crain's New York Business*, November 3, 2007; Stephanie Armour, "Job Opening? Work at Home Moms Fill the Bill," *USA Today*, July 20, 2005; John Micklethwait and Adrian Wooldridge, *A Future Perfect: The Challenge and Promise of Globalization* (New York: Random House, 2000), p. 320.

58. Alvin Toffler and Heidi Toffler, *Creating a New Civilization* (Atlanta: Turner Books, 1994), p. 87.

59. Joseph P. Fuhr and Stephen Pociask, "Broadband Service: Economic and Environmental Benefits," American Consumer Institute, October 31, 2007, p. 11.

60. William H. Frey, "Metro America in the New Century: Demographic Shifts Since 2000," Brookings Institution, September 2005; Frey, "Married with Children"; "Migration of the Young Single and College Educated: 1995 to 2000," U.S. Census Bureau, November 2003.

61. Pat Riley, interview by author.

62. "Best Cities for Business," Michael Shires, Praxis Stratgy Group, April 13, 2009.

63. Mike Shultz, interview by author; demographic analysis of American Community Survey data 2004–06 by Praxis Strategy Group. Cited in Joel Kotkin, "Austin's Secrets For Economic Success," http://www.newgeography.com, May 11, 2009.

64. Sharon Graham Niederhaus and John L. Graham, *Together Again: A Creative Guide to Successful Multigenerational Living* (Lanham, Md.: Evans, 2007), p. 144.

65. Kelly Greene, "It Takes a Village," *Wall Street Journal*, November 15–16, 2008.

66. Annie Gowen, "Brave New Boomers," *Washington Post*, September 16, 2007; William R. Frey, "Mapping the Growth of Older America: Seniors and Boomers in the Early 21st Century," Metropolitan Policy Program, Brookings Institution, May 2007; Victor Hull, "Retirement Choices Stretch Beyond Florida," HeraldTribune.com, June 11, 2006; Chip Jacobs, "Here to Stay," *Los Angeles Times*, July 1, 2007; Jeff Lee, interview by author.

67. Linda Baker, "Retirement Homes Go High-Rise and Urban," *New York Times*, April 1, 2007; "Empty Nesters Flock to Cities," CBS News, July 9, 2004; "NAHB Study Finds Boomers Aren't Downsizing by Much," Buildingonline.com, March 5, 2008; "Baby Boomer Survey Shows Big Appetite for Real Estate," National Association of Realtors, 2006; Al Heavans, "Active-Adult Boomers Still Favor Suburbs," *Realty Times*, October 14, 2004; Peg Tyre, "Seniors and the City: An Urban Retirement," MSNBC.com, April 7, 2007; Gary V. Engelhardt, "Housing Trends Among Baby Boomers," Research Institute for Housing, 2006; William R. Taylor, *In Pursuit of Gotham: Culture and Commerce in New York* (Oxford, U.K.: Oxford University Press, 1992), p. xvii; "Second and Urban Homes Not a Big Lure for Baby Boomers," *National Building News Online*, December 11, 2006; Gail Marks Jarvis, "Second Thoughts About Second Homes," *Chicago Tribune*, November 12, 2006; William H. Frey, "Boomers and Seniors in the Suburbs," Center on Urban and Metropolitan Policy, Brookings Institution, January 2003; Joel Hirschhorn, "Sprawl Politics Traps Americans in Blandburbs," *Newtopia Magazine*, January 1, 2006.

68. Jennifer Lisle, "Active-Adult Builders Target Urban Locales," *Wall Street Journal*, January 29, 2005; Nicole Stelle Garnett, "Suburbs as Exit, Suburbs as Entrance," *Michigan Law Review* 106 (November 2007); Michael Derus, "Generation Has High X-pectations: Buyers Born Between 1965 and 1979 Redefining What's Crucial in a House," *Milwaukee Journal-Sentinel*, January 10, 2006; "Fast Facts: Baby Boomer Statistics on Empty Nesting and Retiring," *Del Webb Backgrounder* (Del Webb Corporation, 2005); Sandra Rosenbloom, "The Mobility Needs of Older Americans: Implications for Transportation Reauthorization," Center on Urban and Metropolitan Policy, Brookings Institution, July 2003, pp. 1–11.

69. Tomoeh Murakami Tse, "Hefty Appetite for Supersize Homes," *Washington Post*, September 3, 2006; Daniel Miller, "Builder Betting on Urban-Suburban," *Los Angeles Business Journal*, June 18, 2007.

70. Randall Lewis, interview by author.; David Wessel, "Older Staffers Get Uneasy Embrace," *Wall Street Journal*, May 15, 2008.

71. Jarvis, "Second Thoughts."

72. "The Emerging Influence of the 'Micropolis,'" *Innovation Briefs*, January-February 2005; June Kronholz, "The Coming Crunch," *Wall Street Journal*, October 13, 2006.

73. Jeffrey K. Hadden and Josef J. Barton, "An Image That Will Not Die: Thoughts on the History of Anti-Urban Ideology," in Irving Lewis Allen, ed., *New Towns and the Urban Dream: Ideology and Utopia in Planning and Development* (Port Washington, N.Y.: Kennikat Press, 1977), p. 50; Charles F. Longino and Don E. Bradley, "A First Look at Retirement Migration Trends in 2000," *Gerontologist* 43 (2003), pp. 904–7.

74. Frey, "Mapping the Growth of Older America"; Matt Gouras, "Unfilled Jobs Abound Out West," *Los Angeles Daily News*, August 25, 2007; John Leland, "Off to Resorts, and Carrying Their Careers," *New York Times*, August 13, 2007.

75. Hull, "Retirement Choices Stretch"; "Reviving Small Towns: America the Creative," *Economist*, December 19, 2006; Matthew Grimm, "The Cloning of Austin, Texas," *American Demographics*, December 29, 2005; "Size Doesn't Matter," *American Demographics*, May 1, 2001.

76. Laura Daily, "Good-Bye, Bingo Hello, Blue Books: Why Just Retire When You Can Retire with Class(es)?" December 2008, AARP.org.

77. Ivonne Audirac, "Information Technology and Urban Form: Challenges to Smart Growth," *International Regional Science Review* 28, no. 2 (April 2005), pp. 119–45; John Leland, "Off to Resorts, and Carrying their Careers," *New York Times*, August 13, 2007; Jim Sylvester, "The Migration Behavior of Great Plains Residents," Bureau of Business and Economic Research, University of Montana–Missoula, April 12, 2002; "Perceptions of Rural America," W.K. Kellogg Foundation, n.d., pp. 1, 5.

78. Tomas Alex Tizon, "Cold Case Cowboys Ride Again," *Los Angeles Times*, January 29, 2004; "Volunteering 61 Million Strong; Need and Momentum Grow," *eSight Community News*, August 13, 2008, Tabinc.org.

79. Arthur Hertzberg, *The Zionist Idea* (New York: Doubleday, 1959), p. 455.

80. "Volunteering 61 Million Strong."

81. Carol Lloyd, "Farmer's Markets Nurture a Need for Open Space," *San Francisco Chronicle*, January 14, 2007; Rod Walton, "Business Model, Community Supported Agriculture: Pair's Farm Has Strong Backing," *Tulsa World*, August 8, 2007; "Community Supported Agriculture in Wisconsin," Center for Land Use Education, July 2007; Joe Rodosevich, "Community Supported Agriculture Grows," *Twin Cities Daily Planet*, July 7, 2007.

82. Richard Reep, "Farmer's Markets: Reviving Public Space in Central Florida," NewGeography.com, December 13, 2008.

83. Traci Vogel, "My So-Malled Life," *Metro: Silicon Valley's Weekly Newspaper,* November 7–13, 2002.

84. Becky Nicolaides, "How Hell Moved from the City to the Suburbs," in Kevin M. Kruse and Thomas J. Sugrue, eds., *The New Suburban History* (Chicago: University of Chicago Press, 2006), p. 97; Steven Flusty and Michael Dear, "Invitation to a Postmodern Urbanism," in Robert A. Beauregard and Sophie Body-Gendrot, eds., *The Urban Moment: Cosmopolitan Essays On the Late 20th Century City* (Thousand Oaks, Calif.: Sage, 1999), p. 33; Andrew Kirby, "The Production of Private Space and Its Implications for Urban Social Relations," *Political Geography* 27 (2008), p. 81.

85. Edward J. Blakely and Mary Gail Snyder, *Fortress America: Gated Communities in the United States* (Washington, D.C.: Brookings Institution Press, 1997), pp. 3–14, 71, 132.

86. Andrew Kirby et al., "Examining the Significance of Housing Enclaves in the Metropolitan United States of America," *Housing, Theory and Society* 23, no.1 (2006), pp. 19–33; Andrew Kirby et al., "A Multitude of Particular Little Societies: An Examination of Housing Enclaves in Metropolitan Phoenix," draft paper; Steven Greenhut, "Picture Imperfect? A Question for the New Urbanists," *Orange County Register,* June 26, 2005; *Social Capital Benchmark Survey* (Harvard University, 2000), p. 2; Kirby, "Production of Private Space," p. 82.

87. Mariana Mogilevich, "Big Bad Buildings: The Vanishing Legacy of Minoru Yamasaki," *Next American City,* no. 3 (October 2003); Alexander von Hoffman, "Why They Built the Pruitt-Igoe Project," in John F. Bauman et al., eds., *From Tenements to the Taylor Homes: In Search of an Urban Housing Policy in Twentieth-Century America* (University Park: Pennsylvania State University Press, 2000).

88. Benjamin Schwartz, "A Vision in Concrete," *Atlantic,* July-August 2008; "France Reexamines Grim Housing Projects," Associated Press, November 23, 2005.

89. Katrina Herron, "From Bauhaus to Koolhaas," *Wired,* July 1996; Francis Morrone, "When Buildings Stopped Making Sense," *Wall Street Journal,* November 23, 2007; Jane Jacobs, *The Life and Death of Great American Cities* (New York: Vintage Books, 1961), pp. 388–89.

90. Andrew Haeg, "Farm Towns Look for Ways to Survive," Minnesota Public Radio, July 10, 2001; Patricia Leigh Brown, "If This Is the Swap Meet, Then It Must Be Monday," *New York Times,* April 28, 2002; Stephanie Rosenbloom, "To Save Gas, Shoppers Stay Home and Click," *New York Times,* July 19, 2008.

91. Sidney E. Mead, "The Nation with the Social of a Church," in Russell E. Richey and Donald G. Jones, eds., *American Civil Religion* (New York: Harper & Row, 1974), p. 45; K. Connie Kang, "Immigrants Fertile Soil for Mennonites," *Los Angeles Times,* April 30, 2005; Fielding Buck, "Religious Diversity Works to Define 21st Century America," *Facsnet,* May 7, 2005.

92. Stan L. Albrecht and Tim B. Heaton, "Secularization, Higher Education and Religiosity," *Review of Religious Research* 26, no. 1 (September 2004); "U.S. Stands Alone in Its Embrace of Religion," Pew Research Center, December 19, 2002.

93. Jackie Calmes and John Harwood, "Bush's Big Priority: Energy Conservative Christian Base," *Wall Street Journal,* August 30, 2004.

94. James Cusick, "The Disunited States of America," *Sunday Herald* [Scotland], November 11, 2004; Dale McConkey, "Whither Hunter's Culture War: Shifts in Evangelical Morality, 1988–1998," *Sociology of Religion* 62, no. 2 (Summer 2001).

95. Phil Zuckerman, interview by author; Phil Zuckerman, "Atheism: Contemporary Rates and Patterns," unpublished paper, Pitzer College; Judy Mandell, "New Life for Old Churches," *Christian Science Monitor,* May 11, 2005; Carolyn Marshall, "Their Churches Shut and Now Sold, Parishioners Fight On," *New York Times,* April 2, 2006.

96. McConkey, "Whither Hunter's Culture War"; Stuart Silverstein, "Colleges Fail to Encourage Spiritual Ideas, Study Finds," *Los Angeles Times*, November 21, 2003.

97. Arthur Brooks, "Our Religious Destiny," *Wall Street Journal*, August 20, 2007; Phil Zuckerman, "Is Faith Good for Us?" www.secularhumanism.org/index.php?section=library&page=pzuckerman_26_5; Zuckerman, "Atheism."

98. Naomi Schaefer Riley, "God on the Quad: At Religious Colleges—Which Are Growing Fast—Student Life Is Different," *American Enterprise*, March 2005.

99. Julian Walker, "Dwindling Membership Bedevils Many Religions," *Northeast Times*, August 2, 2005.

100. "A Moment with Robert Wuthnow," *Princeton Alumni Weekly*, October 10, 2007, http://www.paw.princeton.edu/; Riley, "New Generation of Young and Restless."

101. Laurie Goodstein, "Religious Voting Data Show Some Shift," *New York Times*, November 9, 2006; K. Connie Kang, "Christianity's Image taking a Turn for the Worse," *Los Angeles Times*, October 13, 2007.

102. Forrest G. Wood, *The Arrogance of Faith: Christianity and Race in America from the Colonial Era to the Twentieth Century* (New York: Knopf, 1990), pp. 345–55.

103. Daniel J.Wakin, "Following the Shifting Flock: As Some Churches Falter and Others Grow, Catholic Church Plans Overhaul," *New York Times*, October 23, 2003; Michael Paulson, "Many Parishes Seem Closure Candidates," *Boston Globe*, December 10, 2003; Howe, *World of Our Fathers*, pp. 47–49; Leonard J. Arrington, *Great Basin Kingdom* (Lincoln: University of Nebraska Press, 1958), p. 5; William J. Stern, "How Dagger John Saved New York's Irish," *City Journal*, Spring 1997; Shannon, *American Irish*, pp. 34–35.

104. Anthony M. Stevens-Arroyo, "Building a New Public Realm," in Margaret E. Graham and Alberto Vourvoulas-Bush, eds., *The City and the World: New York's Global Future* (New York: Council on Foreign Relations, 1997), pp. 147–53.

105. Marilyn Elias, "Spirituality Will Be Key to Boomers, but Religious Revival Is Unlikely," Gannett News Service, November 2001; "How Many Faith Groups Are There in the U.S.," Religioustolerance.org; Anna Greenberg and Jennifer Bertktold, "Evangelicals in America," Greenberg Quinlan Rosner Research, April 5, 2004; Wade Clark Roof, *Spiritual Marketplace* (Princeton, N.J.: Princeton University Press, 1999), pp. 54–55, 62–63, 250–51; Neela Banerjee, "A Fluid Religious Life Is Seen in U.S., With Switches Common," *New York Times*, February 26, 2008.

106. Christian Smith, *Christian America: What Evangelicals Really Want* (Berkeley: University of California Press, 2002), pp. 200, 204: Chris Anderson, *The Long Tail: Why the Future of Business Is Selling More of Less* (New York: Hyperion, 2006), p. 190.

107. Marilyn Elias, "Spirituality Will Be Key to Boomers, but Religious Revival Is Unlikely," Gannett News Service, November 2001; *Social Capital Benchmark Survey* (Harvard University, 2000), p. 2; Justin Taylor, "How Many Americans Really Attend Church Each Week," Theologica.blogspot.com, August 2, 2005.

108. Andrew Greeley, "The Other Civic America: Religion and Social Capital," *American Prospect*, May-June 1997; Gregg Easterbrook, "Religion in America: The New Ecumenicalism," *Brookings Review* 20, no.1 (Winter 2002), pp. 45–48.

109. Easterbrook, "Religion in America."

110. Reverend Don Gebert, interview by author and Colin Drukker; Roger Galatas and Jim Barlow, *The Woodlands: The Inside Story of Creating a Better Hometown* (Washington, D.C.: Urban Land Institute, 2004), pp. 71–79.

111. Galatas and Barlow, *Woodlands*, pp. 71–79.

112. Ibid., pp. 71–78.

113. Al Toffler, *Future Shock* (New York: Random House, 1970), p. 452.

114. Robert H. Nelson, "Does 'Existence Value' Exist? An Essay on Religions, Old and New," discussion paper, Competitive Enterprise Institute, May 1996.
115. Ibid.; Paul Watson, "The Beginning of the End of Life as We Know It on Planet Earth," SeaShepard Conservation Society, May 4, 2007.

CHAPTER SEVEN: AMERICA IN 2050

1. Quoted in David Hamer, *New Towns in the New World: Images and Perceptions of the Nineteenth Century Frontier* (New York: Columbia University Press, 1990), p. 207.
2. Edward Bellamy, *Looking Backward 2000–1887* (New York: Penguin, 2000).
3. Charles Beard and Mary Beard, *The Rise of American Civilization* (New York: Macmillan, 1930) vol. 2, p. 800.
4. John Gunther, *Inside USA* (New York: New Press, 1997), p. 920.
5. Philip K. Dick, *Do Androids Dream of Electronic Sheep?* (New York: Doubleday, 1968); John Helfers and Martin H. Greenberg, eds., *Future Americas* (Daw Science Fiction, 2008); Michael Chabon, "The Omega Glory," *Details*, January 2006.
6. Immanuel Wallerstein, *The Decline of American Power* (New York: Norton, 2003), p. 306; Parag Khanna, "Waving Good-bye to Hegemony,"*New York Times Magazine*, January 27, 2008; Fred Kaplan, "War Stories," *Slate*, January 26, 2005.
7. Robert J. Lieber, "Falling Upwards: Declinism, Box Set," *World Affairs*, Summer 2008.
8. "Europe's Demographic Collapse," *American Enterprise*, October-December 2005; "Half a Billion Americans?" *Economist*, August 22, 2002; Matthew Brunwasser, "In Shrinking Bulgaria, Where Are the People?" *New York Times*, October 10, 2006; Elisabeth Rosenthal, "European Union's Plunging Birthrates Spread Eastward," *New York Times*, September 4, 2006; Paul Treanor, "All Ten Million Europeans," http://web.inter.nl.net/users/Paul.Treanor/nohumans.html, June 2007.
9. Frederick Kempe, "Demographic Time Bomb Ticks On," *Wall Street Journal*, June 6, 2006; Niko Karvounis, "Not Out of the Woods," New America Foundation, June 2009.
10. Padma Desai, "Running Out of Russians," *Wall Street Journal*, May 22, 2006; Ben J. Wattenberg, *Fewer: How the New Demography Will Shape our Future* (Chicago: Ivan R. Dee, 2004), p. 45; Mitra Toosi, "A Century of Change: The U.S. Labor Force, 1950–2050," *Monthly Labor Review*, May 2002; "Working After Retirement: The Gap Between Expectations and Reality," Pew Research Center, September 21, 2006; "Banking the Demographic Dividend," Rand Policy Brief, 2002; George Melloan, "Putin's KGB Instincts Serve Russia Badly," February 14, 2006; Mara Hvistendahl, "No Country for Young Men," *New Republic*, June 29, 2008; Stephanie Fitch, "Gilt Edge Pensions," *Forbes*, February 16, 2009.
11. Allan Carlson, "The Family Factors," Touchstonemag.com, January-February 2006.
12. Chabon, "Omega Glory."
13. Phillip Longman, *The Empty Cradle: How Falling Birthrates Threaten World Prosperity* (New York; Basic Books, 2004), p. 139.
14. John Allen, "Child-Free by Choice," *Waco Tribune-Herald*, August 9, 2003; Elizabeth Warren, "The New Economies of the Middle Class," testimony before the Senate Finance Committee, May 10, 2007.
15. Warren Wagar, *A Short History of the Future* (Chicago: University of Chicago, 1989), p. 157; Alan Weisman, *The World Without Us* (New York: Thomas Dunne Books, 2007); Frank Furedi, "Confronting the New Misanthropy," *Arts & Letters Daily*, April 18, 2006.
16. Arthur Herman, *The Idea of Decline in Western History* (New York: Simon & Schuster, 1997), pp. 416–23; Longman, *Empty Cradle*, p. 133; Donella Meadows et al., *The Limits to Growth* (New York: Potomac Associates, 1972), pp. 25–87.

17. Colleen Heenan, "Global Population and the Resulted Demands from Earth," Greenornot .experience.com, August 18, 2008.

18. Peter Kareiva, "Children and Their Carbon Legacy: A Way to Be an Eco-Hero?" *Cool Green Science*, Blog.nature.org, March 11, 2009.

19. Peter Ozment, *When Fathers Ruled: Family Life in Reformation Europe* (Cambridge, Mass.: Harvard University Press, 1983), pp. 49, 152; Simon Schama, *An Embarrassment of Riches* (New York: Vintage, 1987), pp. 484–85, 495; Peter Ozment, *Ancestors: The Loving Family in Old Europe* (Cambridge, Mass.: Harvard University Press, 2001), p. 47; Theodor Mommsen, *The History of Rome* (New York: Meridian Books, 1958), pp. 549–50.

20. Sarah-Kate Templeton, "Two Children Should Be the Limit," Women.timesonline.co.uk, February 1, 2009; "U.K. Population Must Fall to 30m, says Porritt," Timesonline.co.uk, March 22, 2009.

21. John Holdren, Anne Ehrlich, and Paul Ehrlich, *Human Ecology: Problems and Solutions* (San Francisco: W. H. Freeman, 1973), p. 3. Holdren, science adviser to President Obama and a former protégé of Paul Ehrlich, has long argued that population and economic growth are driving the earth to a crisis state. A population of 280 million Americans, he says, would be unsustainable. His solution has been to call for the "de-development" of the United States as well as other advanced countries.

22. David E. Bloom and David Canning, "Booms, Busts and Echoes: How the Biggest Demographic in History Is Affecting Global Development," *Finance and Development* 43, no. 3 (September 2006).

23. Paul D. Gottlieb, "Growth Without Growth: An Alternative Economic Development Goal For Metropolitan Areas," Brookings Institution, February 2002.

24. Longman, *Empty Cradle*, p. 41; "Banking the 'Demographic Dividend,' " Rand Policy Brief, 2002.

25. Jeremy Rifkin, *The European Dream: How Europe's Vision of the Future Is Quietly Eclipsing the American Dream* (New York: Penguin, 2004), p. 3; Tony Judt, "Europe vs. America," *New York Review of Books*, February 10, 2005.

26. David Rosnick and Mark Weisbrot, "Are Shorter Work Hours Good for the Environment?" Center for Economic and Policy Research, December 2008.

27. Longman, *Empty Cradle*, p. 41; Peter Burke, *Venice and Amsterdam* (Cambridge, U.K.: Polity Press, 1994), p. 139; George Cowgill, "Onward and Upward With Collapse," in Norman Yoffie and George L. Cowgill, eds., *The Collapse of Ancient States and Civilizations* (Tucson: University of Arizona Press, 1997), p. 271. Numbers in the late Roman Empire are somewhat disputed; those of early modern Holland are probably more reliable.

28. Mike Wendling, "Is Too Few People the New 'Population Problem'?" *Grist*, December 14, 2005; Phil Longman, "Population Bombing," *National Review*, May 19, 2008.

29. Robert Wiebe, *Businessmen and Reform: A Study of the Progressive Movement* (Cambridge, Mass.: Harvard University Press, 1962), p. 224.

30. Daniel Bell, *The Coming of Post-Industrial Society* (New York: Basic Books, 1973), pp. 360–65.

31. Herman Kahn and Anthony J. Weiner, *The Year 2000: A Framework on the Next Thirty-three Years* (New York: Macmillan, 1967), p. 62.

32. Kenichi Ohmae. "New World Order: The Rise of the Region-State," *Wall Street Journal*, August 16, 1994; Finlo Rohrer, "Are Cities the New Countries?" BBC News, July 14, 2006.

33. Arthur C. Brooks, "A Nation of Givers," *American*, March-April 2008; Arthur C. Brooks, *Who Really Cares: America's Charity Divide Who Gives, Who Doesn't and Why It Matters* (New York: Basic Books, 2006), pp. 120–22.

34. Wendell Cox, "America Is More Small Town Than We Think," Newgeography.com, September 10, 2008; Andres Duany, Elizabeth Plater-Zyberk, and Jeff Speck, *The Rise of Sprawl and the Decline of the American Dream* (New York: North Point Press, 2000), pp. 227–28.

35. William Sullivan, "Making Civil Society Work: Democracy as a Problem of Civic Cooperation," in Robert K. Fullinwider, ed., *Civil Society, Democracy, and Civic Renewal* (New York: Oxford University Press, 1999).

36. Richard T. Pascale, Mark Milleman, and Linda Gioja, *Surfing the Edge of Chaos* (New York: Crown Business, 2000), p. 271; John Micklethwait and Adrian Wooldridge, *The Company: A Short History of a Revolutionary Idea* (New York: Modern Library, 2003), p. 129; John Micklethwait and Adrian Wooldridge, *A Future Perfect* (New York: Random House, 2000), p. 320; Stefan Theil, "Europe's Philosophy of Failure," *Foreign Policy*, January-February 2008; Sharon Jayson, "Gen Y Makes a Mark and Their Imprint Is Entrepreneurship," *USA Today*, December 8, 2006; Jim Hopkins, "Microbusinesses Find Huge Benefits in Outsourcing," *USA Today*, December 11, 2006.

37. Tom Martin, "Layoffs Tempt Some Entrepreneurs," Associated Press, February 1, 2009; "Top 5 Reasons Entrepreneurs Will Succeed in This Recession," *Published Daily*, April 7, 2009.

38. Charlie Wilson, interview by author.

39. Brooks, *Who Really Cares*, p. 32.

40. "U.S. Stands Alone in Its Embrace of Religion," Pew Research Center, December 19, 2002; Stephanie Coontz, "Too Close for Comfort," *New York Times*, November 7, 2006.

41. Ward Harkevy, "The Numbers Behind the Bling," *Village Voice*, January 4, 2004; Alan Wolfe, *One Nation, After All: What Middle Class Americans Really Think About* (New York: Viking, 1998), p. 185.

42. Barbara Ehrenreich, *Nickel and Dimed: On (Not) Getting By in America* (New York: Owl Books, 2001), p. 79.

43. Stephen Rose, "What's (Not) the Matter with the Middle Class?" Prospect.org, September 4, 2006; David Wessell, "Fed Chief Warns of Widening Inequality," *Wall Street Journal*, January 7, 2007; Brad Knickerbocker, "Is a Bigger Nation Richer?" *Christian Science Monitor*, September 12, 2006.

44. Irving Kristol, "Income Inequality Without Class Conflict," *Wall Street Journal*, December 18, 1997.

45. Greg Ip, "Wages Fail to Keep Pace with Productivity Increases, Aggravating Income Inequality," *Wall Street Journal*, March 27, 2006; Louise Story, "After an Off Year, Wall Street Pay Is Bouncing Back," *New York Times*, April 26, 2009.

46. Elizabeth Warren, "The New Economies of the Middle Class," testimony before the Senate Finance Comttee, May 10, 2007; John W. Schoen, "Who or What Is Middle Class," MSNBC.com, October 17, 2007.

47. *The State of Working America, 2006–2007*, Fact Sheets, Economic Policy Institute, Stateofworkingamerica.org; David Wessel, "In Poverty Tactics, An Old Debate: Who Is at Fault?" *Wall Street Journal*, June 15, 2006; "The Rich, the Poor and the Growing Gap Between Them," *Economist*, June 15, 2006; Greg Ip, "Income-Inequality Gap Widens," *Wall Street Journal*, October 12, 2007; Conor Dougherty, "High-Degree Professionals Show Power," *Wall Street Journal*, September 10, 2008.

48. David Wessel, "As Rich-Poor Gap Widens in U.S., Class Mobility Stalls," *Wall Street Journal*, May 13, 2005.

49. Ellen Wulfhost, "Job Losses Hitting Men Harder than Women," Reuters, January 22, 2009; Greg Ip, "The Declining Value of Your College Degree," *Wall Street Journal*, July 17, 2008; Steven Greenhouse, "Many Entry Level Workers Feel Pinch of Rough Market,"

New York Times, September 4, 2006; Bob Herbert, "Here Come the Millennials," *New York Times*, May 13, 2008; Laurence Mishel and Elise Gould, "Inhospitable Job Market to Greet College Graduates," Economic Policy Institute, May 14, 2008; Michael Mandel, "What the Income Report Tells Us About College Grads," *Business Week*, September 4, 2007; David Wessel, "College Grad Wages Are Sluggish Too," May 18, 2006; Niko Karvounis, "Not Out of the Woods," New America Foundation, June 2009.

50. Rose, "What's (Not) the Matter"; "The Rich, the Poor and the Growing Gap Between them," *Economist*, June 15, 2006.

51. "Crisis of the Spirit," *American Enterprise*, October-December 2005; "Because of the economy have you lost faith in getting ahead through hard work," *USA Today*, October 7, 2009.

52. Hartmut Kaelble, *Historical Research on Social Mobility*, trans. Ingrid Noakes (New York: Columbia University Press, 1981), pp. 36–37; Paul Wilken, *Entrepreneurship* (Norwood, N.J.: Ablex, 1979), p. 207.

53. Rowland Berthoff, "Independence and Enterprise: Small Business in The American Dream," in Stuart Buchey, ed., *Small Business in American Life* (New York: Columbia University Press, 1980), p. 33.

54. Walter LaFeber, *The New Empire: An Interpretation of American Expansion, 1860–1898* (Ithaca, N.Y.: Cornell University Press, 1963), pp. 7–8.

55. Jane Allen Shikoh, "The Higher Life in the American City of the 1900s: A Study of Leaders and Their Activities in New York, Chicago, Philadelphia, St. Louis, Boston, and Buffalo," Ph.D. diss., New York University, October 1972, pp. 5–8, 81–85; Richard Hofstadter, *The Age of Reform* (New York: Knopf, 1955), p. 305.

56. Daniel R. Fusfeld, *The Economic Thought of Franklin D. Roosevelt and the Origins of the New Deal* (New York: Columbia University Press, 1956), p. 124.

57. Franklin D. Roosevelt, *Looking Forward* (New York: John Day, 1933), p. 22; Michael Lind, "Progressives, New Dealers and the Politics of Landscape," Newgeography.com, August 11, 2008.

58. "The Missing Rungs of the Ladder," *Economist*, July 16, 2005; Wendell Cox and Jean Love, *The Best Investment a Nation Ever Made: A Tribute to the Dwight D. Eisenhower System of Interstate and Defense Highways* (Washington, D.C.: American Highway Users Alliance, June 1996), pp. 1–15.

59. "The Economic Effects of Federal Spending on Infrastructure and Other Investments," congressional budget office (June 1998); Average Real Income Levels and Shares 1979–2001, http://www.calvert-henderson.com/income-table4.htm (accessed August, 2006a); Infrastructure Capital Stock, 1950–1999, http://www.calvert-henderson.com/infra-table1.htm (accessed August, 2006b).

60. Nathan Glazer, "The Mosaic Persuasion," *New Republic*, July 27, 2007.

61. William Neuman, "New York Transit Failings Similar to Those in 2004," *New York Times*, August 9, 2007; Harry Siegel, "Maybe Bloomberg Should Try Getting Angry," *New York Observer*, August 10, 2007; Nicole Gelinas, "NY's Sick Transit," *New York Post*, April 24, 2007.

62. "Funding," California Infrastructure Coalition, Calinfrastructure.org.

63. Alvin Toffler and Heidi Toffler, *Creating a New Civilization* (Atlanta: Turner Publishing, 1994), p. 69; Richard Florida, "The New American Dream," *Washington Monthly*, March 2003.

64. Richard Florida, "Financial Recovery Needs Money—and a Massively Different Mindset," *Toronto Globe & Mail*, November 29, 2009.

65. Paul Glader, "Monuments to Labor," *Wall Street Journal*, August 10, 2004.

66. David Brooks, "Greed and Stupidity," *New York Times*, April 3, 2009; David Wessel, "A Source of Our Bubble Trouble," January 17, 2008.

67. Analysis of figures from U.S. Department of Commerce, International Trade Administration, by Mark Schill, Praxis Strategy Group.

68. Quoted in Rachel Layne, "GE's Immelt Accepts Responsibility as Shares Fall," Bloomberg, March 3, 2009.

69. Eamonn Fingleton, *In Praise of Hard Industries: Why Manufacturing, Not the Information Economy, Is the Key to Future Prosperity* (Boston: Houghton Mifflin, 1999); Eamonn Fingleton, "In Praise of Hard Industries," nytimes.com, July 18, 2007.

70. Peter G. Gosselin, "Suddenly a Bright Future for Old-economy Companies," *Los Angeles Times*, May 25, 2008; Pete Engardio, "China's Eroding Advantage," *Business Week*, June 15, 2009.

71. Martin Weiner, *English Culture and the Decline of the Industrial Spirit, 1850–1980* (Cambridge, U.K.: Cambridge University Press, 1981), pp. 129, 141.

72. Richard Deitz and James Orr, "A Leaner, More Skilled U.S. Manufacturing Workforce," *Current Issues in Economics and Finance* 12 (February–March 2006); Mark Trumbull, "Small, 'Inner Sunbelt' Cities Grow," *Christian Science Monitor* 99 (July 2007), pp. 2–4; Richard Dietz, "Restructuring in the Manufacturing Workforce: New York State and the Nation," Federal Reserve Bank of New York, Buffalo Branch, Winter 2004.

73. *2005 Skills Gap Report—A Survey of the American Manufacturing Workforce*, National Association of Manufacturers, the Manufacturing Institute, and Deloitte Consulting, 2005; Timothy Aeppel, "Firms' New Grail: Skilled Workers," *Wall Street Journal*, November 22, 2005.

74. Jerry Jasinowksi, "In Search of Skilled Employees for America's Future," National Association of Manufacturers, Center for Workforce Success, May 24, 2005.

75. Joel Popkin and Kathryn Kobe, "U.S. Manufacturing Innovation at Risk," Council of Manufacturing Associations and the Manufacturing Institute, February 2006; Barbara Hagenbaugh, "Wanted: Factory Workers," *USA Today*, December 5, 2006.

76. Joellen Perry and Stephen Power, "A Shortage of Skilled Labor Pinches Eastern Europe," *Wall Street Journal*, July 10, 2007.

77. David Knox, "The Very Things that Define the Middle Class Slipping Out of Reach for Many Ohioans," *Beacon Journal*, March 16, 2008; Frederick Merk, *History of the Westward Movement* (New York: Knopf, 1978), pp. 447–50.

78. Peter S. Goodman, "In N.C., A Second Industrial Revolution," *Washington Post*, September 3, 2007.

79. Louis Uchitelle, "Private Cash Sets Agenda for Urban Infrastructure," *New York Times*, January 6, 2008.

80. Rebecca Smith and Daniel Machalaba, "As Utilities Seek More Coal, Railroads Struggle to Deliver," *Wall Street Journal*, March 15, 2006; officials at Basin Electric, conversation with author, Bismarck, N.D.

81. "Daniel Yergin, "The Katrina Crisis," *Wall Street Journal*, September 3, 2005.

82. ASCE 2006 Report Card, http://www.asce.org/reportcard/2005/page.cfm?id=25# conditions, accessed September 2006; "NERC Acts to Strengthen Grid Reliability," North American Electric Reliability Council, February 2004.

83. Jim Carlton, "One Tiny Town Becomes Internet-Age Power Point," *Wall Street Journal*, March 7, 2007; "Servers as High as an Elephant's Eye," *Business Week*, June 12, 2006; John Markoff and Saul Hansell, "Hiding in Plain Sight, Google Seeks More Power," *New York Times*, June 14, 2006.

84. "Siting Critical Energy Infrastructure: An Overview of Needs and Challenges," National Commission on Energy Policy, White Paper, June 2006.

85. Ian W. H. Parry and Joel Darmstadter, "The Costs of U.S. Oil Dependency," Resources for the Future, November 17, 2004.

86. Joshua Kurlantzick, *Charm Offensive: How China's Soft Power Is Transforming the World* (New Haven, Conn.: Yale University Press, 2007), p. 208; Alan Murray, "Ascent of Sovereign-Wealth Funds Illustrates New World Order," *Wall Street Journal*, January 28, 2008; Tony Hayward, "A Compromise Energy Policy Is Within Reach," *Wall Street Journal*, February 26, 2009.

87. Frank Furedi, "Confronting the New Misanthropy," *Arts & Letters Daily*, April 18, 2006.

88. Leo Marx, *The Machine in the Garden: Technology and the Pastoral Ideal of America* (Oxford, U.K.: Oxford University Press, 1964), pp. 149, 203; Kevin Roazario, "Making Progress: Disaster Narratives and the Art of Optimism in Modern America," in Lawrence J. Vale and Thomas Campenella, eds., *The Resilient City: How Modern Cities Recover from Disaster* (Oxford, U.K.: Oxford University Press, 2005), pp. 27–31.

89. David E. Nye, *America as Second Creation: Technology and Narratives of New Beginnings* (Cambridge, Mass.: MIT Press, 2004), pp. 294–95.

90. Amy Kaleita with Gregory Forbes, "Hysteria's History: Environmental Alarmism in Context," Pacific Research Institute, n.d.; Daniel Yergin, "It's Not the End of Oil Age: Technology and Higher Prices Drive a Supply Buildup," *Washington Post*, July 31, 2005.

91. Brad Knickerbocker, "The Environmental Load of 300 Million: How Heavy," *Christian Science Monitor*, September 26, 2006.

92. Florida, "Financial Recovery Needs Money," Richard Florida, "The Creativity Exchange," April 4, 2007; "Shelter or Burden?" *Economist*, April 16, 2008.

93. Al Ehrbar, "The Housing Boom: Another Twenty Years of Growth," Stern Stewart consulting; "The State of the Nation's Housing 2001," Joint Center for Housing Studies, Harvard University, 2001, p. 11; Florida, "Creativity Exchange"; "Shelter or Burden?" *Economist*, April 16, 2008. Frank Magid and Associates survey on Millenial Attitudes, http://www.newgeography.com/content/00119-a-return-avalon.

94. http://www.newgeography.com/content/00937-projecting-30-45-year-olds-united-states.

95. Jeffrey K. Hadden and Joseph E. Barton, "Thoughts on the History of Anti-Urban Ideology," in William Allen Whyte, ed., *New Towns and the Suburban Dream* (Port Washington, N.Y.: Kennikat Press, 1977), pp. 53–54; John Micklethwait and Adrian Wooldridge, *The Right Nation: Conservative Power in America* (New York: Penguin Press, 2004), p. 331.

96. "The Future of Homes and Housing," *Christian Science Monitor*, January 5, 2005.

97. Jordan Rappaport, "The Shared Fortunes of Cities and Suburbs," Federal Reserve Bank of Kansas City, third quarter 2005.

98. Jim Carlton, "Many Voters Agree to Raise Money for Green Space," *Wall Street Journal*, November 7, 2003; Tom Martison, *American Dreamscape: The Pursuit of Happiness in Postwar Suburbia* (New York: Carroll & Graf, 2000), p. 228.

99. James Martin, *The Wired Society* (Englewood Cliffs, N.J.: Prentice Hall, 1978), pp. 181–92; Andrew Bolger, "Broadband Spurs Techno-commuters Rise," *Financial Times*, September 2, 2007.

100. Margaret Wallace and Elena Safirova, "A Review of the Literature on Telecommuting and Its Implications for Vehicle Travel and Emissions," Resources for the Future, 2004; Joseph P. Fuhr, "Broadband Services: Economic and Environmental Benefits," American Consumer Institute, October 31, 2007; Ted Balaker, "The Quiet Success: Telecommuting's Impact on Transportation and Beyond," Reason Foundation, July 2005; Sam Dillon,

"High Cost of Driving Ignites Online Classes Boom," *New York Times*, July 11, 2008; Ann Bednarz, "Sun Sheds Light on Telework Savings," *InfoWorld*, June 30, 2008; Ted Sansom, "Give Telecommuting the Green Light," *InfoWorld*, June 7, 2007.

101. Fred Hirsch, *Social Limits to Growth* (Cambridge, Mass.: Harvard University Press, 1976), p. 39; Andrea Coombes, "Seeking Loyal, Devoted Workers? Let Them Stay Home," *Wall Street Journal*, September 11, 2007.

102. Dan Fost, "Where Neo-Nomads Ideas Percolate: New Bedouins Transform a Laptop, Cell Phone and Coffehouses into Their Office," *San Francisco Chronicle*, March 11, 2007; Ilana DeBare, "Small Businesses Helped SF During Dot-com Bust: Layoffs Less Likely When Employer Knows Workers," *San Francisco Chronicle*, August 9, 2006; "Sustaining Our Prosperity" ICF International, for Mayor's Office of Workforce and Economic Development, City of San Francisco, November 1, 2007.

103. Dan Blake, CSU Northridge, interview with author.

104. Bowles and Kotkin, op. cit.

105. Peter Smirniotopoulos, "In Search of the Middle Class," *Urban Land*, October 2004.

106. David G. Littman, "The Forgotten Refugees," *National Review*, December 3, 2002; Jonathan Eric Lewis, "Iraq's Christians," *Wall Street Journal*, December 19, 2002.

107. Jonathan Becker, "Putin and the Dawn of the New Authoritarianism," *Globalist*, November 30, 2007.

108. Joshua Kurlantzick, *Charm Offensive: How China's Soft Power Is Transforming the World* (New Haven, Conn.: Yale University Press, 2007), pp. 36–37; George Melloan, "Putin's KGB Instincts Serve Russia Badly," *Wall Street Journal*, February 14, 2006; Joshua Cooper Ramo, "The Beijing Consensus," Foreign Policy Centre, Spring 2004.

109. Clive Cookson, "U.S. Widens Gap with Europe on R&D," *Financial Times*, October 30, 2006; Chris Giles, "A Productivity Prescription: How the U.S. Has Pulled Away from Europe and Japan," *Financial Times*, January 25, 2006; David Rennie, "Red Tape Turning Best Firms Away from Europe," *Financial Times*, January 21, 2006; Grace Sung, "Ageing Europe Forced to Open Door to Immigrants," *Straits Times*, March 3, 2004.

110. Prakaj Mishra, "The Myth of the New India," *New York Times*, July 6, 2006.

111. Fred Kaplan, "A CIA Report Predicts American Global Dominance Could End in Fifteen Years," *Slate*, January 26, 2006; Parag Khanna, "Who Shrank of the Superpower," *New York Times Magazine*, January 27, 2008; Andrew Browne, "China Girds for Future Shock," *Wall Street Journal*, April 4, 2005; Howard W. French, "China Scrambles for Security as Its Workers Age," *New York Times*, March 22, 2007.

112. Ben Feller, "U.S. Immigrants Lag Behind in School, but Gaps Are Bigger in Other Nations," Associated Press, May 15, 2006; Sung, "Ageing Europe Forced."

113. Census of Canada, 2001; U.S. Census, 2000.

114. David Cannadine, *Ornamentalism: How the British Saw Their Empire* (Oxford, U.K.: Oxford University Press, 2001), p. 170; Pankaj Ghemawat, "The Myth of Globalisation," *Australian Financial Review*, March 16, 2007.

115. Rifkin, *European Dream*, p. 255; Phillippe Legrain, *Immigrants: Your Country Needs Them* (Princeton, N.J.: Princeton University Press, 2006), pp. 157–58; Marcus Walker, "Berlin Cracks Immigrant Door," *Wall Street Journal*, August 27, 2007; Richard Bernstein, "A Quiz for Would Be Citizens Tests German Attitudes," *New York Times*, March 29, 2006; Bob Sherwood, "The Uneasy Cosmopolitan: How Migrants Are Enriching an Ever More Anxious Host," *Financial Times*, September 21, 2006; Jeff Chu, "How to Plug Europe's Brain Drain," *Time*, January 26, 2004; Philip Thornton, "Britain Tops 'Brain Drain' League," *New Zealand Herald*, October 24, 2005.

116. Jeffrey Fleishman, Ralph Frammolino, and Sebastian Rotella, "Outraged Europeans Take Dimmer View of Diversity," *Los Angeles Times*, September 5, 2005; "An Uncertain Road: Muslims and the Future of Europe," Pew Forum on Religion and Public Life, December 2004; Jan Rath, "The Politics of Recognizing Religious Diversity in Europe: Social Reactions to the Institutionalization of Islam in the Netherlands, Belgium and Great Britain," *Netherlands Journal of Social Scientists* 35, no.1 (1999), pp. 53–68; James P. Gannon, "Is God Dead in Europe?" *USA Today*, January 8, 2006; Bob Sherwood, "The Uneasy Cosmopolitan: How Migrants are Enriching an Ever More Anxious Host," *Financial Times*, September 21, 2006.

117. Cannadine, *Ornamentalism*, pp. 126, 132; Paul Kennedy, *Preparing for the 21st Century* (New York: Random House, 1993), p. 23.

118. Cornelia Butler Flora, "Immigrants as Assets," *Rural Development News* [North Central Regional Center for Rural Development] 28, no. 3 (2006); "Brain Drain," *Economist*, July 10, 1999; Andrew Sum, Paul Harrington, and Ishwar Khatiwada, "The Impact of New Immigrants on Young Native Born Workers," Center for Immigration Studies, August 2006; "Foreign Students in Higher Education by Continent of Origin," UNESCO, 1999; Kareb W. Anderson, "A Decline in Foreign Students Is Reversed," *New York Times*, November 13, 2006.

119. Joshua Kurlantzick, *Charm Offensive: How China's Soft Power Is Transforming the World* (New Haven, Conn.: Yale University Press, 2007), p. 9; Legrain, *Immigrants*, p. 196; "Population Paradox: Europe's Time Bomb," *Independent*, August 9, 2008.

120. Somini Sengupta and Larry Rohter, "The Changing Church," *New York Times*, October 14, 2003; Russell E. Richey and Donald G. Jones, "The Civil Religion Debate," in Russell E. Richey and Donald G. Jones, eds., *American Civil Religion* (New York: Harper & Row, 1974), p. 6; "Vive le Difference," *American*, March-April 2008.

121. Quoted in David E. Nye, *America as Second Creation: Technology and Narratives of New Beginnings* (Cambridge, Mass.: MIT Press, 2004), p. 147.

122. Gunther, *Inside USA*, p. 920.

INDEX